PRAISE FOR *OCCUPY WORLD STREET*

"Many wri

the human future.
Ross Jacks· ·iary, yet practical,
program c ·f all, he draws on
his distinc· r to outline sound
proposals ₂ and finance that
currently c ːal collapse. This is
a truly imr

—**David Korten**, cofounder of *YES!* magazine, author of *Agenda for a New Economy*

"*Occupy World Street* is a masterpiece that deserves to get wide circulation and commitment by world leaders. Never has the kind of 'breakaway' Ross Jackson envisages been more necessary to our prospects for survival."
—**Maurice Strong**, Secretary-General of the UN Earth Summit, Rio 1992

"Ross Jackson's proposal for post-collapse strategy is the first plausible, constructive scenario I have seen; an excellent text, even amazing. It is comprehensive, original, and very well written."
—**Dennis Meadows**, coauthor, *The Limits to Growth*

"*Occupy World Street* breaks through the barriers that have shackled us. It is a monumental and inspirational call to action—and a long-awaited blueprint for how the actions should be implemented. Ross Jackson's insights empower us to dream a new dream and give it the energy required to materialize a truly Gaian world order."
—**John Perkins**, author of *Confessions of an Economic Hit Man*

"*Occupy World Street* has the potential to unite hundreds of NGOs and millions of ordinary citizens in the streets behind a single simple proposal that could change the current dysfunctional game."
—**Hazel Henderson**, author of *Ethical Markets: Growing the Green Economy*

"In *Occupy World Street* Ross Jackson tenderly brings us to understand how *capitalism*, *patriarchy*, and *empire* are three suicidal paradigms. These chapters are obligatory. But the last third of *Occupy World Street* is absolutely mind blowing—pure creative genius. Jackson was struck by lightning and disciplined enough to transform the brilliance into a practical action plan. He has cleared the mists and his trumpets announce we do not have to go the way of the dinosaurs if we choose not to. *Occupy World Street* is the Aha! moment launching heartbroken activists into an immediate global collaboration which we could not implement without his ideas. Here they are. Let's go."
—**Clinton Callahan**, author of *Directing the Power of Conscious Feelings*

"*Occupy World Street* is a profound and urgently needed roadmap for the future of human civilization. Unlike most books emerging today on the global crisis, *Occupy World Street* challenges fundamental social and cultural assumptions that are driving the crisis, and stretches beyond painful symptoms to practical solutions. Integrating forty years of leadership in business, science, ecology, philanthropy, and social activism, author Ross Jackson is a true servant of humanity who has engaged in high finance and business without ever losing touch with his concern and compassion for the entire human family. Few analysts have the requisite depth of insight, radical honesty, systemic expertise, and sheer courage to propose such far-reaching reforms of today's world order. *Occupy World Street* is a break*through*. Read it, find your unique role to play in its sweeping vision forward, and then if you haven't already, breakaway!"
—**Will Keepin**, author of *Divine Duality*

"*Occupy World Street* is a breakthrough book! Ross Jackson is one of the world's wise elders, and he sees clearly the collapse of the world system that is already underway. More importantly, he looks beyond breakdown to describe a new world with 'Gaian institutions' far better suited to the reality of an integrated world system. *Occupy World Street* offers creative leverage points and new approaches for moving beyond the obstacles of collapsing institutions and then, with deep insight, Jackson describes a range of new global institutions that can give birth to a world of sustainable prosperity."
—**Duane Elgin**, author of *The Living Universe*

"Ross Jackson has written the definitive analysis of why the current system cannot reform itself and why a completely new system must be born. The corruption of the global financial system, combined with the magnitude of the escalating crisis of climate change, warrants no less than a complete human rebirth. *Occupy World Street* points the way." —**Jim Garrison**, chairman and president, State of the World Forum

"A brilliantly detailed template for how to materialize enlightened global society. Radical shifts include natural phases of instability and unpredictability. Instead of becoming lost in the gaps that are forming between the death of the old and the birth of the new, Ross Jackson shows us how we can direct our energy toward positive change. *Occupy World Street* helps us understand the anatomy and developmental stages of our contemporary crises. Most importantly, it shows us how we can transform and move beyond them."
—**Llyn Roberts**, author of *Shapeshifting into Higher Consciousness*

"*Occupy World Street* is a welcome addition to the growing chorus calling on us humans to grow up and start acting like adults and live together in a finite world more maturely. The longer we wait to change our ways the more difficult and challenging it will be for our descendants. Ross Jackson offers practical solutions to the course correction so sorely needed today." —**John Renesch**, author of *Getting to the Better Future*

"*Occupy World Street* provides both a brilliant analysis of the imminent dangers that threaten to lead to a collapse of our global civilization and a bold and visionary design of global governance that embraces local sovereignty within an international framework for stewardship." **—Peter M. Pruzan**, coauthor of *Leading with Wisdom*

"*Occupy World Street* is an important, timely, and courageous piece of work."
—Thomas H. Greco Jr., author of *The End of Money and the Future of Civilization*

"Economic disasters, climate change, species extinctions, social and political collapses—What next? Realistic solutions would help. And here they are, large enough in conception and sensitive enough in detail, courageous in facing the defining challenges, even exterminating angels of our times, and realistic enough to have a fighting chance.

"That's what you get in Ross Jackson's *Occupy World Street*. We need to break away from the infinite-growth economics that threaten practically everything. Says he, we need to reshape economics and create new institutions, admit that nature has its rules for people, too, and we need to acknowledge that the politics of genuine democracy and sustainability must rule business and economics, not the other way around."
—Richard Register, author of *Ecocities: Rebuilding Cities in Balance with Nature*

"Ross Jackson has been both a successful financier and an inspirational grassroots innovator. This new book brings his wealth of experience to bear in a powerful and pragmatic response to our social, ecological, and economic malaise."
—Helena Norberg-Hodge, author of *Ancient Futures*

"We are as skaters out on thin ice, humming a waltz in our heads. When suddenly we break through, it shocks us to the bone, and in that instant changes everything. If you have seen the Occupy Wall Streeters but can't quite fathom either what they are trying to say or how they might actually succeed, Ross Jackson has something to tell you. Here is a book that lays the Occupy world out in a clear and complete way, from drug-resistant superbugs to Wikileaks, from neoliberal capitalism to the Tunisian Spring. Put your Keynesian monetary theory back in its box. Jackson weaves a story of a world separated too long from nature but now returning by fits and starts to the real world."
—Albert Bates, author of *The Biochar Solution*

"Brilliantly informative, timely and prescriptive, this book has global solutions for the Occupy movement. Simply the best strategy I have seen, and because Jackson himself started with grassroots community seeding, his strategy is well grounded. The Occupy movement will grow and blossom; it will inevitably require a global strategy and here it is! All levels of the global economy must be healthy if we are to have a reasonable human life on this planet, and as Jackson says, the longer it takes for people to wake up and act the more painful it will be. So spread this book and get going!"
—Elisabet Sahtouris, author of *EarthDance: Living Systems in Evolution*

Occupy World Street

*A Global Roadmap for Radical
Economic and Political Reform*

Ross Jackson, PhD

Foreword by Hazel Henderson

CHELSEA GREEN PUBLISHING
WHITE RIVER JUNCTION, VERMONT

Project Manager: Bill Bokermann
Developmental Editor: Ian Baldwin
Copy Editor: Cannon Labrie
Proofreader: Helen Walden
Indexer: Peggy Holloway
Designer: Peter Holm, Sterling Hill Productions

Printed in the United States of America
First printing January, 2012
10 9 8 7 6 5 4 3 2 1   12 13 14 15 16

Chelsea Green Publishing is committed to preserving
ancient forests and natural resources. We elected to print
this title on 30-percent postconsumer recycled paper,
processed chlorine-free. As a result, for this printing, we
have saved:

20 Trees (40' tall and 6-8" diameter)
8 Million BTUs of Total Energy
2,073 Pounds of Greenhouse Gases
9,348 Gallons of Wastewater
592 Pounds of Solid Waste

Chelsea Green Publishing made this paper choice because
we and our printer, Thomson-Shore, Inc., are members
of the Green Press Initiative, a nonprofit program dedicated to supporting authors, publishers, and suppliers
in their efforts to reduce their use of fiber obtained
from endangered forests. For more information, visit:
www.greenpressinitiative.org.

Environmental impact estimates were made using the Environmental Defense Paper Calculator.
For more information visit: www.papercalculator.org.

Our Commitment to Green Publishing

Chelsea Green sees publishing as a tool for cultural change and ecological stewardship. We strive to
align our book manufacturing practices with our editorial mission and to reduce the impact of our
business enterprise in the environment. We print our books and catalogs on chlorine-free recycled
paper, using vegetable-based inks whenever possible. This book may cost slightly more because we
use recycled paper, and we hope you'll agree that it's worth it. Chelsea Green is a member of the Green
Press Initiative (www.greenpressinitiative.org), a nonprofit coalition of publishers, manufacturers, and authors working to protect the world's endangered forests and conserve natural resources.
Occupy World Street was printed on Joy White, a 30-percent postconsumer recycled paper supplied by
Thomson-Shore.

Library of Congress Cataloging-in-Publication Data
Jackson, J. T. Ross.
 Occupy World Street : a global roadmap for radical economic and political reform / Ross Jackson ;
foreword by Hazel Henderson.
     p. cm.
Includes bibliographical references and index.
 ISBN 978-1-60358-388-6 (pbk.) -- ISBN 978-1-60358-408-1 (ebook) 1. Sustainable development-
-International cooperation. 2. Human ecology. 3. Gaia hypothesis. I. Title.

HC79.E5J295 2011
338.9'27--dc23

                    2011039163

Chelsea Green Publishing Company
85 North Main Street, Suite 120
White River Junction, VT 05001
(802) 295-6300
www.chelseagreen.com

FSC
www.fsc.org
MIX
Paper from
responsible sources
FSC® C013483

CONTENTS

ABOUT THE AUTHOR

Ross Jackson has for many years been an innovative leader in both the business and NGO worlds. His business career has been as an independent IT consultant and software designer, specializing in international finance. Among other things, he cofounded in 1971 Simcorp, which is today a leading global financial-software company and listed on the NASDAQ OMX Nordic Exchange. In 1988, he founded the first international hedge fund dealing exclusively with interbank currency trading. He is chairman of Gaia Trust, a Danish-based charitable entity he cofounded in 1987 to promote a more sustainable and spiritual world. Gaia Trust has financed hundreds of sustainability projects in more than thirty countries, as well as several "green" startups in Denmark, and continues to support two major international NGO initiatives—the Global Ecovillage Network and Gaia Education. His undergraduate degree was in engineering physics in Canada, followed by a master's degree in industrial management at Purdue University and a PhD in operations research, the science of problem solving, at Case Western Reserve University. Born a Canadian, he has since 1964 lived in Denmark, and became a Danish citizen in 1972. His current business interests include Urtekram, the leading organic-foods wholesaler in Scandinavia, of which he is the major shareholder. He lives with his Danish wife, Hildur, on an organic farm near Copenhagen.

FOREWORD

Ross Jackson, my longtime colleague, has worked his entire career in the business and financial world. That experience, coupled with his macro view of today's flawed globalization model, led him to reject the unreality of global finance and the neoliberal economic system behind it. After years as a foreign-exchange advisor and currency-fund manager, he cofounded the nonprofit Gaia Trust with his partner, Hildur Jackson, which has supported hundreds of sustainability projects around the world, particularly his and Hildur's ecovillage movement and education for sustainability.

Ross's experience also led him to some conclusions I share: global finance has become a casino disrupting every local ecosystem and social system and must be downsized. Many observers have pointed out that the current economic/political system is simply not working for the majority of people on the planet, but most have been short on solutions. The Occupy Wall Street and 99% movements have energized our efforts for reform. Ross makes a unique contribution in *Occupy World Street* by presenting a radical and comprehensive global solution. As someone who has focused for decades on sustainable development and socially responsible business and investment practices—to create a more livable future—I am eager to see Ross's strategy embraced around the world.

My own critique of economics appeared as early as 1978, in *Creating Alternative Futures: The End of Economics*. In 1995, I helped organize the Global Commission to Fund the UN and coedited its report, *The UN: Policy and Financing Alternatives,* which proposed a financial transaction tax (FTT) on all commercial exploitation of the global commons: oceans, atmosphere, forests, biodiversity, Antarctica, the electromagnetic spectrum, and space, as well fines and penalties for abuses. Ross joined as one of over fifty commissioners and experts worldwide. Vilified then by the World Bank, the International Monetary Fund (IMF), and most economists and financiers, the FTT is now widely supported. It is backed by Germany, France, and other European Union–countries whose economies were decimated by the financial crises of 2008–9 and who see it as a good way to restore their budgets after their foolish bailouts of banks with their taxpayers' money.

Globalization must be reshaped to build networks of self-reliant, local "eco-communities" at every level from urban to rural. These communities are now linking around the world via today's communications tools from the Internet to alternative TV, radio, print, and all media.

As we face the specter of another meltdown of the still-untamed global casino, these local communities can provide safety nets. Local complementary currencies are proliferating worldwide—including in Greece—for use domestically alongside the euro. In Brazil, the central bank has authorized over 200 cities to issue their own locally circulating currencies to fully employ their citizens in businesses meeting local needs. In the United States, the movement to install public banking based on the successful model of the Bank of North Dakota is on the agenda in Oregon, Massachusetts, Washington, Maryland, Virginia, Hawaii, Louisiana, Illinois, and other states, covered by the Public Banking Institute, chaired by lawyer Ellen Brown, author of the *Web of Debt* and other books.

Nation-states that have the greatest power to bring about change are dominated by corporate power and corrupted by money and special interests. They are also the ones benefiting most from the current system. They have no incentive to change, except when their own people revolt as in Tunisia, Egypt, other Arab states, Europe, and North America. Ross's innovative and visionary proposal can break this political logjam. He proposes that change must come from a small group of nations prepared to break away from the old dying political/economic structures like the World Trade Organization (WTO), the IMF, the World Bank and the UN and form a new trade organization, a new "Gaian Congress," a new "Gaian Clearing Union," and a new development bank based on principles that will work for everyone in a just and sustainable world—creating thereby a veritable template for a new global civilization that others can join when they are ready.

Ross intends to follow up publication of this book by initiating a dialogue on the proposal with a few potential nation-states that may be prepared to take on a leadership role at this critical time. I intend to help him as my company, Ethical Markets Media, covers innovations in reforming markets and metrics while growing the green economy globally, and our affiliate Mercado Etico focuses on Brazilian initiatives. Brazil is now a world leader as the seventh-largest economy, a green giant in its natural wealth and in its influence in the G-20 and the United Nations (UN). As a member of the international board of Instituto Ethos, the influential association of ethical Brazilian companies, I know personally of Brazil's enormous potential.

Occupy World Street has the potential to unite hundreds of NGOs and millions of ordinary citizens in the streets behind such a proposal that could change the current dysfunctional game. We see how Latin American countries have rejected the "Washington Consensus," forging their own paths to development. Brazil is providing such leadership. China is leading the world in exporting green technologies and offering new models for reforming financial markets.

What is so inspiring about *Occupy World Street* is its holistic vision of globalization—rejecting the either/or, black-and-white logic of some anti-globalization groups. It is no longer possible, in my view, to espouse a wholesale return to local, self-sufficient communities or to espouse without question all indigenous cultural norms (since many are repressive, sexist, and dogmatic). At the same time, I share Ross's rejection of today's narrow, ideologically based forms of economic and technological globalization. The social and environmental destruction is too visible—culminating in climate disruption and species extinction. Thus, I have promoted the concept of "glocalization," where local communities themselves analyze to what extent they wish to maintain links with national and international economies and in which ways they will de-link and pursue strategies of self-reliance. The Green Transition Scoreboard® highlights this self-reliance by reporting on trillions of dollars in private investments since 2007 in cleaner, greener, locally sourced technologies worldwide.

The oldest question for human society is reemerging: how will we balance individual freedom with communal—and now global—responsibility? Grasping this nettle in the global context, Ross floats many bold proposals for linking like-minded communities and countries in a new kind of global governance with the goal of promoting diversity, localism, and sustainable forms of development. These are similar to the initiative on Transforming Finance, a call to reaffirm finance as a global commons endorsed by some 100 experts worldwide. They are also similar to my own proposals for over-hauling the rules of the WTO (see "Principles of Sustainable World Trade," *Ethical Markets: Growing the Green Economy*, 2007). Ross also cites the inspiring new examples in Latin America, as most countries in that region replace the "Washington Consensus" with homegrown models of more human-centered development.

Ross Jackson's proposals, now endorsed by many of my friends and colleagues, will be debated by many as too sweeping and idealistic. Yet, we are already in the midst of a whole-system transition, and old paradigms in economics and finance are failing to address our problems—falling back on "rearview mirror" approaches of "bond vigilantes" calling for auster-ity, budget cuts, and shrinking governments rather than making smarte policy for our common human future. *Occupy World Street* is both visionary and profoundly practical in facing and dismantling the destructive rules and practices of today's globalization. I commend the author and intend to collaborate with him in all possible ways to achieve our shared goals.

HAZEL HENDERSON, President
Ethical Markets Media (USA and Brazil)
December 2011

ACKNOWLEDGMENTS

I wish to acknowledge first and foremost my debt to my good friend and colleague Helena Norberg-Hodge, who has a better grasp of the dynamics of how the world really works than anyone I know. We actually collaborated on an earlier version of this work, as we had both independently envisioned the breakaway strategy as a novel solution to the crisis. But instead of a joint work, she produced an excellent film, *The Economics of Happiness*, while I put my ideas into this volume.

I owe a lot also to my longtime colleague Hazel Henderson, who has long been on the front lines of the struggle for radical reform, and is truly an inspiring example for all who would work for a more just and sustainable world.

I would also like to thank Clinton Callahan for his encouragement and his detailed proofreading and constructive criticisms of the first draft. Special thanks go also to Ian Baldwin, Margo Baldwin, and Joni Praded of Chelsea Green for their thorough and always constructive criticisms and recommendations. Finally, I would like to thank my life partner, Hildur, for her enthusiasm and forbearance in a time that has been rather difficult.

INTRODUCTION

"The people who are crazy enough to think they can change the world, are the ones who do."

—STEVE JOBS

The spontaneous emergence of Occupy Wall Street in New York in September of 2011 struck a chord that resonated around the world. Like a bolt of lightning out of the blue, the demonstrators in Zuccotti Park—chanting "We are the 99 percent!"—expressed in words and action the suppressed anger and frustration with the status quo felt by millions of ordinary citizens around the world. By October 15, Occupy Wall Street went viral over the social networks, morphing into Occupy World Street when the citizens of 1,500 cities across the planet took to the streets in one of the biggest demonstrations in history to express their dissatisfaction—and with good reason. It is the ordinary citizens of the world who have been paying the price of an economic/political corporatocracy that has used financial speculation, which has no redeeming social value and only serves the interests of the 1 percent, to exploit the rest of society. The result has been an enormous transfer of real wealth from the middle class and the nonprofit sectors of society—the environment, communities, and social structures—to the already wealthy. Susan George, honorary president of ATTAC, calls the phenomenon "one of the greatest hold-ups of ours or any generation." It is a process that has been accelerating for over thirty years and has reached the point where an explosive reaction to colossal social failure had to happen.

The demonstrators were quickly criticized by some observers for the wide range of issues they bring to the table and for their lack of any coherent alternative. This should not surprise anyone because the issues are indeed complex, interrelated, and actually quite a bit broader than most of the demonstrators and their critics even realize. Nor is an alternative a simple thing to formulate, as it involves—as this book will illustrate—a radical revamping of our global economic and political structures if we are to go to the root of the problem and propose real, workable solutions that can respond to the real needs of the demonstrating citizens. The corporatocracy is not only the cause of an inequitable wealth distribution. It is also a threat to democracy, to human rights, and to the rights of sovereign states to self-determination, as I will show. But most important, the reigning economic/political establishment is a major threat to the very survival of our civilization.

The failure of the 2009 and 2010 UN Climate Conferences to deal decisively with the looming danger of climate change raises a worrisome thought—it may not be politically possible to deal with the many global crises that our civilization faces. While this thought will strike many as absurd, it is unfortunately a very real possibility. And it is not just about climate change. The problem goes much deeper. We are facing a multitude of serious threats to life as we know it at this time, threats that were not relevant for previous generations—overload of the ecosystem, overpopulation, unsustainable growth, species extinction, growing inequality, global injustice, and more recently, global warming and peak oil.

There has been no lack of hard evidence and good analyses from numerous sources, no lack of worthy initiatives from thousands of NGOs and others to raise awareness and to suggest solutions, but to what avail? Things seem to be getting worse rather than better. For example, in May 2011 the International Energy Agency reported that energy-related CO_2 emissions are now higher than ever before, in spite of the Kyoto Protocol and other initiatives.

Many people have tried to respond to the rising threats, and in many different ways. In my own case, I have focused on helping the ecovillage movement grow and on increasing the quality of, and access to, education about sustainability. Others have focused on other important issues, like raising awareness, or changing consciousness, or global warming, or social justice, or sustainable agriculture, or saving the rainforests, and so on. Then why is so little being done about these obviously critical issues by the ruling powers that sometimes seem to be living on a different planet? Why the constant resistance? Why is it so difficult?

Parallel with the evolution of this untenable situation, economics has evolved into an irrelevant and abstract tool of the ruling elite, based on the dubious assumption that natural resources are without limit and are there to be used for the sole benefit of those who control them. While modern economists like to consider their field to be a branch of science, value-free and independent of politics, a more realistic view, critical to understanding the crux of the problem, is that put forward by American economist Hazel Henderson, who characterizes economics as "politics in disguise." Economics has always served its political masters.

The current global structure is dysfunctional, undemocratic, corrupt, and exploitative of the environment, the developing countries, and even the citizens of the wealthiest nations. The ruling elites are apparently quite satisfied with the status quo and have no interest in finding global solutions, which can only weaken their relative position in the hierarchy. The current political leadership's inflexible focus on economic growth makes it impossible to deal effectively with global issues like climate change, ecosystem damage, peak oil, and rationing of resources. Meanwhile, thousands of NGOs and millions, if not billions of ordinary citizens are dissatisfied with the status quo and are crying out for change. The dilemma seems to be: those who can, will not; those who will, cannot.

My purpose in this book is threefold: to analyze the root causes of the current political/economic logjam and the barriers that are preventing real solutions from being implemented; to propose global solutions, including new institutions that deal specifically with the identified problems and that work for everyone; and to put forward a strategy to get us there.

We have been far too slow in realizing the true nature of the threats facing us. It is vital that we deal with these global issues on an urgent basis. It is probably too late to avoid a collapse of civilization as we know it due to an obsession with economic growth on a finite planet that cannot tolerate much more without collapsing. I do not believe we can survive in the longer term as a global civilization without major reforms of the type proposed in the latter part of this book.

Personally, I have been straddling two very different worlds for the last thirty or so years. On the one hand, I have been at the very center of the evolving world of financial derivatives, hedge funds, and foreign-exchange fluctuations, both as adviser and manager. On the other hand, I have been an active reformer in the NGO world, very much aware of the unsustainability of our current path and the need for a major shift in lifestyle. This book is thus my attempt to draw upon my experience in these apparently incompatible areas of interest to show a possible way forward toward a more sustainable and just global civilization, with a major focus on economics, since misguided assumptions about unlimited economic growth are central to the crises facing us. Thus, *Occupy World Street* is about collapse and renewal of our human civilization, about danger and opportunity, suffering and vision.

Part 1—"Planet Under Siege"—presents evidence that our civilization is already in the middle of a global collapse that will continue for several decades. It is a collapse that was inevitable, and should not be seen as entirely negative, although it is, and will continue to be, very painful. Collapse has happened many times in the past for regional civilizations, but happens only once for the entire planetary civilization—the time at which the limits to physical growth begin to have serious global consequences. There is hard evidence that we are heading for a major discontinuity brought about by an overloading of the ecosystem as we hit the wall that limits further growth.

For our planet, the climax will be unique in one significant respect. In a dramatic coincidence, the driver that explains 75% of the enormous economic growth of the past 100 years—oil and gas—is about to peak and go into permanent decline during this period of ecological stress. The result of these two phenomena—ecological overload and peak oil—happening at almost the same time is going to result in the bursting of what I call the "growth bubble" and lead into a period of severe energy descent. When that happens, economic growth is going to turn negative rather suddenly for an indefinite period and with wide-ranging and painful consequences for everyone.

In part 2—"Drivers of Destruction"—I will explain why the collapse is happening, with particular emphasis on understanding the dominant world-view that produced both unprecedented growth and an economic/political system that made a collapse inevitable.

In part 3—"The Empire"—we will look at what has been happening in the United States over the past 60 years, acknowledging that the United States is no longer a true democracy, but has mutated into something else, where a "corporatocracy" controls, with a firm hand, all the vital sectors, including Congress, the financial institutions, the military, industry, and the media in what has become a global empire, but one on shaky ground.

Part 4—"New Values, New Beliefs"—describes the shift in values that is already happening and will eventually form the foundation of a new civilization. The impetus for radical change will be the realization that we have been living a lie, dominated by the cruel illusion of unending growth that simply cannot continue. It is time to reinvent ourselves as a sustainable and far more desirable civilization based on a new worldview and universal human values. Such a vision has been gradually emerging for several decades all across the world beneath the radar of the dominant culture—in NGOs, in the business world, in governments, in academia, and in the minds of people everywhere who dream of a better world. A deeper understanding of the coming crisis can give us the opportunity to make that vision a reality. To do so requires that we learn from the errors of the past in order to design a new kind of economics and a new kind of politics that will revolutionize every aspect of our lives.

In part 5—"Toward a Gaian World Order"—I outline the new international institutions that are a logical necessity if we are to realize the vision of a sustainable and just future that works for everyone. I call the result of this restructuring effort the Gaian World Order to reflect the focus on the oneness of all planetary life in the emerging holistic worldview. A key component of the required restructuring lies in a revolutionary reform of the economic, monetary, trade, and financial system, as well as the political structure under which the international community operates. If we allow the vision to manifest, then future generations will function under a far more appropriate form of global governances and within the framework of an economic system that is protective of the environment and the social needs of all world citizens, without sacrificing the democratic institutions and personal freedoms that are two of the most positive characteristics of our time. But it will not happen by itself. Resistance from the dying culture will be formidable.

It is not enough to put forward a vision without a plan to achieve it. Therefore, in part 6—"Getting There"—I will describe a strategy to bring about the desired end result based on a peaceful cooperation between bottom-up grassroots supporters of the vision from across the world and a handful of small nations that are prepared to take on a leadership role at this critical time. The coauthor of an earlier draft of this work, Helena Norberg-Hodge, and I call it the Breakaway Strategy. It's about breaking away from a dysfunctional and dying political/economic system that is holding us in bondage. The task of the initiators is to found a prototype of the Gaian World Order in a Gaian League that offers an invitation to all nations to join the project as equal partners when they feel they are ready to partake in an exciting new adventure into a future of great promise that will work for everyone.

PART ONE

Planet Under Siege

If you look at the science about what is happening on Earth and aren't pessimistic, you don't understand data.

—PAUL HAWKEN, 2009 Commencement Address,
University of Portland, Oregon

ONE

The Assault on Nature

Like a parasite, the paradigm of empire is killing its host.
—CLINTON CALLAHAN, *Directing the Power of Conscious Feelings*

Today, crisis is all around us. We are living right on the edge of breakdown, our well-being—if not our very survival—threatened by climate change, resource depletion, toxic pollution, social breakdown, hunger, and a rate of species extinction not seen in 65 million years. Powerful forces are driving our civilization toward a deep abyss. Behind all of them is a single reality: *ecosystem overload.* Too many people with too-powerful technologies are undermining the basis of our existence. As a global population, we are living beyond our means—living off our natural capital, consuming more than Nature can replenish.

What are the possible consequences to humankind when we weaken the ecosystem on which all life depends? How will Nature react to this intrusion—this assault on its integrity? The short answer is that we just do not know. In spite of our advanced technologies and the laudable achievements of modern science, Nature's complexity is orders of magnitude beyond our comprehension. But react it will, and sooner or later the ecosystem will collapse if we continue on this path. That much is for certain. We are carrying out an unprecedented experiment with our very survival at stake.

An analogy would be the case of passengers removing one screw at a time from a jumbo jet. We can predict with certainty that the jumbo jet will crash eventually, but we cannot predict exactly where and when, or which component will be the immediate cause of the crash. Of course, the analogy is a simplification, because Nature is far more complex than a jumbo jet. We can predict with certainty that the ecosystem will terminally fail if our society continues on its current path, but we know far too little about Nature's complexity to predict precisely where, when, and how the critical failure will occur. It could be a consequence of global warming. It could be many other things.

Let's review some of the possible consequences of ecosystem overload that are already beginning to show up. As you read, I ask you to make a judgment as to whether the risks mentioned here are exaggerated, and whether the response of the political and economic leadership to date is sufficient or derelict.

Our Growing Ecological Footprint

A useful quantitative measure of the degree of sustainability of a region is the so-called ecological footprint. While it is a rough measure, it is the most useful tool we have at this time for assessing the impact of human societies on the environment. The ecological footprint measures the amount of land that would be required by the population of a region in order to provide the renewable resources consumed and the sinks to absorb waste products. This measure is now widely used. Figures are published regularly by the World Wildlife Fund for Nature (WWF) for 150 nations in their *Living Planet Report*.[1] The number of hectares per person required in 1961 and 2005 (the most recently available) is shown in figures 1.1 and 1.2 for major world regions.

The average footprint per person increased in this forty-four-year period by 28%. But since population has also been increasing, the total impact has more than doubled. Relative to the world biocapacity, the total footprint

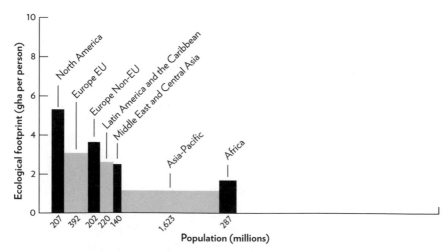

Figure 1.1. Ecological Footprint and Population by Region, 1961. Reproduced with permission from the World Wildlife Fund.

increased from approximately 53% to 130%, as shown in figure 1.3. The 2005 level thus corresponds to an overshoot of roughly 30%.

The available productive land and sea space in 2005 was roughly 2.1 "global hectares" per person for a global population of 6.6 billion, and is, of course, falling as population rises. A global hectare (gha) is one with bio-production averaged out over all regions. The world average actual ecological footprint

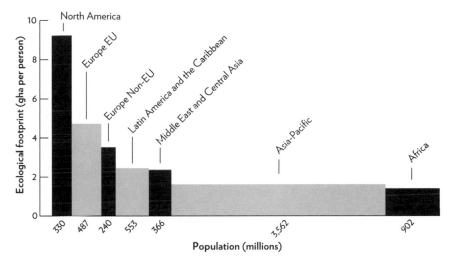

Figure 1.2. Ecological Footprint and Population by Region, 2005. Reproduced with permission from the World Wildlife Fund.

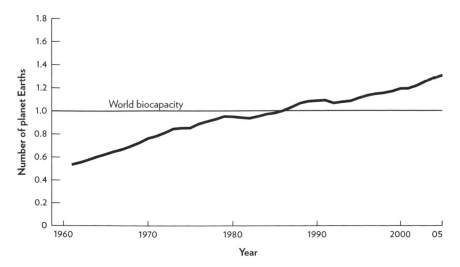

Figure 1.3: Humanity's Global Footprint 1961–2005. Reproduced with permission from the World Wildlife Fund.

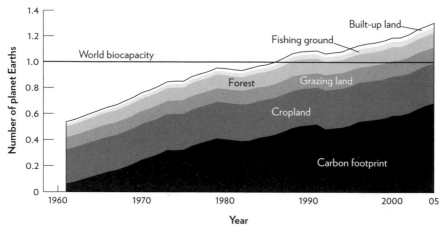

Figure 1.4. Global Footprint by Component, 1961–2005. Reproduced with permission from the World Wildlife Fund.

in 2005 was 2.7 gha per person and is constantly rising as economic growth, urbanization, and population increase. The overshoot is probably just over 40% in 2011. WWF figures are about three years behind for data-collection reasons, but our footprint is thought to be growing by 2% per year.

If we break down the ecological footprint by component, as shown in figure 1.4 from the WWF 2008 report, we see that by far the major contributor in 2005, and the fastest growing component, is the "carbon footprint," or CO_2 emissions—now roughly 50% of the total—as opposed to only about 10% in 1961. In absolute terms the 2005 carbon footprint was roughly thirteen times larger than the 1961 level.

It is therefore not surprising that global warming, which is a direct consequence of rising CO_2 emissions, is currently the most visible example of ecosystem breakdown. Examples of drought, floods, hurricanes, glacial melt-offs, shifting rain patterns, and other consequences of what amounts to about a 1-degree Celsius temperature rise are so numerous now that we all have had some personal experience of what is in store. And this is just the beginning.

North America is by far the greatest consumer and waste producer per capita with a usage of about 9.6 gha per person in 2005, or about 4.6 times its "allocation" of 2.1. Stated in different terms, if the entire world should have the same consumption and ecological footprint as North America, we would need the equivalent of more than three extra planets (360% overshoot). How this will play out is largely uncertain. But at some point, the eroding carrying capacity cannot fail to have dire consequences for the ecosystem on which all life depends.

In other words, there is no way that other regions can ever attain the same level of consumption as North America, even if North America voluntarily froze consumption at current levels. It is just not going to happen. Nor is North America going to be able to continue its current level of overconsumption for very much longer. U.S. president George W. Bush once said "The American way of life is not negotiable," but a more correct statement would be that "Negotiating with Nature is not possible."

Overpopulation

Population growth is a sensitive issue, rife with many taboos and misunderstandings. Some observers claim that we do not have to worry about population growth, and their arguments tend to fall into three camps. Some say population will fall in developing countries once their standard of living reaches that of the industrialized countries. Others contend that the density of people is still quite small, so there is living space for a much higher population. Still others insist food productivity—a key concern when contemplating expanding human numbers—can continue to increase to match the needs of an increasing population.

The first two postulates are correct, but the claim that there is no problem is incorrect. The problem with the first claim is that there is no way that the developing counties will ever match the present standard of the industrialized countries. Before they get to the point where a decline in population might set in, the ecosystem will have collapsed due to overload. The problem with the second statement is that it is not living space that is the limiting factor on population growth, but humanity's impact on the ecosystem.

The third claim is more subtle, as we don't know what the future may bring, but strong evidence suggests that the conclusion here is also wrong. What we do know is that advances in crop yields over the last several decades have been dependent on an abundant supply of cheap oil to drive efficiency gains in industrial agriculture, where oil is a major component in all phases of production and distribution, including fertilizers, pesticides, machinery, irrigation, packaging, and transportation. That access to abundant, cheap oil is soon going to end, as we will see when we discuss the implications of "peak oil" in chapter 2. Another factor that indicates these yield increases are unsustainable is that they are due in large part to the consumption of natural capital in the form of depletion of soil quality and water aquifers.

Population growth is a major factor contributing to ecological collapse, since the global ecological footprint increases in direct proportion to increased population. In this connection, it should be noted that the marginal impact of one additional person born in North America is roughly twelve times the impact of one additional person born in India. Most of the population growth is in the developing countries, which generally have a below average footprint, while population in many industrialized countries is falling. Taken together, this is good news, but the objective fact is that the overall impact on the environment is growing inexorably with increasing population. There is no doubt that if world population today were 1 billion rather than 6.8 billion, all of the crises facing us would either be nonexistent or easily dealt with.

Global Warming

The burning of fossil fuels seemed like a reasonable thing for humans to do once oil and natural gas resources were discovered and the necessary technologies developed in the late nineteenth and early twentieth centuries. Few, if any, guessed that this seemingly innocent act was going to cause Nature to react in an unexpected and potentially disastrous way one hundred years later. Unintended consequences are typical when we mess with complex systems that we do not thoroughly understand. We are likely to experience many more such surprises in the future.

Today, the threat of global warming is the most visible of all the threats facing us at this time. An irreversible increase in temperature could—in the worst case—put an end to human life on the planet. For many years, the economic/political establishment ignored the warnings from many environmental organizations and scientists. However, a major shift in perception among average citizens, the media, and politicians took place in 2006 and early 2007. The acceptance of man-made global warming and its threat to our civilization became widespread and politically correct for the first time, not least due to the solid scientific evidence and analysis of the thousands of participants in the Intergovernmental Panel on Climate Change (IPCC). No longer was the threat of global warming the exclusive domain of climatologists and environmental activists. Former U.S. vice president Al Gore's highly visible Oscar-winning film, *An Inconvenient Truth*, provided convincing evidence for millions who had not thought so much about it before. Even the few remaining hard-core skeptics were having second thoughts after experiencing the warmest January ever in northern Europe in 2007, when flowers that normally bloom in May appeared in January. Nature was clearly confused.

Global warming, the most visible effect of ecological overload, is so far the one global threat that is at least being talked about at the highest political levels. Unfortunately, the UN Climate Conference in Copenhagen in December 2009 was almost a caricature of the fundamental problem of the current model of global governance to deal with global issues. The two major polluters, the United States and China, both stood firm on nationalistic policies and would not budge. The Chinese have a good case in pointing out their right to cumulatively pollute as much per capita as anyone else, and feel they should not be penalized just because they came later into the game. They can also point out that much of their CO_2 emissions are for producing exports to the rich countries, who should logically be charged with these emissions as final consumers. The American problem is grounded in the same political fantasy as the Chinese of unending economic growth.

Extinction of Species

A substantial majority of scientists agree that the world is currently undergoing the sixth known extinction of species, the most recent being when the dinosaurs were wiped out by a meteor crashing into the earth.[2] While the previous five extinctions were spurred by volcanic eruptions, meteor impacts, and other exogenous causes, the current one has been brought on by human actions. Species extinction is another example of ecosystem reaction to overload, and is potentially fatal for humankind, as we are dependent on other plant and animal species for our own survival. A number of biologists have predicted that up to one-fifth of all living species could disappear within 30 years, and that if present trends continue, one-half of all species of life on earth will be extinct in less than 100 years, including one-third of the mammal population as a result of habitat destruction, pollution, invasive species, and climate change. Daniel Simberloff, a University of Tennessee ecologist and prominent expert in biological diversity, says, "The speed at which species are being lost is much faster than any we've seen in the past— including those [extinctions] related to meteor collisions."

One of the major direct causes is loss of habitat as humans take over more and more of the space previously occupied by other species as population grows. Hunting, logging, overfishing, and pollution have also caused significant losses. Many species of birds, frogs, and other animals sensitive to toxins have fallen to pollution. Other life-forms can be very sensitive to subtle changes caused by increasing CO_2 levels. For example, coral reefs are dying on account of a complex of factors, including small temperature and acidity changes in the oceans, while the polar bear's time is running out as the arctic ice melts. Many plants and insects are disappearing without us even noticing, as are many microorganisms in soils that are depleted by chemical agriculture.

These extinctions are going to have serious consequences for humanity. It is impossible to predict specifically how this ongoing mass-extinction event will affect the human population other than to say that it will be severely negative. The problem is that natural systems are complex, deeply interconnected, and far beyond our capability to understand. A species that disappears may have unpredictable effects on the whole food chain, all the way up to humans at the top. Biodiversity is not just about pleasant experiences of humankind in nature, but is about resilience, robustness, and redundancy in the face of change—it is nature's immune system. When we weaken biodiversity, we increase the likelihood of some aspect of nature going off in an entirely unexpected direction that is potentially fatal for humankind, for example, mutations and cell crossovers leading to new kinds of dangerous bacteria and viruses, or perhaps fatal attacks on crops or domesticated animals that we are dependent upon for food.

Genetic Engineering

The topic of genetic engineering is controversial, but relevant as a potential major threat to humankind according to some experts. Mae-Wan Ho, a leading British expert in biochemical genetics at the Open University, UK, claims that genetically modified organism (GMO) supporters are victims of reductionist thinking—a mentality that "misinforms both practitioners and the public." According to Dr. Ho, GMO promoters are grossly overstating the case for the ability of GMOs to alleviate world hunger and are grossly underestimating the mortal dangers that they are introducing to an unsuspecting and misinformed world society.[3]

While her opinions are controversial and by no means a consensus view, they reflect the views of a large number of NGOs who have no commercial interest in the matter, as opposed to the GMO promoters, who mostly have a financial interest. Dr Ho emphasizes that the most serious danger, which could be catastrophic for humankind, is unexpected virus recombination and subsequent gene transfer in wildlife, even extending to humans, particularly so-called "naked DNA," where viruses have their protective coating stripped off. Genetic engineering biotechnology depends on developing artificial "highways for gene transfer and recombination where previously there was only restricted access through narrow, tortuous paths." [4]

We are interfering with the optimal adaptations to the environment found by billions of years of experiments by nature, and are thereby disabling nature's security system. This opens up new possibilities hitherto not allowed by natural evolution, just as disabling your computer's firewall makes you vulnerable to unwanted hacking. Bacteria and viruses are extremely good hackers with millions of years of experience. They are cooperative and clever at sharing genes wherever possible, and when something is possible, it is only a question of time before it occurs.

Dr. Ho claims that commercial pressure has led to regulatory guidelines that are based not on scientific evidence, but "largely on assumptions, *every one of which has been invalidated by scientific findings.*" We continually underestimate the ingenuity of microorganisms, which continually find ways to do things previously thought impossible. In the worst case, such unintended gene transfers could result in infertility or uncontrollable epidemics that could threaten our very survival. Therefore, Dr. Ho concludes, "Genetic-engineering biotechnology is an unprecedented alliance between bad science and big business." [5]

Supporters of GMO foods often claim that the critics' negative views are not based on studies published in recognized scientific journals. An explanation for the paucity of scientific criticism was published in *Scientific American* in a shocking exposé in August 2009. It seems that the corporations selling GMO seeds demand an "end-user agreement" with buyers that forbids any independent research on their products. The authors write: "Only studies that the seed companies have approved ever see the light of a peer-reviewed journal." Elson J. Shields, an entomologist at Cornell University, writing to the American Environmental Protection Agency on behalf of a group of twenty-four insect researchers, complains that "as a result of restricted access, no truly independent research can be legally conducted on many critical questions regarding the technology." [6]

Antibiotic-Resistant Bacteria

The increasing and excessive use of antibiotics over the past half century has had the effect of forcing the development and frequency of antibiotic-resistant bacteria, which take over the space vacated by their dying colleagues—another example of nature's reaction to human interference. Health researchers are in a constant battle to stay one step ahead of these extremely innovative and cooperative bacteria; like methicillin-resistant *Staphylococcus aureus* (MRSA), vancomycin-resistant *Enterococcus* (VRE), and multi-drug-resistant *Mycobacterium tuberculosis* (MDR-TB), and the newest threat—bacteria that produce the NDM-1 enzyme, which can exist within other common bacteria like *E. coli*, and cannot be treated by the current antibiotic of last resort—carbapenems. Examples of the types of bacteria that have become resistant to antibiotics include the species that cause skin infections, meningitis, and respiratory-tract infections such as pneumonia.

When antibiotics don't work it may mean longer or more complicated illnesses, frequent doctor or veterinary visits, the use of stronger and more expensive drugs with potentially serious side effects, and more deaths related to bacterial infections. Resistant bacteria are very worrying, as they could potentially wipe out billions of people in the worst case scenario. The trend toward greater resistance is in part due to the common practice of preventative use of antibiotics in industrial production of hogs, cattle, and poultry as well as overmedication of humans.[7]

Recent trends are alarming. For example, in 1990 almost all cholera isolates in New Delhi, India, were sensitive to the cheap, first-line drugs furazolidone, ampicillin, co-trimoxazole, and nalidixic acid. Now, formerly effective drugs are largely useless in the battle to contain cholera epidemics.[8]

A Japanese woman recently developed a strain of drug-resistant gonorrhea, triggering a worldwide alert about the spread of untreatable sexually transmitted diseases, when she was found to be infected with a new strain, HO41, which is resistant to almost all antibiotics. The research team that made the discovery said the strain was "likely to transform a common and once easily treatable infection into a global threat to public health."[9]

Monoculture

A major part of the Industrial Revolution was the industrialization of agriculture, as traditional crop-rotation techniques, diversity of production, and local self-sufficiency were gradually replaced by monoculture—specialization in enormous single crops, supported by the intensive use of chemical fertilizers, herbicides, insecticides, heavy farm machinery, irrigation, and long-distance transport. There are a number of problems with monoculture techniques, including energy inefficiency, increased rate of soil erosion, compacting of earth, waterlogging (saturation of soil by groundwater), destruction of aquifers, salination of soils, and the destruction of vital microorganisms in the soil, not to mention the negative social effects: increased unemployment among small farmers and related secondary industries and the breakdown of rural communities.

But the main problem from a risk perspective is the effect of the intensive use of pesticides, which not only forces the development of new strains of insecticide-resistant pests, but also often destroys natural pest predators in the process. Because of the lack of biological diversity, such a new strain can wipe out entire crops in devastating attacks with enormous financial and food losses. The likelihood of this happening is increasing year after year.

Few are aware that industrial farming is a major contributor to global warming. Twenty-three years of ongoing research at The Rodale Institute Experimental Farm provides strong evidence that organic farming helps combat global warming by capturing atmospheric carbon dioxide and incorporating it into the soil, whereas conventional farming exacerbates the greenhouse effect by producing a net release of carbon into the atmosphere.

The key difference lies in the handling of organic matter (OM): because soil organic matter is primarily carbon, increases in soil OM levels will be directly correlated with carbon sequestration. While conventional farming typically depletes soil OM, organic farming builds it through the use of composted animal manures and cover crops. Rodale Institute claims: "If only 10,000 medium-sized farms in the U.S. converted to organic production, they would store so much carbon in the soil that it would be equivalent to taking 1,174,400 cars off the road."[10]

Endocrine Disruptors

Endocrine disruptors are foreign substances that act like hormones in the endocrine system and thereby disrupt the physiologic function of hormones. Many studies have linked endocrine disruptors to adverse effects in animals, particularly related to a range of reproductive problems, giving rise to concerns that low-level exposure—no more than what is already found in the environment—at an early stage of fetal development could be damaging to later development. In some reported cases, similar doses had no discernable effect on adults. This is important because traditional tests on new chemicals for approval normally test only for cancer effects in adults. Thus, many chemicals that are potentially dangerous for a fetus in low dosages are being allowed to enter the ecosystem even after traditional testing. Endocrine-disrupting compounds encompass a variety of chemical classes, including hormones, plant constituents, pesticides, compounds used in the plastics industry and in consumer products, and other industrial by-products and pollutants. Some are pervasive and widely dispersed in the environment.

More than two decades ago, Theo Colborn's *Our Stolen Future* warned that low-level concentrations of endocrine-disrupting chemicals (so-called phthalates) present in animal and human fetuses posed threats to fertility and intelligence—by interfering with complex cellular communications and specialization in the very early stage of development. Phthalates are a class of widely used industrial compounds—for example, they can seep into food from the plastic lining of cans, and are now present in dangerous quantities in mothers' milk all over the world.

The effects of endocrine disruptors are controversial and subject to much ongoing research. I include them as a potential threat to humanity because of some indications that they may be affecting fertility levels, though this is far from conclusive at this time. At an international conference on fertility in June 2007, one of the world's leading fertility researchers, Niels Skakkebæk of Denmark, sounded an alarm concerning the phenomenon of declining male fertility due to estrogen-like endocrine disruptors and pesticide residues in mother's milk, a threat he declared was every bit as serious as global warming.

Unheeded Warnings

There has been no lack of warnings of the dangerous path our civilization is taking, but they have all been ignored, with the possible exception of global warming, where there is some movement. There have been different types of warnings concerning our relationship to nature.

For example, several scientists have warned us about the unintended consequences of new biotechnologies. One of the earliest was Rachel Carson, whose *Silent Spring* in 1962 highlighted the increasing threats to our health from pesticides and herbicides from industrial agriculture. Almost a decade later, Barry Commoner's *The Closing Circle* pointed out how a shift from natural to synthetic products was stressing and polluting nature with unprecedented speed. Commoner's book was especially relevant for me because I was not previously aware of how dangerous our technologies had become. These are just two early examples of the many studies, books, and articles that have appeared over the last five decades, all warning us about the path we were following.

In November 1992, some 1,700 of the world's leading scientists, including the majority of Nobel laureates in the sciences, issued a quite general warning with the following appeal: "We the undersigned, senior members of the world's scientific community, hereby warn all humanity of what lies ahead. A great change in our stewardship of the earth and the life on it is required, if vast human misery is to be avoided and our global home on this planet is not to be irretrievably mutilated."[11] There has been no lack of warnings since, but for the most part societies around the world have failed to act quickly and completely upon them. The end result is that we are now dealing with the aftermath of problems that could have been diverted long ago.

Take the case of the historic *Limits to Growth*, published as a report to the Club of Rome in 1972. Based on a study that used a groundbreaking nonlinear computer model to simulate the long-term interactions between global trends in population, industrial production, pollution, resources, and new technologies, the book showed that we were heading for a major crisis, possibly even a major collapse, in the twenty-first century if we did not take action to live within the physical limits of our planet. I was particularly impressed with this work, which used a methodology from my professional field of operations research—a systems-based science of problem solving—in a highly original way. The reason I was impressed was that the authors had used a fairly simple and understandable computer model to illustrate a fundamental problem facing our civilization. It was a work of genius, a study worthy of a Nobel prize. Most technical studies have a tendency to be so mathematically obtuse that the message to the nonscientist gets lost; but not so here.

I sensed immediately the importance of this study, which prompted me to write articles, arrange a conference on the topic, and do whatever I could to raise interest in the subject. The *Limits to Growth* study launched my active involvement with the environmental movement. However, the response to the study was minimal and highly critical, not only in Denmark, where I live, but everywhere. Many mainstream economists, clearly emotionally upset by this incursion on "their turf" by computer scientists, attacked the study vigorously for its failure to acknowledge that prices were relative, and that there was no such thing as absolute scarcity—all the old flawed concepts that defy the laws of physics. They argued that the data was too uncertain and the degree of aggregation was too high, a traditional way to shoot down a simple but essentially correct model. The mainstream economists won the day and did society a major disservice by delaying our understanding of the dynamics of planetary development by several decades. Ironically, a far more detailed regional model with better data was subsequently developed by the Club of Rome, with more or less the same conclusions, but received little attention. The damage had been done.

In subsequent years, I was surprised to see many journalists refer to the *Limits to Growth* study as an example of a pessimistic doomsday scenario that had been proven incorrect, with derisive comments like, "They predicted we would run out of oil by 2000." Of course, the authors predicted no such thing, and the journalists had either not read the book or not understood its message.

In 2004, the authors of the 1972 book—Dennis Meadows, Jorgen Randers, and Donella Meadows—published *The Limits to Growth: The 30-Year Update*. Their major message: things were pretty much in line with what they said 32 years before. The major difference was that we had wasted valuable time and, as a result, had 32 fewer years left to implement the necessary changes. Their message in this second book remains vital to understanding the risks facing us right now, and it has not been understood properly by the media, politicians, or economists, if they are even aware of it.

The authors write: "Most critics believe that our concerns about limits result from a belief that fossil fuels or some other resource will soon be exhausted. In fact . . . we worry that current policies will produce overshoot and collapse." They specifically mention the "dot-com bubble" as an example. "Sadly, we believe the world will experience overshoot and collapse in global resource usage and emissions much the same as the dot.com bubble. The collapse will arrive suddenly, much to everyone's surprise," they write.[12] A major misunderstanding is that the resource crisis will occur when the resources run out. Not so—it will come much sooner than that when prices start to rise rapidly and inexorably. The crisis will be economic in the first instance.

TWO

Energy Descent

Society ignoring peak oil is like the people of Pompeii ignoring the rumblings below Vesuvius.

—JAMES SCHLESINGER, former U.S. energy secretary

The potential threats to humanity reviewed in the last chapter are all in the intermediate term, that is, decades rather than centuries. There is, however, a shorter-term event, years rather than decades away, looming on the horizon that is likely to overshadow concerns about global warming and other problems caused by the assault on nature.

I am referring to the coming peak in global oil production. The subsequent decline in oil supplies is not a threat to survival as such, but is going to cause a more immediate crisis that is a threat to our whole way of life. The basic problem is summarized in figure 2.1, which shows that net additions to global oil reserves have been declining for several decades.

We are consuming more each year than we are discovering. In other words, oil reserves in the ground are decreasing for every year that goes by. Until now, supply has always exceeded demand, but just as reserves are decreasing, demand is increasing, especially from China and India. Thus, it is only a question of time before demand will exceed supply for the first time ever, and there will not be enough oil to go around. When this happens, the consequences will overshadow everything else on the political agenda. Anyone who doubts the validity of the "peak oil" claim should carefully examine the expert comments in table 2.1. The only real doubt among the experts is *when* the peak will occur, if it hasn't already occurred.

Putting an exact date on the peak is tricky because it will not necessarily be a sharp drop-off, but may well be more of a plateau over several years. So we won't know for sure until some time after the fact. A factor that can affect the timing is the market's reaction. As oil prices increase, the economy typically slumps because of increasing production costs and falling profits while demand drops temporarily below supply for a while, oil prices drop a little, and the production peak is delayed—a see-saw phenomenon that could go

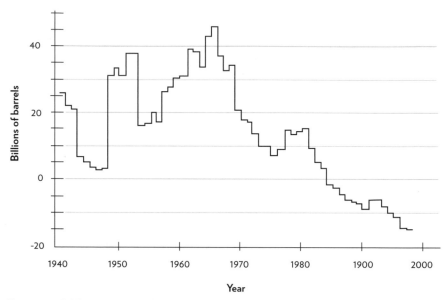

Figure 2.1. Oil Discovery Less Consumption. From Robert L. Hirsch, Roger Bezdek, Robert Wending, "Peaking of World Oil Production: Impacts, Mitigation & Risk Management," U.S. Dept. of Energy (February 2005), p. 15.

on for years. For example, the financial crisis of 2007–9 had the effect of easing oil prices for a while. Improved technology of oil extraction can also delay the peak for a while. But within the life span of the current generation, a traumatic period of energy descent seems inevitable.

While peak oil theory has its doubters, they tend to have a financial interest in denying the threat. For example, OPEC denies that there is any problem at all for fear of seeing increasing investments in alternative energy. Some OPEC members are noted for great secrecy about their actual reserves and tend to grossly overstate them according to most independent oil geologists. Many oil companies and their consultants play a similar game. It is interesting to see that it is only after retirement that many former oil-company geologists have the courage to speak out publicly (see three examples in table 2.1).

Almost all governments are in a state of denial about "peak oil." One reason is the frightening threat of a prolonged economic collapse beyond the control of the political leadership. They hope that the problem will either go away or be dealt with by their successors. Another reason is that The International Energy Agency (IEA), which they generally consider their most reliable source of information, has consistently published far more optimistic forecasts of future oil availability than independent experts. For years, many independent oil geologists have accused the IEA of publishing

Projected Date	Source	Background
2006–2007	Bakhitari	Iranian oil executive (ret.)
2007–2009	Simmons, M. R.	Investment banker
After 2007	Skrebowski, C.	Petroleum journal editor
Before 2009	Deffeyes, K. S.	Oil company geologist (ret.)
Before 2010	Goodstein, D.	Vice provost, Cal Tech
Around 2010	Campbell, Colin J.	Oil company geologist (ret.)
After 2010	World Energy Council	NGO
2010–2020	Laherrere, J.	Oil company geologist (ret.)
2016	EIA	Dept. of Energy, USA
After 2020	CERA	Energy consultants
After 2024	Shell Oil	Major oil company

Table 2.1. Projected Dates of Peak by Experts. From R. L. Hirsch, R. Bezdek, R. Wending, "Peaking of World Oil Production: Impacts, Mitigation and Risk Management," p. 19.

completely unrealistic forecasts of future oil production, but to little avail. In November 2009, however, an explosive UK *Guardian* article validated such criticisms, writing: "The world is much closer to running out of oil than official estimates admit, according to a whistle-blower at the International Energy Agency who claims it has been deliberately underplaying a looming shortage for fear of triggering panic buying. The senior official claims the U.S. has played an influential role in encouraging the watchdog to underplay the rate of decline from existing oil fields while overplaying the chances of finding new reserves." The IEA source added: "The Americans fear the end of oil supremacy because it would threaten their power over access to oil resources."[1]

In February 2011, Wikileaks released cables dating from 2007 to 2009 from the U.S. consul in Saudi Arabia to Washington offering further evidence for the long-held suspicion by independent oil experts that the world's largest oil exporter was grossly exaggerating its reserves. The source was none other than Sadad al-Husseini, geologist and former head of exploration at the Saudi oil monopoly Aramco, who estimated the nonexisting reserves to be an amazing 40% of the government's official number. The motive, he said, was to spur foreign investment.[2]

Jeremy Leggett, convener of the UK Industry Taskforce on Peak Oil and Energy Security, commenting on the leaked cables, said: "We are asleep at the wheel here: choosing to ignore a threat to the global economy that is quite as bad as the credit crunch, quite possibly worse."[3]

Commentator	Statement	Reference
David O'Reilly, chairman, Chevron	"The time when we could count on cheap oil is clearly ending."	CERA Energy Conference, Feb. 2005.
Samuel Bodman, U.S. secretary of energy	"The era of cheap and abundant petroleum may now be over."	Christian Science Monitor, July 8, 2006.
Jeroen van der Veer, chief executive, Shell	"Peak oil does exist for easy-to-drill oil. . . ."	C. Cummins and M. Williams, "Shell's Chief Pursues Simple Goals," Wall Street Journal, Jan. 17, 2006.
Alpha Oumar Konare, chair, African Union Commission	"The era of cheap oil is over."	"Era of cheap oil is over." Reuters, Feb. 4, 2006.
Viktor Khristenko, Russian energy minister	". . . the era of cheap hydrocarbons is over."	C. Hope, "Russia: Era of Cheap Fuel Is Over," Telegraph, June 6, 2006.
Guy Caruso, administrator, EIA (U.S. Dept. of Energy)	"The era of low-cost oil is probably over."	J. Holmes, Four Corners Broadband Edition, Australian Television Program, July 10, 2006.

Table 2.2. The End of Cheap Oil.

The quotes in table 2.2 from a number of leading oil-energy executives and ministers offer firm evidence of the serious nature of the coming peak as cheap oil becomes a thing of the past.

Note in table 2.2 that it is not so much the lack of oil as the exploding prices that worry the oil executives.

The Oil Production Profile

Oil production in an individual field has a very special profile on account of the peculiarities of oil geology—increasing production in early days, rising to a peak, followed by a decline, the whole cycle typically stretching over several decades. By the nature of oil recovery, approximately half of the total available is left when the production peak is reached. At any given time there is a ceiling on how much oil can be taken out of a given oil field. The graph in figure 2.2 ($\cdots$) shows the history of oil production for the United States (lower 48 states), which peaked in 1971.

The graph also illustrates the famous prediction of geophysicist M. King Hubbert in 1956 that U.S. oil production (lower 48 states) would peak in 1971 and go into decline. His bold prediction is shown ($---$), along with his estimate of likely future oil discoveries (——) and total reserves (- - -), all

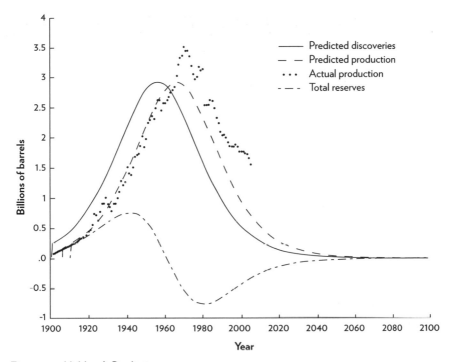

Figure 2.2. Hubbert's Prediction. From Ben Witten, "Evaluating Hubbert's Peak and Improvements?", working paper, "Oil and War," Stanford University (2006).

based only on data available to him in 1956. His prediction was received with ridicule by the oil industry, but proved to be essentially correct fifteen years later and provided the foundation for the much more sophisticated models that today predict a similar peak in global production of conventional oil sometime soon.

Of the 42 states producing 98% of all oil, 30 have already peaked. Total production of countries outside the former Soviet Union and OPEC increased until about the year 2000, but since then total production has been declining. Only a very limited number of these countries are still able to expand production, particularly Brazil and Angola, but not enough to compensate for the declines elsewhere. Both Russia and OPEC are close to peak if not already past, depending on whose analysis you read.

Economic Contraction and Lifestyle Change

If we had twice as many reserves still in the ground, we could probably continue economic growth and the assault on nature for several more decades until the ecosystem collapsed because of overload. But with peak oil so near, it seems more likely that this event rather than ecosystem breakdown will be the prime factor causing the economic growth bubble to burst.

The most significant immediate feature of post-bubble living is likely to be a long period of economic contraction due to the decline in conventional oil production, because our infrastructure, including production, transportation, and settlement patterns in the industrialized countries, has been built up around the unstated assumption of cheap and abundant oil; or alternatively, around a more sophisticated assumption, that by scientific research and technological innovation we can develop a slightly more expensive alternative that will allow us to continue more or less with the same lifestyle and infrastructure. In my opinion, that is not going to happen. Lifestyles will have to change.

Oil geologists tell us that the period of energy descent cannot be avoided simply by investing more money in oil exploration or improved extraction technologies. Geologists have a quite firm grasp on how much oil is likely to be found in the future based on extensive geological surveys and past production figures, as Hubbert illustrated so convincingly in 1956. The big fields have all been found. Production tends to mirror oil discovery with a lag time of about 30 years. No major discoveries have been made for the last 30 years, only minor ones, in spite of much hype about offshore fields in Brazil, Alaska, and the Arctic. The mathematics of oil discovery is well known by oil geologists. Their forecasts of production levels and new discoveries have in fact been quite accurate for over thirty years.[4]

Nonconventional Oil and Gas Sources

Some people pin their hopes on nonconventional oil sources such as the Canadian tar sands and shale gas. However, tar-sands oil production is not only very expensive, but very energy-intensive and has created what some have called the greatest ecological disaster on record. It has been estimated that the energy return on energy invested ratio (EROEI) is barely greater than one for tar sands and may even be less than one.[5] On top of this are two other major problems. There is simply not enough water in the region to satisfy the enormous requirements of large-scale tar-sands oil production. Second, there is an additional energy cost in cleaning up the toxic wastes and reestablishing the original habitat as required by Canadian law. Former U.S. vice president Al Gore calls the tar sands dream "crazy," a huge waste of energy, and an eyesore on the landscape of western Canada. "For every barrel of oil they extract there, they have to use enough natural gas to heat a family's home for four days," Mr. Gore told *Rolling Stone* magazine. "And they have to tear up four tons of landscape, all for one barrel of oil. It is truly nuts. But you know, junkies find veins in their toes. It seems reasonable, to them, because they've lost sight of the rest of their lives." [6]

In recent years, a potential, but very expensive, source of nonconventional energy—shale gas—has attracted a lot of attention in the United States on account of improved "fracking" technologies that allow previously inaccessible natural gas reserves to be tapped. However, the amount extractable is hotly disputed, as is the safety of the methods used to extract the gas, including possible contamination of groundwater and triggering of seismic activity. Some companies are claiming as much as a 100-year supply for the United States at current usage rates. However, Art Berman, a geological consultant with considerable practical experience with the technology, claims that the optimists have grossly exaggerated the potential, and claims 7 years' supply to be a "pretty darn realistic estimate." [7] Commercial shale-oil operations may require oil prices of over $200 per barrel to be profitable.

A Type I Ecosystem

Biologists define Type I ecosystems in nature as those that spring up to take advantage of suddenly abundant resources. They use up these resources as quickly as possible, multiplying in the process. When the resource is exhausted, they move on to the next opportunity, if there is one. They perform a useful function in nature, cleaning up waste and recycling nutrients. An example would be the maggots that decompose cadavers. A problem arises, however, if there is nowhere else to go. Suppose you put a few bacteria in a test tube full of rich nutrients and seal it. The bacteria will multiply rapidly as they consume the nutrients and when the food runs out the population will inevitably collapse and die out.

Our oil-based economy is just such a phenomenon, with fossil fuel as the food. Oil, coal, and natural gas deposits are one-off energy sources that have not yet completed their decay cycle. Once discovered by humanity they were available to fuel material production and to feed an exploding population, similar to bacterial growth in a nutrient. Industrial agriculture literally turns oil into food, and can obviously not be sustained, nor can the resulting increase in population.

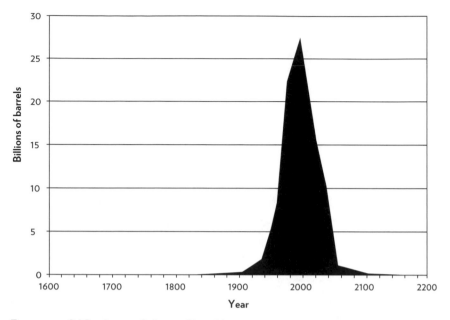

Figure 2.3. Oil Production (billions of barrels). From Richard Heinberg, *Powerdown: Options and Actions for a Post-carbon World* (London: Clairview Books, 2004), p. 35.

If we look at total oil production historically, we see that it represents a relatively short-lived source of abundance in geological time, exploitable by a Type I ecosystem. It is no coincidence that population growth has followed oil production upwards. Without oil, the world population level would probably have remained considerably below today's 7 billion.

A Type I biological system is short-lived and very different from a Type III ecosystem, which forms what biologists call a "climax community." A Type III ecosystem comprises a complex group of plants and animals that live in a long-term, stable, and cooperative relationship. A classic example is the rain forest. A biological maxim, which has been ignored during the twentieth and early twenty-first centuries, is that growth cannot continue forever. Biology tells us that growth will always lead to one of two possible outcomes—collapse, or a sustainable climax community.

Fantasies and Reality

According to most "business as usual" forecasts that neglect supply limits, demand for oil is expected to continue to increase by about 1.5%–2% per annum in the coming years, not least to satisfy the needs of China and India. But even without increasing demand, the falling supply will trigger a crisis. Thus the "business as usual" path is a fantasy in the heads of ungrounded growth fanatics. The reality is that we are heading for a major economic crisis in a few years, with demand for oil permanently exceeding supply and with the shortfall increasing year after year.

By the nature of oil recovery, we will have used up approximately half of the total available when we hit the peak. It has been estimated that, if we continue to produce oil at the maximum rate, we will run out, for all practical purposes, within about 50 years. Since the global-warming effect is largely due to burning fossil fuels, there is no way we can burn the remaining half of our oil deposits in 50 years if we take global warming seriously. If we do not cut back on CO_2 emissions through oil rationing, taxation, or some form of CO_2 sequestering, global warming will most likely get out of control in the coming decades.

Other Energy Sources

A second fundamental energy problem facing us is that oil is a highly concentrated, easily transportable energy source with no substitute that comes even close. The Oil Age of roughly 200 years (1850–2050) will probably be seen by our descendants as an anomaly. The increase in population in the twentieth century was in part explainable by us "eating" oil. For example, if we take into account the oil used in chemical-based industrial agriculture for fertilizer production, farm machinery, transportation, irrigation, livestock raising (exclusive of feed), and pesticide production in the United States, over 400 gallons of oil per year are used to feed each American. This figure does not include packaging, refrigeration, or transportation to retailers.[8] How are we going to feed 7 billion people when oil production goes into permanent decline? How are we going to maintain a society of megacities and an oil-based automobile and aviation culture when oil prices quadruple? These are the issues that will soon be at the top of the political agenda.

But what about coal, nuclear, solar, wind, hydro, geothermal, biogas, wave energy, and other energy technologies? Can they not replace oil so we can continue our high-consumption society? Leaving aside for the time being the problem of ecosystem overload, none of these can replace oil. They are all substitutes in the sense that they are types of energy, but none has the low-cost access or concentrated energy of oil that has allowed us to build up

Resource	Energy Return
Oil	19
Natural gas	10
Coal	50
Nuclear	1.1–15
Wind	18
Solar PV	3.7–10
Hydrogen	< 1

Table 2.3. Energy Return on Energy Invested (EROEI). From Richard Heinberg, "Searching for a Miracle," www .postcarbon.org (September, 2009), p. 55.

a highly technological, centralized, automobile-based society. In the future, when considering alternative strategies, we will have to think much more in energy conversion terms rather than economic calculations based on distorted pricing.

The key question we have to keep asking regarding useful energy production is how much energy do we put in and how much do we get out? It costs energy to produce useable energy. The source has to be mined, the raw product refined and transported before it can be used at the point of need. Table 2.3 shows roughly how much energy we can usefully get out of various energy sources for 1 unit of energy put into production, the so-called EROEI (energy return on energy invested). A figure below 1 means that we use more energy on the input side than we get on the output side. Figures are based heavily on the analyses of Charles A. S. Hall, systems ecologist and professor at the State University of New York.

Figures can vary depending on the resource quality. Oil and natural gas will both run out in this century. The time frame of availability of oil, natural gas, and uranium (to power nuclear plants) can all be measured in terms of decades rather than centuries. None can provide a long-term solution.

Although some optimists claim that there are coal reserves for at least 130 years at current usage rates and quality, there are strong indications that economically available quantities are much lower. The one country that has (almost) finished the complete cycle of coal production is the UK, where it turns out that historically estimated useable reserves were grossly overstated. Dave Rutledge of Caltech has developed a more accurate model of useable coal based on actual historical production data rather than government estimates, and concludes that traditional estimates, including the IPCC's, overestimate useable reserves by 4 to 6 times. Rutledge estimates that 90% of all

Biomass Type	EROEI
Corn	0.78
Switch grass	0.69
Wood biomass	0.64
Soybeans	0.79
Sunflower plants	0.46

Table 2.4. Biodiesel and Ethanol Energy Efficiencies. From David Pimentel and Tad W. Patzek, "Ethanol Production Using Corn, Switchgrass, and Wood; Biodiesel Production Using Soybean and Sunflower," *Natural Resources Research* (March 2005).

useable coal will have been burned by 2070.[9] Others are even more pessimistic, as increasing costs of mining suggest that the EROEI of coal will slide substantially within a few decades, making coal much less efficient within a relatively short period.[10]

A good deal of the current debate is related to how we can maintain our automobile culture in the face of declining oil production. Three major alternatives are under discussion and study—ethanol, biodiesel, and hydrogen. There has been an enormous amount of hype and disinformation circulating recently on these topics, much of it about the optimistic views of hopeful entrepreneurs and other interested parties angling to get a portion of the coming government subsidies. However, if we stick to peer-reviewed scientific studies, we get a clearer picture. Ecologist David Pimentel of Cornell University and Tad Patzek, professor of civil and environmental engineering at the University of California–Berkeley, recently published the results of their detailed analyses of the energy ratios for producing ethanol from corn, switch grass, and wood biomass as well as the ratios for producing biodiesel from soybean and sunflower plants. Their conclusion: "There is just no energy benefit to using plant biomass for liquid fuel. These strategies are not sustainable." Their conclusions are controversial and not universally accepted. However, their opponents tend to have a political or economic interest in biofuels. Pimentel and Patzek claim that biodiesel and ethanol energy can only be kept alive with massive government subsidies and by ignoring the environmental and social costs. Their output-to-input energy ratios are as shown in table 2.4.

These figures are actually overly optimistic as neither the cost to taxpayers of government subsidies nor the costs of environmental damage, which can be considerable, are taken into account. In a separate study, Patzek argues that up to 6 times more energy is required to make ethanol than the final product delivers, corresponding to an energy ratio of only 0.17.[11]

The much-hyped "hydrogen economy" is not a viable solution either. Like biodiesel and ethanol, it takes more energy to produce hydrogen than the hydrogen contains. But hydrogen does have the advantage that it can be stored in fuel cells and used to power electric cars. The problem is, where do we get the energy to produce the hydrogen? Do we use the declining supplies of nonrenewable sources like natural gas, coal, and nuclear power? That is certainly not a sustainable policy. Should we use the limited sources of renewable energy, like wind and solar? First, that would mean diverting them from other more critical uses, and second, there is simply not enough energy available from these sources in the intermediate term. And besides, what is available is expensive. The best we can hope for is to maintain the automobile culture for a while longer, but eventually we will likely be faced with a choice between starvation in parts of the world or large-scale use of automobiles. Whether hydrogen production will be the best way to use the limited energy available in a post-peak-oil world is highly questionable.

Nuclear energy is only viable with huge government subsidies to cover hidden costs that are never mentioned by the promoters. Take, for example, the United States. The first hidden cost to taxpayers is due to a cap on possible insurance claims against private corporations at $10 billion per accident—as mandated by the Price-Anderson Act. The risk of a major accident, typically claimed by promoters to be negligibly small, is simply too high for private insurance companies to accept. This raises an interesting question: who is most credible on risk evaluation, the promoters of nuclear energy or the insurance companies? I vote for the insurance companies. Thus, anything above $10 billion must be paid by the payer of last resort—namely, the taxpayer. In the meantime, the corporate owners can pay out their yearly dividends, knowing that if worst comes to worst, they will be bailed out, just like the "too big to fail" American banks were bailed out in 2008. We are talking big numbers here. It is impossible to put a precise cost figure on a nuclear accident because of the individual circumstances and the long-range generational effects and the human costs, but the numbers can be astronomical.

The second subsidy is the cost of disposing of nuclear wastes, some of which will be around for over 100,000 years. There is still no adequate solution to the disposal problem after decades of research. The only certain way to destroy the dangerous waste products is through nuclear bombardment in a cyclotron, which would be so costly that it will probably never be undertaken in practice. It is impossible to put an upper limit on what nuclear energy waste products will have cost humanity when the final record is written.

The third hidden cost is public research funds. In the IEA countries in the three decades between 1974 and 2002, nuclear energy received 58% of energy research funds, or $175 billion, and fossil fuels 13%. Wind energy received only 1%. In EU budgets for the coming five years, nuclear research continues to get over 50% of the total energy research budget.[12] In a world of no subsidies and full-cost accounting—including CO_2 emission costs— nuclear power plants would never be competitive.

The Fukushima nuclear incident of March 2011 has already forced a lot of countries to reconsider their nuclear power policies. Germany was the first country—in May 2011—to reverse policy and promise to phase out nuclear energy. Also in May, ministers and other delegates from eight European countries (Austria, Portugal, Latvia, Malta, Lichtenstein, Luxembourg, Greece, and Ireland) issued a declaration on the need to phase out nuclear power, stating that nuclear power "is not compatible with the concept of sustainable development and . . . does not provide a viable option to combat climate change." Italian voters rejected nuclear power in a national referendum in June. Also in June, Switzerland's lower house voted in favor of a gradual plan to shut down the country's five nuclear reactors by 2034. In July, the Prime Minister of Japan, Naoto Kan, recommended the phasing out of nuclear energy. At the time of writing, no decision has been made.

Looking forward to the twenty-second century, when the useable oil, natural gas, uranium, and coal have run out, we will probably be left with solar, wind, and hydro as the most promising alternatives. Solar technology is getting closer and closer to parity with oil every year as demand increases and costs decrease. When oil prices start to rise again because of supply constraints we are likely to see a rapid increase in the efficiency and competitiveness of solar energy in subsequent years. Regarding other sources, geothermal energy is certainly available in Iceland, and may be a suitable solution for some other locations, but aside from natural springs, the technology is still unreliable at great depths. Wave energy has theoretical potential if the technological problems can be solved. Large-scale hydro is clearly limited and already exploited for the most part. Micro-hydro can be a useful supplement locally, like biogas. Nuclear fusion energy has been the ultimate energy dream for fifty years but is still far from any practical application in spite of the enormous funds put into research. There are no simple solutions and certainly none we know of that can produce the amounts of energy provided by traditional fossil fuels in the intermediate term. We can look forward to a decades-long period with much less energy available at much higher prices.

Total Oil and Gas Projections

British petroleum geologist Colin J. Campbell was one of the first to warn of the coming peak in global oil production already in the early 1990s.[13] Campbell uses a very pragmatic approach, building upon Hubbert's and other more recent oil geologists' models. He projects a decline in oil production (including all conventional and nonconventional sources) of about 3% per annum after the peak, corresponding to a decline of almost 60% in the period 2010–50. Figure 2.4 shows his projection as of November 2009 of conventional oil production by region, and nonconventional production by type, including tar sands, heavy oils, deep-water oil, polar oil, and natural gas liquids. His work suggests that the production of conventional oil peaked in 2005 and the peak of all liquid categories occurred in 2008. Campbell expects natural gas production to peak soon after oil and go into a similar, but slightly slower decline.[14]

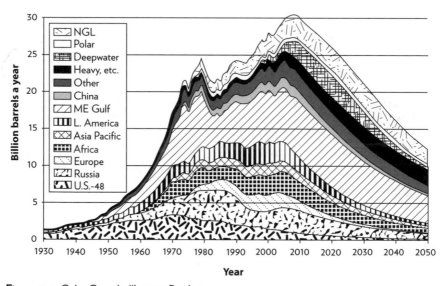

Figure 2.4: Colin Campbell's 2009 Prediction. (Letter to the *Guardian* [UK], November 2009).

Dealing with Energy Descent

Our civilization is about to enter an unprecedented discontinuity, the most critical event in its history, and the world economy is likely to unravel very quickly. The current political debate features religious conflicts, unemployment, threats to the welfare state, bank rescue packages, the balance of power in the Middle East, sovereign debt crises, consumption stimulus strategies, and much more, as if things were going to continue on a "business as usual" path forever. Global warming is also on the agenda now, and the economic and political leadership will try to deal with it *as long as their actions do not jeopardize continuing economic growth*. But we are all in for a rude awakening. The issues mentioned above will all pale in significance with what will soon be at the top of the political agenda.

The coming period of energy descent is going to be a time of great turmoil. With not enough oil and gas to fulfill global demand, a totally new and unprecedented situation will suddenly be upon us. How will the scarce fossil fuel resources be allocated? Will the "market" alone determine who goes without? Will the strong forcefully exploit the weak as they attempt to maintain their energy-intensive lifestyle for a little while longer? Will the international community think longer term and find a way to peacefully cooperate and ration resource usage in a fair and equitable manner? How will the hordes of unemployed and starving masses react as banks, household name multinationals, and countries go bankrupt? We will undoubtedly see quite different reactions in different parts of the world. No one can foresee how the energy-descent scenario will play out, other than to say it will be a traumatic and painful experience for everyone. But I would like to point out one important factor that we should bear in mind no matter what else we do in this period—the risk of falling into an "energy trap."

A fatal energy trap could condemn humanity to become a permanent subsistence civilization if we are not very careful with how we use the remaining fossil fuel resources. The production of alternative energy sources like solar power plants, windmills, wave, and geothermal energy all require fossil fuel energy. It takes energy to mine the metals and manufacture the necessary inputs in order to build alternative-energy power plants. Today this energy can only come from one source—fossil fuels. Imagine for a moment what will happen when the oil and gas run out in a matter of decades at current usage rates. Not enough fossil fuel energy will be available to build or maintain windmills and solar power plants. Unless some unforeseen energy breakthrough occurs, humankind will be doomed to a subsistence-level low-energy future with a much smaller population. This is the energy trap we must avoid at all costs.

If we plan carefully, we should be able to fulfill our energy needs without fossil fuels in the long run. An IPCC report in May 2011 estimated that we could meet 80% of our global energy needs with renewables by 2050 while keeping the CO_2 concentration in the atmosphere under 450 ppm. The major problem, as the IPCC also points out, is political will.[15]

Avoiding the energy trap may well be the greatest challenge facing humankind in the coming decades. Solar energy is the key to a long-term solution because of the enormous amounts that strike the planet every day and will continue to do so for at least a billion years. But in the long term, solar power plants, whether based on solar-thermal or photovoltaic technology, must become self-replicating, i.e., be produced 100% from solar energy without fossil fuels. Until we reach that point, we cannot relax. From that point on, we can always produce more energy than we need. If we continue to use fossil fuel energy for running cars, heating houses, and producing nonessential products, we may not make it out of the trap. Escaping the trap will require sophisticated rationing and prioritizing the use of the remaining fossil fuel energy.

The combination of an oil shortfall and skyrocketing fossil fuel prices due to excess demand is an explosive cocktail. Indeed, we may well be looking at the collapse of civilization as we know it. Therefore, it may be instructive to take a look at the experiences of previous societies that have collapsed.

THREE

The Collapse of Civilizations

Every time history repeats itself, the price goes up.
—GRAFFITI WISDOM

Can the major discontinuity that seems to be ahead of us be compared to previous collapses of civilizations? Let us look at the evidence. The collapse of civilizations is nothing new. It has been going on for at least 12,000 years. Archaeologists and historians can cite dozens of well-known examples of this recurrent phenomenon. The most familiar to modern society is the Roman Empire, but there are many others. The lesson from the past is that civilizations are fragile, ephemeral things. In the evolutionary timescale, none lasts for very long. We would be wise to acknowledge that ours is subject to the same forces that have destroyed other civilizations. Why do civilizations collapse? This question has occupied historians for centuries, and many theories have been put forward. However, now for the first time, we can combine a recent quite general theory of collapse with a recently developed economic measure of the true state of the economy—a combination that leads to a rather shocking conclusion.

Numerous books addressing this question have appeared in recent years. The key factor in William Kötke's *The Final Empire* is the tendency of civilizations to destroy the ecological foundation of life by cutting down forests and destroying topsoil, which results in short-term gains but inevitably leads to long-term disasters. He presents so many historical examples that one asks oneself: How can people be so stupid? Will we never learn? But the same practices go on and on, even in our supposedly intelligent modern twenty-first-century society. Kötke mentions as a prime reason the fact that the responsible political leaders typically live in towns and cities far from the areas being destroyed. "Civilized people's lives are focused within the social system itself. They do not perceive the eroding soils and the vanishing forests," he writes. A related factor is the human failure to adjust population to match the level that is sustainable. An example is Ethiopia, which has one of the world's highest death rates and a devastated environment, yet population continues to rise, driven by each family's attempt to survive. Kötke identifies the human characteristic at the root of this self-destructive dynamic as the "conflicts/competition value imbedded in the cultural mind with material wealth and control as the objects of the struggle." Kötke sees an immanent global collapse as the natural result of thousands of years of this dynamic in action.[1]

In *Collapse*, Jared Diamond puts forward a list of countries comprising the world's worst political "trouble spots," racked by civil war and at risk of collapsing, and a second list of the countries suffering from the worst environmental stress and overpopulation. His lists are identical, namely Afghanistan, Bangladesh, Burundi, Haiti, Indonesia, Iraq, Madagascar, Mongolia, Nepal, Pakistan, the Philippines, Rwanda, the Solomon Islands, and Somalia. His point is that this is completely consistent with the lessons from history—environmental degradation is a prime cause of collapse, if not *the* prime cause. But Diamond claims he is not an "environmental determinist," pointing out that many past collapses might have been avoided if not for human failure to take action, even when a serious problem had been identified. Why was no action taken? Examples would include psychological denial of the problem's existence because the consequences are too painful to contemplate (e.g., living just beneath a large dam); the inability to sacrifice personal freedom for government planning that would be in the common interest (e.g., the well-known "tragedy of the commons"); conflicts between the interests of the ruling elite and the rest of society (typical of most dictatorships); the lack of incentive of major societal forces in the long-term preservation of the civilization (e.g., commercial corporations).[2]

Tainter's Theory

Historian Joseph Tainter, in *The Collapse of Complex Societies*, goes a step further than Kötke and Diamond by formulating a general theory that includes earlier theories as special cases. His theory, which has impressive explanatory powers, is particularly interesting to our task in this book as it specifically relates civilization collapse to *economic* factors.[3]

Tainter sees societies as problem-solving organizations with a tendency to solve problems by creating greater complexity. Generally speaking, greater complexity means "more parts, different kinds of parts, more social differentiation, more inequality, and more kinds of centralization and control." The path from less to more complexity typically involves "change from small, internally homogeneous, minimally differentiated groups characterized by equal access to resources, shifting, ephemeral leadership, and unstable political formation, to large heterogeneous, internally differentiated, class-structured, controlled societies in which the resources that sustain life are not equally available to all." We recognize our modern society immediately in this description, but it is also a fair description of many previous civilizations that have collapsed. Tainter points out that this kind of society is actually an anomaly of history, requiring constant legitimization of the leadership structure for continued survival. If and when citizens lose confidence in their leaders' ability to act in their interests and there are no real benefits *at the local level*, then the society enters the danger zone of collapse.

According to Tainter, the prime, overriding reason for collapse is economic. More specifically, collapse is an example of the law of diminishing returns, i.e., declining benefits to the population. Now, the word "complexity" has for systems theorists a very specific meaning relating to the behavior of nonlinear systems. Tainter uses the word differently, in an everyday sense. When he talks about increasing "complexity," he really means increasing *costs* relative to benefits. Thus, each time a civilization introduces a new level of "complexity" to solve its problems, the cost is greater, and the payoff, or marginal return, is smaller relative to the cost. This follows logically from the fact that society will always choose the least costly alternative first and more costly solutions later. An important aspect of the theory is the role of energy. It is only energy that can sustain a civilization. Every time a civilization increases complexity, more energy is required to maintain the same level of benefits.

In ancient times, the only sources of energy were the sun—which provided food and biomass through photosynthesis—and manual labor. So, barring the discovery of a new energy source, the only way to sustain a civilization of increasing complexity was to expand territory, gaining access to new food sources or exploitable labor through conquest. In some cases, a growth in population within the same territory might be sufficient, provided new citizens were net contributors to the economy and not a net burden. A more complete analysis must include the efficient use of energy and labor, but this can at best postpone the eventual crisis. At some point, each society solving its problems with increasing complexity will reach the point where adding more complexity will yield a negative marginal return.

Negative Marginal Returns

When a civilization reaches the stage of negative marginal returns, a number of things may happen to trigger the inevitable collapse. There is little or no surplus to meet contingencies. Fixed costs are high and difficult to reduce. Taxes are likely to rise with a consequent greater burden on citizens. Money may be debased to meet expenses, fueling uncontrollable inflation. Increasing dissatisfaction of the populace with the system is typical. A sense of apathy develops. A revolution may take place, leading to implementation of simpler and less costly social structures and greater decentralization. Some regions may see it in their interest to break away from the central authority entirely and manage their own affairs locally, further weakening the center in a downward positive-feedback spiral. The economic decline may also make the civilization less defensible and encourage enemies to move in. This is what happened with the Roman Empire when it was no longer able to defend its widespread territories in spite of increasing military expenses and debasing the currency. In this case, citizens on the periphery actually welcomed a barbarian invasion as the lesser of two evils.

What happens when a civilization collapses? Tainter distinguishes between two cases, depending on whether or not there is a "power vacuum." Where a civilization is relatively isolated with no nearby power strong enough to fill the political vacuum, collapse can be total, with major loss of population and dispersion of citizens. An example is the collapse of the Mayan civilization. Where there is a nearby power, negative marginal returns can result in takeover by the neighbor or slow disintegration with political and military weakness, as happened with the Eastern Roman Empire and the later Ottoman Empire.

Let us consider the theory in light of modern society. Here we can find numerous indications that we have entered the range of diminishing returns in a complex global society. A classic example is the depletion of nonrenewable resources such as oil. We utilize the easily accessible low-cost sources first, and as they disappear, we use more and more complicated and expensive methods—offshore rigs, sonar scanning, tar sands, horizontal drilling, satellite surveys, and not least, military hardware to protect access.

Chemical agriculture and its associated practice of monoculture is another example of a technology that requires greater and greater inputs and complication just to maintain the status quo, while causing long-lasting damage to topsoil, water, and soil quality, increasing the risk of antibiotic-resistant pests, and using up irreplaceable aquifer reserves. For example, an increase in world food production of 34% from 1951 to 1966 required an increase in expenditures of 63% on tractors, 146% on nitrate fertilizers, and 300% on pesticides.[4]

Healthcare is a third example of rapidly increasing complexity and exploding costs with diminishing returns to society. This is closely related to the rising costs and complexity of pharmaceutical research, which increase the price of medicines of marginal value, while often burdening users with side effects that are first discovered long after extensive damage has been done. Proper testing of products before marketing would add even more costs.

Financial Manipulations

The increasing inequities resulting from neoliberal economics—the mainstream economic system that has dominated globally for the last thirty years—is a fourth example of diminishing returns to citizens, as the benefits of a more advanced and more costly information and trade system accrue to a small minority of already wealthy shareholders, large corporations in the industrialized countries, and their allies among the elites in developing countries.

Debasing the currency is a classic ploy of a state with declining marginal benefits and increasing costs, e.g., both the Roman and Ottoman empires. A modern case may be evolving as the Obama administration has created record high debt to stimulate the U.S. economy following the financial crisis of 2007–9. This is coming on top of an already debt-ridden economy due to the previous Bush administration's "war on terror" alongside tax cuts to its wealthiest citizens—all taking place in a period of record trade deficits. The next step may well be cuts in the already low (by European standards) welfare benefits and foreign aid in order to reduce the enormous budget deficit.

The up-and-coming BRIC countries (Brazil, Russia, India, and China)—who are some of the largest holders of U.S. treasury bills in their central bank reserves—are worried about the long-term stability of the dollar in the face of record trade deficits, lack of savings, and the enormous financial bailout. They met in June 2009 to discuss currency cooperation and the eventual development of a new international reserve currency less dependent on the U.S. dollar. This could be the beginning of a long-term decline in the value of the dollar and the wealth of the largest economy. For some time now the stage has been set for a very dissatisfied American public, which can look forward to further job losses due to outsourcing, a drop in consumption as imports become more expensive, fewer welfare benefits, restrictions on their civil rights under the USA PATRIOT Act, and an even greater income inequality with all its negative social consequences. Thus the recent emergence of the "Occupy" movement should surprise no one.

Complexity and Fragility

The tendency to solve problems by increasing complexity is common in the business world, often with corporate benefits but with no net benefits to society as a whole. The driving factor in the postmodern business world is the desire to increase market share. For example, Toyota of Japan developed the highly sophisticated "just in time" strategy in the 1970s to cut inventory costs, improve production quality, and reduce customer-response time using logistics and computer technology, and thereby captured a larger share of the American car market. Competitors were then forced to do the same just to keep up. Their market share has not recovered, but their costs are permanently higher. A further evolution of this concept led to supply-chain management in many industries with even more sophisticated computer-based logistics models. Once again, the early innovators increased market share, and everyone was forced to increase their overhead costs, with only marginal benefits to society. The innovator often gets an insurmountable lead. Market share is what is driving twenty-first-century business.

A factor often overlooked in this kind of innovation is that increased complexity usually goes hand in hand with increased fragility and vulnerability. In the above example, a failure of a single link in the supply chain can disrupt the whole production process and, in the worst case, even destroy a company. In other words, there is less redundancy, and thus less margin for error and for unforeseen developments than before. There were examples of this in connection with the "Y2K" or "millennium bug" issue in 2000. Some companies were actually forced out of business on account of computer failures. Fragility is a general characteristic of complex systems that lack diversity and redundancy.

The financial crisis of 2007–9 was another example of what can happen with increasing risk taking combined with increasingly complex financial products such as off-balance-sheet credit default swaps, securitized subprime mortgages, and new forms of financial derivatives. We will look specifically at the recent financial crisis and its relation to the resource crisis in a later chapter.

Tainter does not think that individual nations today will collapse, because there is no power vacuum anymore. In other words, if the conditions for collapse were present and if a nation were no longer sustainable, either we would see slow disintegration or else some other nation or group of nations would step in and take over. The new leadership would introduce reforms, which would undoubtedly involve simplification of overly bureaucratic and costly solutions that had been adopted by the failing society. No nation would be allowed to collapse totally, just as major banks are rarely allowed to collapse. The risk today, however, is that the whole *system* could break down simultaneously, with all nations collapsing together like a house of cards.

Competition Drives Resource Consumption

Tainter's comments on the risk of collapse in modern society are especially interesting with regard to the issue of competition. He sees competition between nations as the driving factor in the current world scene, which is characterized by what he calls "competing peer polities." The rules of the game, as defined by the neoliberal World Trade Organization (WTO), encourage an upward spiral of competitive investment and cost reduction, from which no one nation dares withdraw—at least, not yet. In this environment, as new technologies are developed, corporate competition and instant communication drive everyone to follow suit, with the result that a higher level of complexity and vulnerability is reached, market share shifts to the innovators, and the benefits to citizens at the local level are hard to see, if they exist at all. With each advance, the world becomes more fragile and more expensive to maintain.

We are caught in a trap of competition that "drives increased complexity and resource consumption regardless of costs, human or ecological," and benefits the strong over the weak. The historical outcome of this type of scenario has always been mutual collapse (e.g., Mayan and Mycenaean societies). In our world, this would mean global economic collapse as we all go down together. Exceptions historically have occurred only where there was discovery of a new energy source (e.g., republican Rome, warring Chinese states). However, there is no such outlook at present. On the contrary, we are about to enter the post-cheap-oil era with substantially higher energy costs and correspondingly diminishing returns. Things are likely to get much worse very soon.

Catastrophe or Relief?

While most people automatically think of collapse as a catastrophe, Tainter's theory is not that simple. Collapse should rather be seen as an "economizing process" that occurs when it becomes necessary to restore a positive marginal return on organizational investment. Collapse is simply a better economic alternative than continuing the old ways. Indeed, it is the most rational, most appropriate response to the crisis. For the population involved, it may well be experienced as a positive change to a simpler existence with both economic and administrative gains. "Collapse is not," writes Tainter, "a fall to some primordial chaos, but a return to the normal human condition of lower complexity." [5]

The opposite of complexity is simplicity, so what we are really talking about here is a return to a simpler, more satisfying, more sustainable lifestyle.

This is not to say that the change will not be experienced as catastrophic by some members of the collapsing society. These are important points that we should keep in mind when considering the crisis of modern society and the alternative paths that lie before us. The word "collapse" is normally associated with something falling apart instantly. But when speaking of the collapse of civilizations, a time span of several decades is more the norm. From a geological viewpoint a century is a very brief moment in time, so the analogy still holds in a longer-term perspective.

The real significance of Tainter's theory is that it links the start of a collapse to an economic concept that should in principle be possible to measure quantitatively. This raises a number of questions. Do we have such a measure? If so, can we identify the time when a global collapse actually starts?

Measuring Growth

Traditional economists use growth in the gross domestic product (GDP) as their measure of economic growth, which the public automatically assumes is the same as a measure of how well we are doing as a nation this year relative to last year. But this is not what it measures, and it was never intended to do so. Nevertheless, when politicians and businessmen and journalists discuss "progress," GDP growth is the standard measure used both for historical analyses and forecasts. How is the public supposed to know that the number everyone is throwing about is not measuring "progress" but something quite different? What citizen John Doe is interested in is his well-being and the well-being of society. He wants to know if he will be better off next year.

The problem is that GDP is a measure of total activity. Much of what is included in GDP is decidedly of *negative* value. In other words, economic growth, as measured by a larger GDP, is not necessarily of positive value for society. Some items included are definite *costs* to society and logically ought to be deducted rather than added, for example: environmental cleanup (e.g., Chernobyl, Love Canal, Exxon Valdez, Bhopal, BP in the Gulf of Mexico, Fukushima), highway accidents, prison costs, costs of treating social problems, effects of global warming (increasing frequency of violent storms, larger insurance premiums), unemployment costs, and many health costs. Other items that ought to be included are left out, primarily the informal economy, which is outside the marketplace but is particularly important in the developing countries.

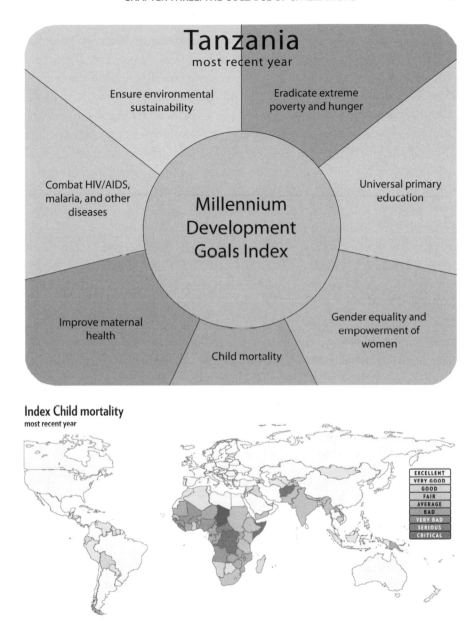

Figure 3.1. Examples of "Dashboard" Reports. From http://esl.jrc.it/envind/dashbrds.htm.

GDP is not an appropriate measure for the effectiveness of economic policy. What we really need for that purpose is a measure of well-being, i.e., the net human results of all the economic activity. This point of view is slowly gaining converts in academic circles, but GDP is still heavily entrenched among mainstream economists.

A good deal of research has been carried out in recent years by ecological economists on the question of developing measures of well-being that would correct for the deficiencies in GDP. For example, the UN Development Index, Canada's Index of Well-being, Bhutan's Gross National Happiness, and the Calvert-Henderson Quality of Life Indicators.[6] All are trying to measure the nonmonetary aspects of the human condition in one way or another.

There are indications that ordinary citizens are clearer about the weaknesses of GDP as a measure of well-being than are politicians and economists. In 2010, almost 12,000 people across industrialized and developing countries were interviewed by the public opinion and global survey firm GlobeScan in collaboration with the green media company Ethical Markets. The poll revealed that more than two-thirds of the people interviewed think that economic statistics like GDP are an inadequate way of measuring national progress. Sixty-eight percent believe that health, social, and environmental statistics are as important as economic data, and that governments should also use those to measure national progress.[7]

In recent years, an alternative way of presenting multidimensional measures of a state's performance—economic, social, and environmental, is gaining in popularity. It is called the "dashboard" report, and is now available as a free software package that can display a whole range of visual quality-of-life indicators on a single Web site, as in the examples in figure 3.1 for Tanzania and Child Mortality.

A Sign of Collapse?

One of the earliest and most illustrative indicators for our purposes is the genuine progress indicator (GPI) based on the work of the think tank Redefining Progress, and shown in figure 3.2 for the United States for the period 1950–2002 on a per capita basis and compared with the more traditional GDP measure.

In Tainter's terms, GDP represents the total costs to society, while GPI represents the corresponding benefits, or well-being. The GPI indicator adjusts GDP for a number of categories of negative factors, including crime and family breakdown, household and volunteer work, income distribution, resource depletion, pollution, long-term environmental damage, changes in leisure time, medical and repair bills from auto accidents, commuting costs, lifespan of consumer durables and public infrastructure, and dependence on foreign assets.

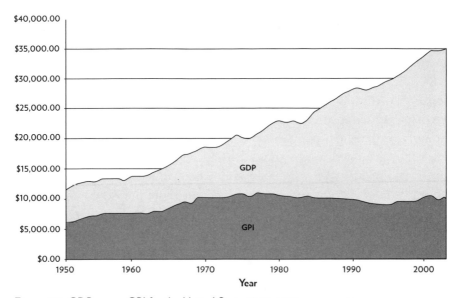

Figure 3.2. GDP versus GPI for the United States 1950–2002. From www.redefiningprogress.org.

Note that the two indicators evolved in parallel until the 1970s. At that point, the marginal costs (slope of the GDP curve) and marginal benefits (slope of the GPI curve) were roughly equal. However, rather than stopping there, the American economy continued to grow, while GPI began to decline. The point of zero slope of GPI around the late 1970s suggests that the optimal size of the economy had been reached. The gap between costs and benefits has been growing ever since. By 2002 the Redefining Progress authors calculated that the American GDP overestimated beneficial production by about $25,000 per person, a really significant difference.[8]

Prior to the 1970s, it could be argued that GDP was a reasonable measure of American well-being. But this is certainly no longer the case. Nevertheless, GDP remains the standard measure of choice for mainstream economists and politicians in their economic forecasting and reporting. The deterioration of well-being over the past thirty years in the face of apparent growth illustrates the need for a total overhaul of the economic system, whose growth fixation is driving our society toward ruin. It would be folly to ignore the powerful message that the synthesis of Tainter's theory of collapse and GPI are sending us. In Joseph Tainter's language, the marginal costs have exceeded the marginal benefits for about thirty years in the United States, suggesting that a collapse may have begun already back in the 1970s.

Other Countries and Measures

In the mid-1990s, the "barefoot economist," Manfred Max-Neef of Chile, based on his observations of a large number of national economies, put forward a "threshold hypothesis" of a national economy's evolution. His theory was that economic growth contributes positively to the quality of life up to a threshold point, beyond which quality of life goes into decline even though growth may continue. This claim was quite the opposite of the claims of many growth enthusiasts who claimed that once "we could afford it," the environment and hence the quality of life would improve. In effect, his idea was to specifically identify the point when marginal costs exceed marginal benefits, which happens to correspond to Tainter's point of beginning collapse, although Max-Neef was apparently not aware of Joseph Tainter's theory at the time.

Max-Neef had no specific tools to test his theory, but they were on their way in the parallel work of another economist. At about the same time, Herman Daly of the World Bank independently proposed just such a measure, which he called the Index of Sustainable Economic Welfare (ISEW). His goal was the same as Redefining Progress, and the resulting index differed in technical details but had many similarities to GPI. The result for the United States is shown in figure 3.3 for gross national prod-

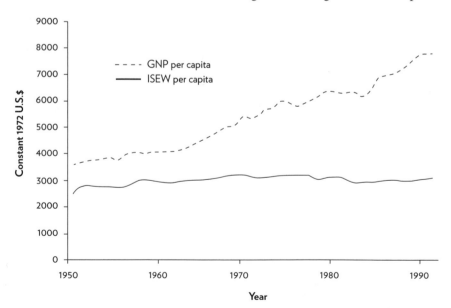

Figure 3.3. GNP versus ISEW for the United States 1950–1989. From C. W. Cobb and C. J. Cobb, *The Green National Product: A Proposed Index of Sustainable Economic Welfare* (Lanham, MD: University Press of America, 1994).

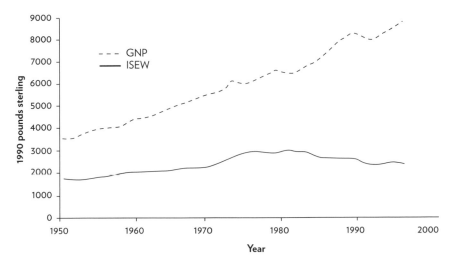

Figure 3.4. Well-Being in the UK. From Ed Mayo, Alex MacGillivray, and Duncan McLaren, "More Isn't Always Better, a Special Briefing on Growth and Quality of Life in the UK," Friends of the Earth (July 2001), www.foe.co.uk.

uct or GNP—an alternative measure of total economic activity similar to GDP—versus ISEW.

The ISEW curve is very similar to the GPI curve with a flat or slightly declining measure of progress since the mid-1970s. ISEW measurements have since been made for other countries as well, including the UK, Sweden, Germany, Austria, and the Netherlands, which all show the same general pattern of declining quality of life since the mid-1970s. Figure 3.4 shows the result for the UK.

The one exception to the pattern identified to date is Italy, which has realized an increasing quality of life over the last thirty years but with an increasing gap between economic growth and "net progress." The gap indicates that citizen benefits are increasing more slowly than economic growth but have not yet gone into decline.[9]

After the Collapse

The evidence strongly suggests that our global civilization is undergoing a collapse that will continue to play out over several decades. In a geological timescale, the collapse is quite rapid—almost instantaneous—like an implosion. We are the generation experiencing this implosion in slow motion as things fall apart around us. The signs are unmistakable, yet most people are still unaware of what is happening and try to carry on as best they can in difficult times. There can be little doubt that we are on a journey toward a different kind of world for the simple reason that this one is on an unsustainable path. But what kind of world are we heading for? Can we affect the next phase in the evolution of our civilization, or is our role to be passive bystanders as events unfold? As the major intention of this work is to propose a grand design for a different kind of society—one that is sustainable and more in touch with reality and the basic needs of its citizens—then it is vital to understand the dynamics of the factors that are driving the planet toward an abyss, and not to repeat the same mistakes.

PART TWO

Drivers of Destruction

An organism that thinks only in terms of its own survival will invariably destroy its environment and, as we are learning from bitter experience, will thus destroy itself.

FRITJOF CAPRA, *The Turning Point*

FOUR

The Evolution of Economic Beliefs

Economics has always been nothing more than politics in disguise.
—HAZEL HENDERSON, *The Politics of the Solar Age*

So what is driving our civilization toward ruin? Ecosystem overload, over-population, unsustainable growth, species extinction, growing inequality, global injustice, global warming, peak oil—we are so familiar with all of these things that it does not occur to us to ask ourselves if there is a common thread linking them. Instead we tend to focus on one issue at a time, often the one that was the headline in yesterday's news. It is my contention that there is a common thread linking all of the above phenomena—a deep underlying link that is not obvious. It has to do with our so-called worldview—the "taken for granted" way that we look at the world. When a child begins to discover the world, he or she accepts the current worldview unquestionably as in "That's just the way things are."

Worldviews

A worldview is not a fixed mental concept, though it tends to be stable for long periods. Occasionally it changes very rapidly in a "paradigm shift," a term coined by physicist Thomas Kuhn in his seminal work—*The Structure of Scientific Revolutions*—which some have called "the most important book of the twentieth century."[1] His book deserves this accolade because it goes to the heart of the causes of the crises enveloping us. Unfortunately, Kuhn's original concept of paradigm shift has been overused and abused to describe everything from a new advertising concept to next year's car design. I use the term in Kuhn's original sense of describing the long-term evolution of science, because it is such a valuable tool to help understand what is happening in the world. You don't have to be a scientist to be affected by a worldview. Changes in the scientific view of the world permeate all of society deeply and for long periods after a true paradigm shift.

The problems we face in the world today are not distinct illnesses, but rather symptoms of a common underlying disease. It is critical that we understand the causes and take appropriate action once we comprehend the interrelationships and what is driving them. Action is required at all levels, from the day-to-day behavior patterns of individual citizens to the way we organize our international relations at the highest level.

To understand what is happening, it is necessary to take a step back for a moment and consider the way a global civilization evolves. At some point in its development, every global civilization will expand until there are no longer new territories available. The civilization will then begin to experience the practical effects of living on a finite planet with finite resources. This is an entirely unique and traumatic experience—happening only once to a given planetary civilization. It is happening to us right now.

Characteristic of this traumatic confrontation with planetary limits is that the rules of the game suddenly and radically change. What worked before does not work anymore. But nevertheless, we continue to follow strategies that have been successful in the past. Evolutionary experience has taught us this normally very sensible principle. However, in this particular case, the previously successful strategies turn out to be disastrous. What previously led to success, now leads to certain catastrophe. But we persist anyway. We have not recognized quickly enough that some fundamental things have changed radically. This is the short answer to why we are experiencing so many related problems right now on planet Earth.

The so-called Cartesian/Newtonian worldview came to dominate the way Western civilization looked at the world from roughly the seventeenth century to the present, and not without good reason. The reductionist, mechanical approach to problem solving inspired by Newton and others, combined with Descartes' concept of the separation of humankind and nature, proved to be a powerful tool in the development of the Industrial Revolution and modern science. It is generally considered to have been a resounding success as one of the key factors in increasing the general standard of living, particularly in the industrialized countries.

However, its successes have not come without costs. Often these costs appear elsewhere in the global system than we might intuitively expect, for example, in damage to the environment and human settlements far removed from, and outside the field of vision of, the centers of the industrialized world of the West. In this regard, it is important to realize that, until recently, the vast majority of people in the world were far less influenced by this worldview, e.g., in China, India, Africa, the Middle East, and South America.

Many of these peoples experienced only the negative effects of this paradigm through colonialism, environmental degradation, and commercial exploitation. In all of these other regions of the planet, more life-based worldviews have always dominated, at least until very recently.

Our civilization has held the Cartesian/Newtonian worldview for too long. The strategies of this paradigm, which seemed to work so well in a "new frontier" society, work no longer in a "spaceship Earth" society. In a world where man is considered to be separate not only from nature but also separate from other humans, it is no wonder that a civilization has evolved that is based on the exploitation of nature and the weaker parts of human society.

The Role of Economics

Central to this evolution is the role of economics. Indeed, if the objective of someone was to drive our civilization to ruin, nothing could do it more effectively than the invention of the currently dominant economic system— neoliberalism. Understanding the economic system is the key to understanding what is happening to our civilization at this time. Therefore, a major objective of my analysis will be to explain the way economic systems work in terms that can be easily understood by anyone.

Economics may seem technical and beyond comprehension to most lay people, but if Joseph Tainter is right, then economics is far too important to be left to economists. It is imperative that all citizens arm themselves with a better understanding of how economics works and the ways that the economic system we choose affects everything in our everyday lives. The economists' way of looking at the world goes a long way to explaining how we got into a situation that is life-threatening for our whole civilization. Note that economics is not something that comes to us from the outside and is beyond our influence, like the forces of nature. To the contrary, economics is an entirely man-made system determining how we organize our relationships and is always capable of reform. Fortunately, the basic principles are really not that difficult to understand, nor do they require great technical knowledge. Therefore, I would like to spend a little time describing how the current economic system evolved, where it went wrong, and where we are today.

This chapter's epigraph by economist and futurist Hazel Henderson reveals a fundamental truth about economics that is not recognized by the general public or even by the great majority of economists. This insight is essential to my contention in this work that reform of the economic system is the key to designing the template for a new form of global governance, and that we cannot separate economic reform from political reform.

There are two equally important aspects to Henderson's very precise formulation. First, economics is inseparable from politics, and thus should be understood as a tool to achieve particular political objectives at a particular time and place. Second, the real role of economics as a political tool is disguised—hidden from the view of a public that is led to believe that economics is an objective science, whose consequences they must passively accept. For example, some modern economists like to claim that the currently dominant "free market" economic system is the natural end result of an evolutionary process. Nothing could be further from the truth. It is a man-made, politically determined system designed to benefit a particular segment of society, and it can be changed.

The Origins

The earliest example of a primitive trade and market economy was probably that of the city-states of Sumer (third millennium BCE in what is now southern Iraq), where the law codes had many attributes still in use today, such as interest rates and commodity prices, and not least normative rules, such as fines in money for "wrongdoing," inheritance rules, laws concerning how private property is to be taxed or divided, and so on.

The earliest known writer on economic issues was probably Chanakya (ca. 300 BCE), who, not surprisingly, was also a politician, being the prime minister of the Maurya emperor Chandragupta in ancient India. His approach integrated economics, political science, military policy, and sociology, as he wrote about monetary policy, international relations, fiscal policy, welfare, war strategies, and the social effects on the Indian lifestyle. His economic writings dealt with such things as opportunity cost, the demand-supply framework, diminishing returns, marginal analysis, public goods, the distinction between the short run and the long run, asymmetric information, and the producer surplus. Over a millennium and a half would pass before Western civilization reached the same level of sophistication in the fourteenth-century work of the North African Ibn Khaldūn, who was proficient in many disciplines besides economics, including history, where his theory of the rise and fall of civilizations later inspired historian Arnold Toynbee.

The word "economy" derives from the Greek *oikonomia*, which originally referred to all aspects of governing a household, later extended to the governing of small businesses. The original concept of household economics was production for personal or community use, not for personal gain. The difference is critical, and the question of economic motive can lead to very different types of societies, even different civilizations. From the viewpoint of the modern reader, this may seem to be a strange claim, as the different political and economic models we are familiar with—such as capitalism, socialism, communism, and Marxism—all assume personal gain as a primary motive. Yet, historically speaking, gain as motive is a relatively recent concept.

Prior to the end of the feudal period in Europe, the behavior of individuals and the production and distribution of goods was determined far more by custom, culture, law, and religious beliefs than by the motive of personal gain. The economic system was a function of social organization. Besides the household economy, the major types of product acquisition were institutionalized in the community organization as reciprocity—barter, gift economy, and so on, often regulated by etiquette and magic and elaborate traditions—and redistribution (a territorial distribution of community production by a central authority to community members according to adopted rules). Markets played no significant role, and whatever markets that did exist were highly regulated by the political leadership.

Socioeconomic issues were related primarily to ethics and politics through most of history, while personal gain was not a motive. It was not until somewhat later in the era of the reductionist Newtonian/Cartesian worldview that gain first became a determining motive, a market economy became important, and economics was considered a separate discipline removed from politics, ethics, and social order.

The Evolution of Markets

One of the best historical treatments of the evolution of economics is by Karl Polanyi, who wrote his classical work *The Great Transformation* during the Second World War.[2] He makes the point that classical economists tend to take as axiomatic the individual's propensity to barter. This assumption, which would seem to be contrary to the historical evidence cited above, led to the nineteenth-century myth that the invention of money transformed society by necessitating the division of labor and the creation of markets, both local and foreign. Polanyi claims that modern research shows to the contrary that the presence or absence of money or markets did not necessarily affect the economic system of primitive societies, for the simple reason that markets did not function within their economies, but without.

Markets were originally meeting places for long-term trade, quite outside the internal organization of the economy, and were not competitive. Nor were they found everywhere. Local markets were of little consequence in this connection. Neither kind of market was intrinsically competitive. Thus, there was no intrinsic pressure to create an internal national market prior to the seventeenth century. Furthermore, local trade in the countryside and long-distance trade in key towns were strictly separated, while according to Polanyi, internal trade among towns and villages was created by the intervention of the state, i.e., it was a top-down political act. In medieval times, local trade in industrial wares was regulated according to the needs of the producers—the craft guilds—while competitive imports were excluded from local markets by the trading towns for the sake of the stability and protection of the local social structure.

These views contrast with the views of most modern economists, who tend to present the gain motive, the market economy, and the integrated market society as the inevitable result of the evolutionary development of the three kinds of trade, international, national, and local. Polanyi argues forcefully that this is not the case; that there have been other arrangements in the past and could be again in the future.

The Mercantile System

The dominant economic system of seventeenth- and eighteenth-century Europe is known as the mercantile system. It was a protectionist system driven by a focus on national sovereignty and the concept of the state controlling the economy with the prime objective of optimizing the use of the nation's resources and creating full employment. The mercantile system recognized the importance of value-added production in creating real wealth, and therefore the merchant class was encouraged to develop domestic production as much as possible to supply the nation's needs, and to export any surplus in return for gold or desired imports. A trade surplus was seen as a primary goal.

The import of finished goods was discouraged, often with import tariffs to protect infant industries that were not yet competitive, while the importing of raw materials for domestic processing was encouraged. The latter policy led to an intense period of exploration and establishment of foreign colonies that could supply the motherland with cheap raw materials. The economy was embedded firmly in the social structure and highly regulated. A major difference between the mercantile system and the later "classical" economic system of the nineteenth and twentieth centuries was that land and labor were not treated as commodities. Wages were regulated by custom and the rules of the guilds and towns. Land was the foundation of political power and off limits for commercial trading. Thus, while commercialism was encouraged, the mercantile system was not a market economy.

The system had negative as well as positive elements. The working class was generally oppressed as the system was designed to primarily benefit the merchant class. With such severe limits on trade, a mercantile system risked developing inefficient industries if it continued for too long. In actuality, most such economic systems were not in existence long enough to experience this particular problem. Whether we approve of it or not, the mercantile system provides us with an excellent example of an economic system specifically designed to fulfill a particular political objective for a limited period of time, and doing it successfully, namely, as a strategy for building a viable economic foundation for a sovereign nation based on competitive industries.

Adam Smith

The Scotsman Adam Smith deserves a special place in the history of economics because of his seminal work *The Wealth of Nations* (1776), which was the first attempt to treat the various aspects of economic activity in a society as an interdependent whole. For this reason, he is often called the "father of classical economics," although he did not use the word "economics," but rather "political economy" for his field of work. Smith can be considered a transition figure between the mercantile system and the era of full-fledged capitalism, which emerged a few decades after his death. He was critical of some aspects of the mercantile system, such as the exclusive focus on domestic production and import tariffs, claiming that greater trade would benefit all parties. But at the same time, he was wary of giving too much leeway to the merchants, whose morals he did not trust. Thus, he supported the mercantile concept of government regulation of the economy to protect the citizens, writing, "People of the same trade seldom meet together, even for merriment and diversion, but the conversation ends in a conspiracy against the public."[3]

Although the concept of "an invisible hand" is not a major part of Smith's work, it suits the neoliberal economists of our day to remember Smith primarily for this idea that an individual acting in his self-interest is automatically acting in the common interest of the entire community ("greed is good"). However, Adam Smith's world was very different from ours. His "invisible hand" operated in an agricultural economy consisting of thousands of small farmers who were unable to affect the prices, which is very different from the monopoly position of many transnational corporations of the twentieth and twenty-first centuries.

Polanyi makes the criticism that there is no evidence prior to Smith's time for his assumption that individual citizens are motivated primarily by the prospect of gain. Polanyi's claim is that for ordinary citizens, personal gain is at best a secondary factor. What really motivates the individual is the maintenance of his or her social standing, a sense of security for the family and the local community, appreciation by others, and the opportunity to use his or her abilities to contribute constructively in some way to the larger society. Material goods are only important to the extent that they further these qualitative goals. Most people, I think, would agree with that assessment. It is as true today as it was prior to Adam Smith. Nevertheless, the highly questionable assumption of personal gain as motive has had an enormous impact on the economic systems that have evolved since Adam Smith's time, perhaps because the assumption resonated with that particular segment of society that was indeed driven by gain—the merchant class. Smith's assumption could be considered an illustration of the tendency of many economists to draw conclusions from abstract theories that are out of touch with reality, a criticism made by ecological economist Herman Daly in *The Common Good* .

Comparative Advantage

Economist David Ricardo introduced in the early nineteenth century the concept of comparative advantage. The basic idea is that every sovereign country has some areas of production where it has an advantage compared to others. Capital and labor will move to the industries and companies within the nation where the advantage of production is greatest and away from those in decline that are no longer competitive. The theory requires the *immobility* of capital across borders. This is an important assumption and a critical point to remember when we come to the design of the necessary global reforms, especially for the developing countries. When capital is mobile, a nation with a very strong capital base could, in principle, dominate all others by foreign investment—as, for example, is the case in today's world of unrestricted capital flow across borders.

Capitalism

Capitalism is a nebulous concept that can take many forms, but the defining characteristic is the commoditization of labor. It arose in the early nineteenth century as a consequence of the Industrial Revolution, which introduced the factory. Prior to this time, merchants organized production and distribution through contacts with many individual suppliers and workers, often working out of their own homes with an anvil or a loom. There was no labor market, and limited risk. The factory system changed all that. The risks of production increased dramatically. It became necessary for the merchant to think in terms of longer-term investment in machines and equipment and establishing a reliable supply of raw materials and workers, and to consider demand for the product, both at home and abroad. For the first time ever, labor became a commodity with a price, and thus part of a market system. The same was true of the other factors of production—land and money.

Polanyi makes the point that these three factors of production are not natural commodities because they are not produced for sale. He called them "fictitious commodities" for this reason. Therefore they require special treatment if the social order is not to suffer. This point was not recognized at the time—indeed, it has never been sufficiently recognized—with the result that the transformation to an industrial-based market economy was a disastrous period for the social order and in particular for the working class, who were forced into utter poverty akin to slavery for a long period until the labor-union movement emerged.

The different forms that capitalism can take are very much determined by how any given society deals with the three "fictitious" commodities—land, labor, and money—and the degree to which the social order is protected from abuse by the unregulated forces of what we might call "raw capitalism." There are infinite ways of dealing with the problem from "laissez faire" (do nothing) on the one extreme to highly regulated totalitarian systems on the other. The problem is in principle a matter of design that starts with the question, what are our goals with this system and what are the constraints? Just as important are these questions: Who is "we" (e.g., a monarch, an elected parliament, a dictator, a global task force, a politburo, a congress of local communities), and in whose interests are "we" doing this?

I would venture to guess that over 80% of all political debates are about, or at least ought to be about, what I call the "design" aspects of the economic system. This is another reason why I do not believe we can separate economics from politics. What do we tax and what does the tax system encourage or discourage? What are acceptable working conditions, minimum wages, and maximum wages for employees? Who issues the currency? Who controls interest rates and the central bank? Who benefits? What are the environmental consequences? Who owns the land and on what conditions? Who owns the businesses? How are they regulated? Should centralization or decentralization be favored—urban life or rural life, private or public transportation? The list goes on and on. To say that one is "against capitalism" is thus a rather empty statement unless a particular instance is specified. There is no one interest group that automatically benefits in a society that commoditizes labor. It all depends on the design. Marxism, for example, can be seen as a particular version of capitalism with a focus on who owns the means of production.

The "Double Movement"

Polanyi argues that prior to the emergence of capitalism, the economy was embedded in society, i.e., subordinated to politics, religion, and social relationships, whereas a truly self-regulating market—the ideal of the merchant class—would essentially extricate the economy from society. Polanyi considered the very idea of an unregulated, self-adjusting market to be a utopia that could not exist for any time without destroying both man and his environment. It should be eminently clear that no market system can exist without government regulations, particularly regarding the "fictitious commodities" of land, labor, and money, which do not behave as real commodities except in the abstract models of the economists. So in practice it is not a question of regulation or no regulation, but how much and what kind of regulation.

Since the emergence of capitalism in the nineteenth century, the dynamic of what Polanyi called the "double movement" has characterized the struggle between the merchant-class supporters of this unobtainable utopia on the one hand and the needs of the citizens for a stable, secure, and satisfying social life, and a supportive natural environment, on the other. The latter is, in its essence, a struggle for local democracy, which is the opposite pole of a self-regulating market society.

Too much power to the "merchants" inevitably results in speculative excesses of unregulated markets leading to periodic market crashes as in 1929, 1998, and 2008, and increasing inequality, which tends to destroy social cohesiveness, citizen security, and satisfaction, and inevitably leads to calls for better regulation, more equitable distribution of income and wealth, and more local democracy, and in the worst case, may even lead to revolution.

The opposite pole—too much local democracy and focus on citizen security and well-being, social cohesiveness, and environmental sustainability would lead to . . . what? Actually, we don't know because it has never been tried. The merchant class would claim that it would lead to slower economic growth, less consumption, and a less dynamic economy that would not be competitive with countries that followed a high-growth, less sustainable path. This claim is true, and the fear of having less consumption than one's neighbor is undoubtedly the reason why no nation has yet dared to try this alternative. But supporters might well ask: Is it not precisely less growth and less consumption we need in order to avoid ecological collapse? And what if other countries agreed to the same priorities in a binding international treaty? What if we focused on cooperation rather than competition? And while unsustainable higher growth may be more competitive in the short run, what about the long-run effects of a degraded environment on the quality of life of our children's grandchildren? Is their well-being not just as important as ours?

Rich and Poor Nations

Why are some nations rich and some poor? Is economic development due to greater industriousness? Or a more favorable climate? Or abundant natural resources? Or free market doctrines? Or better education? Or smarter citizens? Or astute leadership? Or democratic government?

If we look at historical examples since the Industrial Revolution, we see a clear pattern of explanation that requires none of the above. In fact, the necessary and sufficient condition for economic development is quite well established—proactive, goal-oriented government participation in the economy, with subsidies and protectionist policies for key industries. Take Great Britain, for example.

By the mid-nineteenth century, Great Britain was the leading industrial nation. The key components in its strong position were its steel and textile industries. But how did they become so strong? Because Britain was able to combine colonial exploitation and protectionism more effectively than any other nation in this period, not least on account of its military strength and dominance on the high seas. A prime example of this policy was its treatment of India. By the late eighteenth century, India was the world's leading center of manufacturing, producing as much iron as all of Europe combined and having far more advanced steel production and ship-building technology than Britain. In addition, India was a major exporter of cotton textiles. But it had no military to speak of.

The British East India Company had been a major commercial force in India since 1600, but in 1773 the British government, seeing the vast opportunities and magnitude of the task, moved in and forcibly placed the militarily weak India under its colonial rule. In the next half century, India was effectively deindustrialized by Britain. The Indian textile industry was dismantled as India was forcibly converted into a supplier of cheap raw cotton to the new textile factories in England, while India forcibly became a major *importer* of British textiles as Britain built up its industry.

This is the classical technique of colonialism, which locks the colony into being a supplier of cheap raw materials while the exploiting nation gets the value-added and thus far greater profits from a more advanced technology. In the building-up period, it is critical to keep out lower-cost foreign competition that could destroy the infant industry before it is strong enough to withstand the competition. So Britain protected its still inefficient textile production by placing high tariffs on French, Irish, and Indian cotton and woolen imports. A similar strategy was followed with India's steel and ship-building industries, which were dismantled and the technology transferred to Britain without compensation.[4]

Similar protectionist and exploitative policies were followed everywhere where Britain had access for about 150 years from 1700 on, making it by far the major industrial country by the mid-nineteenth century. Then, with India financing 40% of its trade deficit, its industries sufficiently mature to withstand competition, and its colonies having been transformed into captive markets for their exports, it was time for Britain to enter the next logical phase of its economic strategy—a "free market" period; that is, it was time to establish a hypocritical "level playing field" where other countries were pressured to cut their import tariffs and drop their protectionist policies in order to allow the free flow of (British) goods without trade barriers.

The American Experience

If Britain had had its way, America would have gone the same way as India, and would today in all likelihood be in pretty much the same state of poverty as modern India, and would be a major supplier of cheap raw materials to the elites of Europe, primarily to the world's only superpower—Great Britain. It was the American Revolution of 1776 that made all the difference. Unlike India, the thirteen colonies, with help from France, were able to throw off the colonial yoke before it was too late. Abraham Lincoln understood very well the essentials of protectionism and so-called free trade, saying, "When we buy manufactured goods abroad we get the goods and the foreigner gets the money. When we buy the manufactured goods at home, we get both the goods and the money."[5]

Like the good student it was, the United States understood from direct observation the basic rules of the game of how to become a world economic power—proactively support and protect your basic industries, while building up your military strength. Indeed, the pupil became even better at protectionism than its teacher over the next 200 years. The newly formed United States in the late eighteenth century, having learned its lessons well from its former master, successfully blocked British steel with high tariffs and encouraged the buildup of its own steel industry with generous naval contracts to the industry. Later, the government was proactive with government funds in building the railway and high-way infrastructures and the automobile and aerospace industries using American steel and generous subsidies, often disguised as military expenditures. It did the same thing with textiles. High tariffs kept British and other lower-cost producers out of the American market while the country developed its own industry.

Although the United States did not have colonies in the sense of Britain, it accomplished the same result in this critical period through the cheap labor available from slavery and through its Latin American policies. Latin America was earmarked as the United States' "colony" to supply cheap raw materials—a key component in its economic strategy, ensuring that the value added accrued to the exploiter, and not to the poor client state. The United States was strong enough to prevent Latin America from developing competitive industries, while allowing acceptable complementary industries, following the model of British policy in India. With tariffs ranging from 15% to 100% over the years, the United States has been one of the most protectionist of all nations historically, penalizing not only textile and steel imports, but various other manufactured goods as well as wool, iron, hemp, glass, and lead. There have been at times rhetorical support for the principles of "free markets," especially by the founding fathers, but these principles were never implemented in practice. Unlike Britain, the United States had never experimented with a true "free market" policy prior to the late twentieth century.

The Asian Experience

Another historical example of the protectionist principle at work was Japan in the post–World War II period. From a state of devastation after the war, Japan rose to become the world's second largest economy within a single generation by a combination of subsidies for selective manufacturing industries like consumer electronics and computers, combined with diverse protectionist policies to keep out unwanted foreign competition. Japan's success was very much dependent on proactive government intervention and cooperation between different industrial sectors every step of the way, including placing a high priority on the more human aspects of development, exemplified in its well-known lifelong employment policies. Japan also developed "colonies" in its region, but rather than exploiting them, Japan encouraged them to develop in parallel, gradually transferring lower technologies to them while stepping up its own focus on the most advanced technologies having the greatest added value in production. It was an amazingly successful strategy, based on the very opposite of the principles of "free markets."

Other Asian states achieved similar successes, several emulating the Japanese model, but with individual twists—for example, South Korea, Taiwan, Malaysia, Thailand, Indonesia, and Singapore. In all cases, the key ingredients were active state support and subsidies for, and protection of, key industries. In no case did "free market" principles play any role. China too has showed very strong growth in recent decades, in spite of being a closed, protectionist, nondemocratic society with a strong component of state intervention.

In conclusion, there can be no doubt from the historical record that mercantilism—protection of key industries combined with an active, state-directed industry policy, including subsidies where appropriate—is the tried-and-true recipe for early economic development, while the "free market" ideology is typically the way strong, mature economies subjugate weaker, undeveloped economies.

Neoclassical Economics

Prior to the late nineteenth century, the phrase "political economy" rather than "economics" was used to describe the work of Adam Smith and his successors. Political economy was normative, concerned with the factors that caused a particular distribution of resources and income, such as property and political ideology. Political economists were concerned with morals and social structures. What we would call economics today was seen by them as a tool—a means to achieve some political goal.

On the other hand, the new generation of "economists" in the early twentieth century wished to emphasize the separation of their professional field from politics. They were greatly influenced in this regard, by what I have called the Cartesian/Newtonian paradigm of separation. The foundation stone of this paradigm has always been the "hard" sciences—physics and chemistry, where experiments can be replicated, consistent measurements taken, and laws of nature tested empirically. This dominant worldview naturally affected the methodologies of "soft," more human-based areas of research, such as social studies, anthropology, psychology, medicine, and—not least, economics. In all of these areas, an attempt was made to be as quantitative as possible and to introduce the same scientific method used by the physicists. However, the task was severely constrained by the unquantifiable nature of these disciplines, along with the inherent difficulties of replicating experimental results when dealing with human-based systems and human behavior. A tendency evolved naturally in the social sciences and economics to focus on theory rather than experimentation, which was far more difficult to deal with.

The early-twentieth-century economists became more and more abstract and theoretical than their predecessors, with a growing emphasis on mathematics, even though the underlying concepts were often rather fuzzy. As opposed to the "classical economists," they liked to consider their work to be value-free and independent of politics. This approach fit in very well with the dropping of moral, social, and ecological considerations, which were difficult to quantify, and thus became subjects beyond their horizon. A new term was needed for this shift, and thus the expression "neoclassical economics" came into usage around 1900.

Of course, the reality was that they were just kidding themselves. By adapting themselves to the dominant interests and prejudices of society, they in effect became servants of the dominant political elite without realizing it, a phenomenon that Richard Neuhaus called "the worst kind of politics, the politics that refuses to see itself as politics."[6] Keynesian economist

John Kenneth Galbraith commented on this same element of subterfuge as follows: "Neoclassical economics as now taught I do not exaggerate comes perilously close to being a design for concealing the reality of political and social life from successive generations of students."[7]

The Gold Standard

A very important part of any political/economic design is the currency regime. The gold standard was one such regime that regulated economic relationships among the major world powers from roughly the mid-nineteenth century until the First World War, when it began to break down after the major player, Great Britain, went off the gold standard to finance its war effort. The system never fully recovered in spite of several attempts after the war. Historically speaking, it was a relatively short-lived and not particularly successful experiment.

The major characteristic of the gold standard was that the money supply of each participating nation was tied to that nation's holdings of gold via a fixed rate of exchange. There was no such thing as an independent monetary policy, i.e., control of the money supply. Paper money could be exchanged for gold at any time. This was an attractive feature for business, as were the relatively stable prices that followed. Trade deficits had to be paid for by physically transferring gold from the deficit country to the surplus country. There was thus strong pressure on governments to maintain a neutral balance of trade. Imbalances were more or less automatically brought back to normal in a negative-feedback system. The system required a great deal of discipline. Those who did not trust governments to manage their affairs saw this system as beneficial. In terms of Polanyi's double-movement phenomenon, the gold-standard system was definitely far more attractive to the merchant class than to the working class. The adjustments necessary to reestablish equilibrium were very slow and painful—often requiring long-term unemployment—compared to the case where a nation had control of its monetary policy, as is common today.

There were other problems. The amount of gold was not fixed, so new production could cause problems. Perhaps the greatest flaw, seen from a modern democratic perspective, was the subordination of national political priorities to an impersonal mechanism that not only inflicted great pain from time to time, but was a "one shoe fits all" type of system, which drastically reduced the possibilities for the exercise of a nation's democratic right to define other national goals and other priorities than price stability and balanced trade.

Following the Second World War, a hybrid system was adopted that was indirectly dependent on gold. In this system, the United States, which held most of the gold at the time, pledged to exchange anyone's U.S. dollar for gold at the fixed rate of $35 per ounce. The other major nations fixed their exchange rates to the dollar. This system worked for a while, but it too had a limited lifetime, more precisely until 1971, when the United States was forced to renege on its pledge for the simple reason that there was no longer enough gold in existence to reimburse everyone. Since then, the major nations have issued so-called fiat money with no physical backing, and the major currencies have "floated" relative to one another. Most minor currencies are now "pegged" to one of the major currencies, in a variant of the fixed-rate system. Most people realize today that the acceptance of any form of money is, in the last analysis, a matter of trust in the contract between issuer and citizen.

The Keynes Perspective

John Maynard Keynes was one of the most brilliant and influential economists of the twentieth century. He was one of the two chief architects—the other being American Harry Dexter White—of the "Bretton Woods" financial institutions formed at the close of the Second World War, namely the International Monetary Fund (IMF), the World Bank, and the trade organization that became known as the General Agreement on Tariffs and Trade (GATT), which was subsequently replaced in 1995 by the World Trade Organization (WTO).

Keynes' starting point was the observation that unregulated markets fail—a point of which the merchant class does not like to be reminded. They do not always work as they are supposed to in theory. Nor are they self-correcting. Witness the boom-and-bust business cycle, especially the bust phase when high unemployment is a major social problem. No private firm ever developed unemployment insurance or a social security system, reasoned Keynes. Nor would an entirely commercially driven market see any reason to invest in education or long-term fundamental research or environmental protection, or to feed those unable to buy food. Keynes saw, therefore, the need for government intervention in order to smooth out the business cycle and to satisfy social and environmental requirements not fulfilled by the marketplace.

Without such institutions, said Keynes, a country could get into a situation where it lacked liquidity, even though its economy was fundamentally sound. It might then be forced to introduce harsh, punishing legislation, cutting back on public services, putting tariffs on imports, and so on, in order to get through the crisis. Furthermore, Keynes pointed out that economic decisions implemented in one country could have negative repercussions in other countries. He saw, as none before him had, the need for an international body that would have the function of supplying temporary liquidity in the form of loans to tide over a country in temporary trouble and thus ensure international economic stability. In a recession, these funds would enable such a country to take expansionist actions, start up new public works, increase the money supply, reduce unemployment, and run a temporary budget deficit until things were normalized. This would help not only the troubled country, but its trading partners as well, which was a good selling point.

With the international depression of the 1930s foremost in people's minds, there was broad support for Keynes' ideas in the international community. Thus was the International Monetary Fund (IMF) born, as a public institution financed by the taxpayers of the world to provide liquidity when needed, contribute to economic stability, and oversee the functioning of the hybrid gold-based, fixed-rate regime introduced at that time.

Fundamental Flaws in Modern Economics

Since roughly the end of the Second World War the primary goal of almost all nations has been to maximize economic growth, without the least regard for either ecological overload or peak oil. Nor does the reigning political leadership have any regard for whether the net effect of the economic growth is positive or negative. As we saw in chapter 3, it has been negative for over thirty years and has thus been decidedly uneconomic growth. In recent years this one-dimensional focus on economic growth has become indistinguishable from a religion. Critics are considered heretics and are quickly shot down with statements like: "Would you deny the developing countries the same standard of living as us?"

There are two fundamental flaws in the reigning version of economics. Consider the first one: the treatment of the environment as a subset of economics, rather than the reverse—treating economics as a mechanism of resource allocation that operates within the physical restrictions of ecological space. In other words, economists perceive the environment as a collection of resources for humanity's use rather than seeing humanity as an integral part of, and inseparable from, a living and complex organism we call Nature. The consequences of this error are enormous. One of the major consequences is the concept of relative prices of resources. Thus, when one resource gets used up, the economist assumes we can switch to the next cheapest substitute ad infinitum. The price goes up each time, but there are *no limits to growth* in this theory.

The problem with the economists' assumption of relative prices and no limits to growth is that it is in direct conflict with one of the most fundamental and irrefutable laws of physics—the second law of thermodynamics. This law states a fundamental fact about the irreversibility of nature. The nonrenewable resources of our world—minerals, oil, natural gas, etc.—are highly ordered and physically concentrated, having what physicists call low entropy (concentrated). Once these resources are used, the materials and energy are dissipated and are no longer available to do useful work. They are then said to have high entropy (dissipated). The law states that the flow of all processes in a closed system—such as the sun-earth ecosystem—are one-way and irreversible, from low entropy to high entropy. This first flaw allows economists to ignore problems of limited resources, ecosystem overload, and energy descent. It is a truism that we often see only what we expect to see. Economists can literally not see these problems because they are not included in their differential equations. It is as if our civilization is sailing down the Niagara River, and our economist guides, who are servants of the political leadership, have neither compass nor map. They will not see the problems until we go over the waterfall.

The second major flaw in modern economics is the way in which economists model growth. This is especially dangerous because the ruling elite tends to pay more attention to economists than to physicists. I have a different view, perhaps because I studied physics before I studied economics. In the following paragraphs, I will outline what the dispute between economists and physicists is all about as regards growth models, and why the current economic system is one of the main drivers pushing global society toward a major discontinuity.

Growth, Energy, and GDP

When asked about the effect of a decline in oil supply on gross domestic product (GDP), a mainstream economist would go to the national accounts and note that energy accounts for about 5% of GDP. So he would estimate that a 1% drop in energy would result in roughly a 0.05% drop in GDP. Energy descent? Nothing to worry about. A physicist would disagree, and claim that there is indeed a great deal to worry about.

The mainstream economist's theoretical approach to economic growth is to assume that growth is a function of two factors only—capital and labor. Until the 1950s, when reliable national-account data became available in the United States for the first time, little testing of the theory had been possible. That changed with the seminal work of American economist Robert Solow, who used the newly available historical data to test the predictive ability of the classical Cobb-Douglas model for growth. The most striking result of Solow's model is that capital and labor can only account for *one-quarter* of the actual growth in GDP for the United States in the twentieth century. Actual growth was far greater than the model's prediction, as shown in figure 4.1. The error factor was labeled "technological progress" by Solow. However, giving it a name did not make it any clearer just what it was that this residual actually represented. Other economists dubbed it the "Solow residual." Whatever we call it, it is not a well-defined concept, and is not measurable except as a residue.

There are a number of questionable assumptions in the Solow model. It assumes a one-sector economy, which implies that "technological progress"

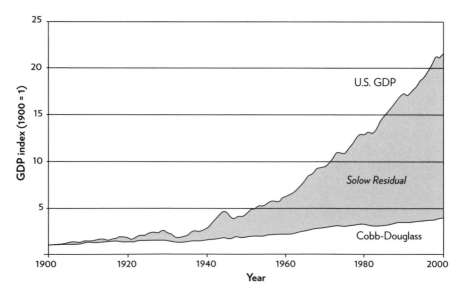

Figure 4.1. Solow: Predicted and Actual U.S. Growth. From Robert U. Ayres and Benjamin Warr, *The Economic Growth Engine: How Energy and Work Drive Material Prosperity* (UK: Edward Elgar, 2009), p. 189.

is not a result of capital and labor, as one might intuitively expect, but rather comes from somewhere outside, for example, "manna from heaven," as some critics sarcastically suggested. Furthermore, the model assumes that the productivities of labor and capital are constant, which is hardly consistent with the idea of technological change. These are dubious assumptions. The model implies that the relative importance to growth is reflected in the monetized value of the two factors as reflected in the national accounts (where labor accounts for about 70% and capital about 30%). Thus, a 1% increase in real labor costs would be expected to bring about a 0.7% increase in GNP. In spite of the obvious oversimplifications and deficiencies of the model, it remains the standard one used by economists to this day. The fact is that economic theory can tell us very little about what determines economic growth.

In recent years, the growth-prediction problem has begun to attract the attention of some physicists, who were shocked to find that economists had no concept of physical resources in their growth models, and thus no concept of limits to growth. The accounting approach to economic growth struck the physicists, with their knowledge of the second law of thermodynamics, as far removed from reality.

One of these is Professor Robert Ayres of INSEAD, a physicist by training, who turned his attention later in his career to economic-growth theories seen from a physicist's perspective. Ayres modified Solow's capital/labor model to include a third factor, which he called "useful work," in a more comprehensive two-sector model. Useful work is calculated by taking the total energy input (in joules) and multiplying by the conversion efficiency at any time to compute useful output for all forms of energy (electricity being the most important). The conversion factor increased dramatically during the twentieth century and provides the sought after explanation for the Solow residual.

Figure 4.2 shows Ayres' prediction versus the actual GDP for the twentieth century in the United States.

The Ayres model was extremely good—a major improvement over Solow's model. The key message with the Ayres model is that *75% of GDP growth*—and not 5% as suggested by the accounting approach—is explained by an increase in net energy use. This is a factor 15 difference, which is enormous! If 75% of growth is due to net energy use, then a 3% annual decline in oil and gas—as forecast by Colin Campbell—can be expected to cause a long-term 2.25% per annum decline in American GDP, and not just 0.15% as in the mainstream economics model. This is major negative growth never seen before in mature economies for a prolonged period, and will come as a shock. This is an important point to keep in mind in understanding the

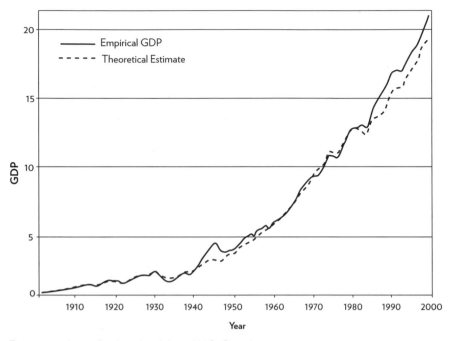

Figure 4.2. Ayres: Predicted and Actual U.S. Growth. From Robert U. Ayres and Benjamin Warr, "Accounting for Growth: The Role of Physical Work," *Structural Change and Economic Dynamics* 16 (2005), p. 196.

complacency of mainstream economists toward peak oil. Ayres concludes: "Economic growth depends on producing continuously greater quantities of useful work" (i.e., more and more net energy).[8] In the coming world of energy descent, the writing is on the wall for all who have the sense to read it.

The Decoupling of Growth and Energy?

Some optimists argue that the above negative growth calculation is exaggerated because economic growth can be decoupled from energy use (and hence CO_2 emissions), with reference to the general trend in many countries—particularly China—toward lower energy use per unit of GDP. Reference is also often made to the widely publicized claim that Denmark was able to increase GDP in the period 1990–2007 by 44% while CO_2 emissions fell by 25%, as shown in figure 4.3.

However, the Danish figures are grossly misleading. First, the CO_2 emissions by the aviation and shipping sectors—Denmark is a major shipping nation—were *excluded* while the rapid growth of shipping income in this period was *included* in GDP. Emissions due to burning biomass were also

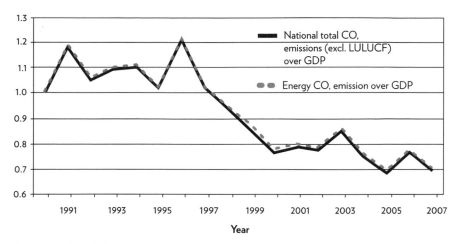

Figure 4.3. Danish Decoupling of GDP Growth and CO_2 Emissions? From E. Lyck et al., "Indicators for Danish Greenhouse Gas Emissions from 1990 to 2007," National Environmental Research Institute, Aarhus University, report no. 754 (December, 2009); see www.dmu.dk.

omitted. These exceptions are standard procedure for the Kyoto Protocol, which tells us something about how deficient this protocol is in practice. According to the Danish Environmental Agency, if shipping and biomass emissions are included, the Danish CO_2 emissions in 2005–7 were actually *up* 62% since 1990, giving a CO_2/GDP ratio of 1.41 for 2005–7 rather than the graph's figure of 0.75, i.e., relative to GDP, CO_2 emissions were *up* 41% rather than *down* 25%—quite a difference![9]

But this is just the beginning of the exaggerations. Also excluded from the graph are the CO_2 emissions due to outsourcing production (mostly to China) and importing the final products rather than producing them domestically. After all, where the emissions occur is not important. It is the final consumer who should bear the costs of CO_2 emissions. For example, in Denmark's case, the WWF has calculated that consumer-based CO_2 emissions *increased* by 40% in the period 2001–6, while the official Danish statistics (not including imported goods) claimed a *decrease* of 4% for the same period. The WWF report concludes: "Danish consumption, in spite of the Kyoto Protocol, is increasing its burden on the global climate because we cause global CO_2 emissions in countries not included in the Kyoto protocol. In this way, we are slowly undermining the purpose of the Kyoto protocol, whilst making it harder for the rapidly developing countries to be included in a global climate deal because an important part of the emissions originating in their countries are in reality caused by consumption in the rich countries." This conclusion is not limited to Denmark. It holds for almost all the OECD countries.[10]

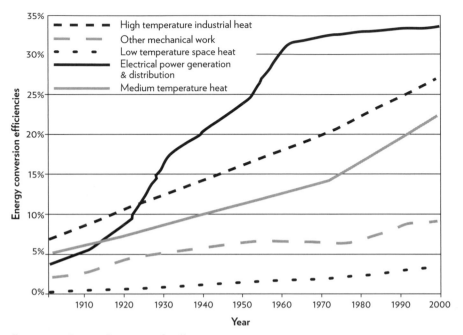

Figure 4.4. Energy Conversion Coefficients, 1900–1998. From Ayres and Warr, "Accounting for Growth," p. 188.

It is correct that not all the CO_2 emitted by Danish ships can be attributed to Danish consumption, and it is also true that some of the domestic Danish emissions were undoubtedly for exported products. But the moral is: be very careful with CO_2 emissions statistics, which can often obfuscate more than elucidate.

A second factor that goes a long way to explaining the apparent declining energy use per unit GDP in recent decades can be deduced from Ayres' model, namely, in the difference between gross and net energy, i.e., useful work. The standard measure typically quoted in energy/GDP ratios is the gross energy, which can decline quite a bit in the short run even as the net energy/GDP ratio remains fairly constant. Figure 4.4 from Ayres illustrates this point. Note how conversion efficiency increased considerably throughout the twentieth century in the United States for several types of energy.

The efficiency of the most important energy source—electric power—increased most, from about 4% to 33% during the twentieth century, corresponding to a an 8-fold drop in gross energy used to produce the same amount of net energy. However, the recent trend is rather flat, suggesting that further increases will be much harder to come by. It is net energy, not gross energy, that explains economic growth according to Ayres, and while it may appear that gross energy use is "decoupled" from economic growth, net energy is not. The primary explanation for the declining ratio of gross energy to GDP is the increasing efficiency in energy conversion. That trend can continue for a while, but not without limit. In the long run, economic growth seems to follow net energy use very closely, in which case a longer-term decoupling of economic growth and net energy use is wishful thinking.

Speculative Bubbles

The most important single factor that is driving our civilization toward ecological collapse is the promotion of greater per capita consumption as the primary goal of every nation state at a time when we are already over-consuming. It does not take a great deal of intuitive insight to realize the fallacy of unending economic growth, as Kenneth Boulding so colorfully pointed out when he said, "Anyone who believes exponential growth can go on forever in a finite world is either a madman or an economist." He was himself an accomplished economist, but obviously, of a different kind, more in the line of Smith, Ricardo, and Keynes, who all had a more sophisticated, more life-based view of economics than the neoliberal economic ideology that currently dominates global society.

Future generations will ask: how was it that such a patently absurd idea as unending physical growth could have become mainstream policy? Part of the answer can be found in the realm of mass psychology operating within a worldview that is focused on satisfying human needs with "more stuff." History is replete with speculative bubbles that have burst. Two of the best known are the "tulip mania bubble" in Holland (1637) and the "South Sea bubble" in the UK (1720).[11] In more recent years the "dot-com bubble" in the United States (2000) is still fresh in our collective memory, while the latest one, the "subprime housing bubble" (2007), led to the worst global financial crisis since the 1930s. Let us review here some of the psychological phases of speculative bubbles in chronological order.

> Phase 1: *Fundamental logic.* Every bubble starts with a concept that is fundamentally sound and leads to apparently sustainable growth. The steady growth begins to attract more and more followers.
> Phase 2: *Promotion by interested parties.* Parties that have a financial interest in continued growth begin to promote the concept aggressively.

Phase 3: *Exaggerated expectations.* Stories with seemingly rational arguments emerge explaining the growth trend, leading to
over-optimism, greed and exaggerated expectations of future
growth. Objections to the logic are countered with the argument that "It is different this time because of . . ."

Phase 4: *Widespread participation.* A consensus of safety begins
to emerge, even among the early skeptics—after all, so far, so
good. The thinking is: "Everyone is doing it, so it must be sound.
I won't be left out." A crowd mentality takes over. Consider, for
example, the comment in 2008 by former Citibank chief executive Charles Prince on why his bank participated in the highly
geared financial speculations that led to the biggest bank bailout in history: He explained: "As long as the music is playing,
you've got to get up and dance."

Phase 5: *Warnings of collapse.* A small but sober minority raises
warning flags that are ridiculed and ignored.

Phase 6: *Overshoot into completely unrealistic territory.* Participants
are out of touch with reality. "Full speed ahead and damn the
torpedoes."

Phase 7: *Collapse.* The fantasy world crashes.

Economic growth has all the classical characteristics of speculative bubbles,
but is unique in the rather long time frame. The focus on economic growth
as a primary political goal goes back roughly to the end of the Second World
War. One result of this long period of success is a strengthening of phase 4,
the crowd mentality. Thus, a shared understanding that everything is OK has
been firmly established in the broad population. This shared understanding has been gradually and successfully transferred to the general populace
by the benefiting commercial interests. The man-in-the-street has bought
into the populist myth and will now only elect politicians that promise even
greater per capita consumption. Actually, one sensible country, Bhutan, has
not gone along with the crowd. They reject economic growth as a goal and
focus rather on "Gross National Happiness." Bhutan is, as far as I know, the
only exception.

The business sector has aggressively promoted economic growth—
almost to the point of a religious movement. The political power of the
business community has been increasing steadily for two hundred years
to the point that today we can no longer separate politics from business,
particularly in the world's dominant economy, the United States. The

combination of powerful business interests, political allies, and popular support makes it almost impossible to stop the growth bubble from bursting either when the ecosystem can no longer take the pressure, or more likely, when the reality of the coming period of energy descent hits the financial markets.

FIVE

The Neoliberal Project

The IMF and the World Bank have arguably done more harm to more people than any other pair of non-military institutions in human history.

DAVID KORTEN, *When Corporations Rule the World*

For thirty-five years after World War II, "Keynesian" economics was the dominant economic system and was generally considered a great success in a period of record growth in international trade and living standards with no major economic crises. By 1980, mainstream economists were in general agreement that financial crises such as in 1907 and 1929 were a thing of the past. Modern economists were confident that they were much cleverer now and knew how to control the money supply and implement countercyclical fiscal policies to prevent a financial crisis. But then something happened that changed everything.

In the early 1980s, a historic shift in the dominant economic system took place with the coming to power of Ronald Reagan in the United States and Margaret Thatcher in the UK, both very much in the clutch of big business—the modern-day successors to the merchant class of the days of Adam Smith and David Ricardo. The shift was not announced publicly, but rather crept into the public domain surreptitiously. Outside of the United States, the new policies acquired the name "neoliberalism," although a more proper name would have been "wealthism," or perhaps "financial colonialism." As opposed to all previous economic ideas, this one was not based on empirical observations and objective testing of models, but was rather a top-down political project with an ideology that fulfilled the wildest dreams of big business and the wealthiest segment of American society for unregulated freedom to operate as they pleased exclusively in their own interests and with little or no social or environmental considerations to worry about.

Neoliberalism can be seen as an extremist version of neoclassical economics where the only thing that counts is money. For this reason, Hazel Henderson has dubbed this development "economism." It can also be considered as an experiment to test Polanyi's postulate that giving total power to merchants, if allowed to persist, would "destroy both man and his environment." After almost thirty years, the conclusions are quite clear to all but the promoters.

The neoliberal ideology is based on the following principles of organizing both national and international economic relationships in an ideal world: (1) the unrestricted movement of capital across borders in a currency regime of floating rates without capital controls; (2) the removal of all restrictions on the free flow of goods and labor; (3) minimum government regulation of markets; (4) the removing of all subsidies, direct or indirect, to domestic industries; and (5) the privatization of state enterprises. The theory is that such a regime would be to the greatest benefit of all world citizens.

The principal instruments for implementing this regime are three international institutions, in which almost all countries are members, but which in practice are under the control of the United States and its closest allies, namely the International Monetary Fund (IMF), the World Bank, and the World Trade Organization (WTO). Thus, the "project" can best be understood as an initiative to project American values and protect American interests across the world. Seen in this light, it is not really important whether or not the theory has any validity. But it is important that the citizens of the United States and its prime allies in the G-7 (UK, Japan, Canada, Germany, France, Italy) accept its principles as political/economic policy guidelines. Therefore, the perception, packaging, and selling of the concept to these citizens is critical to the success of the project. What the rest of the world believes is of less importance, since it turns out they do not have any choice in the matter.

How Did It Come About?

There were two major events in the 1970s that were central to the adoption of what I call "The Neoliberal Project" by the United States. The first was the dropping of the American pledge to back the U.S. dollar with gold in 1971. This meant an end to the fixed-rate currency regime that had been a part of every economic system since the emergence of capitalism. No one was familiar with floating rates and what the consequences would be for economic relations among nation-states. Should capital controls be used or should capital be completely mobile? Should some currencies be "pegged" to others in a kind of fixed-rate proxy system? Should all currencies be allowed to float freely? A completely new situation with new risks and new opportunities was born.

The second event was the oil crisis of 1973, with a drastic hike in prices that shifted world wealth patterns dramatically and instantaneously. The Organization of Petroleum Exporting Countries (OPEC) showed that a consortium of raw-material producers could, by working together rather than competing, play at the same oligopoly game as the G-7, and increase *their* wealth at the expense of the rest of the world. The very thought that other basic commodity producers among the developing countries might form similar cartels sent shivers down the spines of the financial leaders of the industrialized countries. What would be next—coffee, sugar, copper, aluminum? When the Group of 77 developing countries, flexing their muscles a little, called for "a new economic order," the United States knew that something had to be done to keep "the little squirts" in their proper place.

The fear of a coming resource crisis was undoubtedly intensified by the realization that King Hubbert's 1956 forecast of a peak in U.S. oil production in 1971 had indeed come true in spite of all the ridicule from neoclassical economists and the oil industry. A further contribution to panic was the *Limits to Growth* study that sent the same message of coming resource scarcity, which made a greater impression on the CIA than on mainstream economists, for whom the concept of scarcity did not exist.

Making It Happen

Susan George, vice president of the antiglobalization NGO, ATTAC France, attributes the actual carrying out of the strategy to a conscious, systematic effort by the small, but very wealthy American right wing. A generation before it was only a small minority that held neoliberal views. They were considered "wackos" by mainstream economists. No one seriously believed that economics would one day dictate its rules to society rather than the other way around. But the Reagan/Thatcher political leadership of the 1980s unabashedly allied themselves with the wealthiest of the wealthy to achieve their political aims, ignoring the warnings of not only Polanyi and Keynes, but even of conservative economist Milton Friedman who said, "The combination of economic and political power in the same hands is a sure recipe for tyranny."[1]

According to Susan George, the neoliberals "bought and paid for" their success in an "absolutely brilliant" piece of ideological and promotional work. They funded a "huge international network of foundations, institutes, research centers, publications, scholars, writers, and public relations hacks to develop, package, and push their ideas and doctrine relentlessly." Thus, neoliberalism is not an inevitable historical development as they like to describe it, but "a totally artificial construct" created by "people with a purpose."[2] Part of their strategy is to present the whole phenomenon as inevitable and thus not subject to debate.

It should be noted that the project was designed to exploit not only the poor of the developing countries, and to destroy the welfare states of Europe, but also to access the wealth of the poor of the United States! George claims that their purpose was nothing less than a gigantic "transfer of wealth from the public purse to private hands" and "moving wealth from the bottom of society to the top."

Now these are harsh claims, and require evidence. Therefore, in the following, we will look at how the strategy was carried out in practice and what the measurable results were.

Mutation of the IMF

At about the time Reagan came to power in 1981, a mysterious shift in policy occurred within the IMF. There was no official change in the fund's articles, no announcement of any kind, indeed no public debate whatsoever about changing policy, as everything concerning the IMF happens behind closed doors and without any accountability to the public.

An entirely new philosophy, which came to be known as the IMF's "structural adjustment program," emerged to deal with member states that were in need of temporary help. From this point on, IMF loans to developing countries were made conditional upon acceptance of policies dictated by neoliberal ideology. The policies can be summarized in three major categories: trade liberalization—the free flow of goods without government regulation, tariffs or subsidies; financial-market liberalization—the free flow of capital; and privatization—the sale of public monopolies to private corporations. For the typical developing-country client, this meant they had to (1) reduce their tariffs on Western industrial products without compensating tariff cuts by the industrialized countries on the client's exports; (2) devalue their currency and expose it to short-term speculation by gigantic Wall Street hedge funds far larger than their central banks; (3) sell off key public facilities to Western corporations at ridiculously low prices; (4) raise interest rates, throwing hundreds of companies into bankruptcy; (5) remove food subsidies to their poor while being forced to accept the right of the North to dump its subsidized food products on their markets, destroying their small farmers in the process; (6) charge fees for school, resulting in massive school-dropout rates; (7) cut social welfare programs in order to force an unnecessary balanced budget and pay interest on their debt to the IMF; and (8) switch from import substitution to production of export-oriented raw materials and commodities of value to the North. If you are shocked by this and claim that this sounds incredible, it is because this is not the version you will read in the corporate-controlled media of the North. Any country that wanted IMF funds was pretty much forced to accept some variant of these conditions.

As former chief economist of the World Bank Joseph Stiglitz put it, "Founded on the belief that there is a need for international pressure on countries to have more expansionary economic policies—such as increasing expenditures, reducing taxes, or lowering interest rates to stimulate the economy—today the IMF typically provides funds only if countries engage in policies like cutting deficits, raising taxes, or raising interest rates that lead to a contraction of the economy. Keynes would be rolling over in his grave were he to see what had happened to his child."[3]

It was never intended that the IMF should have the power to dictate economic and social policies to member countries, nor have they ever been given that power formally. But, with tacit American approval, the IMF began doing just that in the 1980s by insisting on its narrow, ideological conditions that were often at odds with the client country's economic worldview as well as with the views of economists familiar with developing-country needs.

The IMF's insistence on unrestricted capital flows was particularly arrogant, as IMF members have the right to control their capital flows according to IMF Article VI, section 3. The key phrase is the following: "Members may exercise such controls as are necessary to regulate capital movements." This clause goes back to the founding of the IMF in 1945. For thirty-five years, it was considered standard procedure and necessary for the proper functioning of a modern state. But since the early 1980s, the IMF has routinely insisted that client states relinquish their Article VI rights as a condition for IMF loans. According to Professor Michel Chossudovsky of the University of Ottawa, the IMF has forced over 100 member countries to relinquish their rights, thus exposing their economies to speculative capital flows beyond their control, one of the major causes of all of the recurrent financial crises the world has experienced since, including the 2008 crisis.[4]

The purpose of the shift was to ensure that the developing-country client state would forever be in debt to the rich countries, would be a source of low-cost resources and cheap labor for the United States and its allies, would be amenable to U.S. needs for military sites, and never develop into a potential competitor with independent ideas and priorities.

What we see here is a conscious attempt by the IMF to impose on client states an economic ideology that was by no means universally accepted, and in most cases, not even appropriate. The result was nothing less than a crude transfer of sovereignty from member states to the IMF—and hence to the United States—not *de jura*, but *de facto*. It was not without a certain irony that IMF policy was also called "the Washington consensus." Few developing countries, in critical need of funds, had the option of rejecting the IMF dictates, even though acceptance meant breaking their social contract with their citizens. By its actions, the IMF was in effect taking on a role of global governance, but without being asked and without democratic accountability.

The World Bank

Across the street from IMF headquarters in Washington, D.C., lies the headquarters of the World Bank, the second of the The Neoliberal Project's ostensibly "international" but in reality U.S.-dominated institutions. The World Bank has a different mission—to eradicate poverty. To do this it borrows money on the international financial markets and lends it to developing countries for approved projects. In the early days, after the Second World War, there was not much demand for these loans. Most of the developing countries followed the tried-and-true strategy of nation building based on the very successful mercantile protectionist philosophy, the one used by Great Britain and the United States in their development phases, with a focus on producing as many as possible of their essential goods themselves, minimizing imports, and avoiding too much foreign debt. Seen from the perspective of The Neoliberal Project, there was a major problem here. Such states cannot easily be intimidated or exploited.

Therefore, the World Bank, supported by associated donor countries, such as the Paris Club, adopted an activist policy of lending based on the neoliberal concept of export growth rather than import substitution. Because the money was not really needed in most cases, it was necessary to make an alliance with the wealthy elites and corrupt political leaders of the developing countries, who were allowed to pocket a sizable chunk of the funds for personal use and for their companies, which were awarded lucrative contracts for unnecessary prestige projects. Using local labor was a minor part of the neoliberal strategy. Most of the funds actually returned to the West in the form of contracts with American and European engineering consultancies. U.S. Treasury officials openly admitted that for every $1 contributed to the World Bank, more than $2 came back to U.S. exporters in procurement contracts. Little if any funds trickled down to the rural poor, who became worse off in almost all cases. Anyone in doubt should read Michel Chossudovsky's *The Globalization of Poverty*.

The Neoliberal Project has, since the early 1980s, had as its prime goal the catching of the developing countries in a net of debt that forces them to shift from an import-substitution strategy to an export-oriented strategy in keeping with the G-7's needs for raw materials and cheap labor, and to adopt a foreign policy acceptable to the United States. They are forced to shift policy in order to earn the funds to repay the World Bank loans that their corrupt elites have forced upon their people without their acquiescence, so-called odious debt. Just one example: former chief economist Joseph Stiglitz of the World Bank states unequivocally, "When the IMF and World Bank lent money to the Democratic Republic of Congo's notorious ruler Mobutu, they knew (or should have known) that most of the money would not go to help that country's poor people, but rather would be used to enrich Mobutu. It was money paid to ensure that this corrupt leader would keep his country aligned with the West." Mobutu amassed a personal fortune estimated to be as much as $5 billion. The last thing the West wants to see is developing countries running their own economies the way they want to, growing sustainably and equitably and, in general, running their countries according to their own priorities.

This description of what is really behind the dominant economic system of our day may strike some readers as exaggerated or unbelievable. It is not. It is true that the facts are not known outside of a small group of insiders, and that many well-meaning people are unaware that they are contributing to the mishandling of the developing countries, but the description is not only true, but is consistent with all the known facts. Occasionally, there appears a whistle-blower who exposes behind-the-scenes top-secret policies that were not supposed to reach the general public. John Perkins, former chief economist with the U.S. engineering firm MAIN, is such a person. Perkins, in *Confessions of an Economic Hit Man*, relates how, when he was hired, his boss educated him on the true role of the World Bank when she spelled out for Perkins "the two primary objectives of my job. First, I was to justify huge international loans that would funnel money back to MAIN and other U.S. companies (such as Bechtel, Halliburton, Stone & Webster, and Brown & Root) through massive engineering and construction projects. Second, I would work to bankrupt the countries that received those loans (after they had paid MAIN and the other U.S. contractors, of course) so that they would be forever beholden to their creditors, and so they would present easy targets when we needed favors, including military bases, UN votes, or access to oil and other natural resources."[5]

Perkins adds that these projects "were intended to create large profits for the contractors, and make a handful of wealthy and influential families in the receiving countries very happy, while assuring the long-term financial dependence and therefore political loyalty of governments around the world." Perkins mentions that during his watch, his team often argued that acceptance of IMF/World Bank conditions was necessary to defeat communism. But after the breakup of the Soviet Union, the continuation of the same policies throughout the 1990s made it "apparent that deterring communism was not the goal."

The WTO

The third tool of the neoliberals, the World Trade Organization (WTO) broke into the mainstream public consciousness dramatically on the occasion of the Seattle trade negotiations among member states in November 1999. Unfortunately for the public debate since, the media covering the event chose to focus on the small minority of anarchists and their violent conflict with local police rather than explaining the reasons for the demonstrations. This made exciting news coverage, but did little to inform the public about why more than 700 NGOs from across the world, the leadership of the American labor movement, and 50,000 demonstrators felt it necessary to express their dissatisfaction with the way the WTO was conducting its affairs. This media coverage just happened to be in the interests of their owners, which are almost all among the very corporations being criticized for their antisocial and antienvironmental policies by the demonstrators.

The media message has since been the same when covering subsequent and still ongoing demonstrations against the WTO, IMF, World Bank, the EU leadership and the G-7—correctly perceived by the demonstrators as representing pretty much the same commercial interests—in Washington, Prague, Quebec City, Gothenburg, Genoa, Florence, Copenhagen, Gleneagles, Mexico City, Hong Kong, etc., in a continuing resistance movement. The media message has been that the demonstrators are poorly informed, violent hooligans with no right to be heard, while the basic reason for their protests is misstated or more likely, ignored entirely.

The WTO evolved in 1994 out of GATT (The General Agreement on Tariffs and Trade), which had regulated trade matters since the late 1940s. As trade treaties go, the GATT regime was spectacularly successful: trade volume expanded 87-fold from $124 billion to $10.8 trillion from 1948 to 1997—a period in which controls on capital movements and protectionism were widespread. GATT specifically recognized the need for the "special and differential status" of the developing countries, allowed for well-functioning voluntary bilateral and multilateral trade agreements, and had a satisfactory dispute-settlement procedure. The primary initiative for change came from the United States, under the influence of its newly empowered neoliberal economists. Other industrialized states were ambivalent. The developing countries were directly opposed to the change.

The fundamental problem with the WTO regulations is that they are far more than they appear to be at first glance by an unsuspecting public. They are not just simple trade regulations. They affect every aspect of national sovereignty, including social, environmental, and cultural issues. Trade issues cannot be isolated from the rest of society as if they are sacred, and exist in a vacuum. The WTO is really, without saying so, a first attempt at a formal charter for global governance, as it lays down hard-and-fast rules, with harsh consequences, for resolving conflicts between nations, but without any democratic accountability on the part of those making the decisions. Furthermore, the establishment of the WTO was done almost like a bloodless coup, without any public debate and in a way that primarily served the interests of a tiny minority of humankind—large corporate shareholders. This narrow interest is the whole background for the antiglobalization movement.

Indian physicist and environmental activist Vandana Shiva puts it this way. "Every other constitution has been based on the sovereignty of people and countries. Every constitution has protected life above profits. But the WTO protects profits above the right to life of humans and other species."[6] The WTO is a charter written by corporations for corporations, a charter that puts commercial interests above all, a charter to allow the strong to exploit the weak.

The consequences for the environment, for local communities, for unemployment, for human suffering, are "externalized"—not on the table for discussion—not a part of neoliberal economics. The WTO "free trade" regime is in reality a "forced trade" regime—a term coined by Helena Norberg-Hodge—because the developing countries are forced to accept exploitative conditions that put high tariffs on their otherwise competitive exports, while allowing subsidized Western products to undercut local production. The WTO rules are nothing less than a frontal attack on the welfare state and the environment, making them one of the major drivers of destruction. The consequence of allowing unrestricted capital flows across borders and forbidding protective tariffs on foreign goods gives the competitive advantage to the country with the strongest capital base and smallest social and environmental costs—in what environmental critics have rightly called "a race to the bottom." While the deteriorating environment knows no national boundaries, the commercial advantage goes primarily to the United States, with its special reserve-currency status and low priority on public support for the weakest members of its society and on environmental protection. Effective protection of the environment is impossible in this regime. To the contrary, The Neoliberal Project encourages all countries to trash the environment as quickly as possible. The reason is simple. Any country that unilaterally introduces taxes on environmentally destructive domestic production, for example, a tax on CO_2 emissions, automatically damages the competitiveness of its home industries, and invites foreigners to undercut local producers, because the WTO does not allow tariffs on foreign producers that use environmentally damaging production. In fact, the WTO does not even require disclosure on how exported items, which they can force onto any member state, were produced. Short of leaving the WTO, only a broad international consensus can deal with this problem, but to date it has never been possible to reach any agreement. All it takes is one major country to sabotage the effort. The consequence is that the WTO system encourages the destruction of our natural capital—the very basis of human existence.

Exposing the Myths

The neoliberal, or "free market" belief system is built up around a number of postulates that are all demonstrably wrong, and are nothing but a mishmash of myths and lies intended to mislead the public. This state of affairs has prompted Nobel laureate Joseph Stiglitz to say of neoliberalism: "What is sold nowadays as economics is in reality an ideology or a religion."[7] Let us review some of the dogma.

"Neoliberalism leads to greater growth."

The reality? Economic growth was higher in the prior GATT period. The Center for Economic and Policy Research (CEPR), an independent Washington-based research institute, has published a comprehensive analysis of the growth rates of over 100 countries in recent decades, based on the United Nations Development Program's (UNDP) Human Development Report statistics.[8] Their major conclusion is to note "the failure of the last two decades [the 1980s and 1990s] of globalization, structural adjustment, privatization, and 'market fundamentalism' to raise living standards worldwide, and the dramatic decline in growth, especially in underdeveloped countries." For example, for the whole group of countries, output per person grew by 83% in the pre-globalization era of 1960–80, but only by 33% for 1980–2000. Seventy-seven percent of the countries saw their growth rates fall by more than 5% from the first to the second 20-year period, while only 14% saw them increase by more than 5% in the same period. Looking in more detail at the major swings, Latin America realized a 75% growth rate for 1960–80, but only 6% for 1980–98, a 69% differential. For sub-Saharan Africa the corresponding figures were 36% for the earlier period and –15% for the latter, a differential of 51%. CEPR states: "Even where high growth rates were achieved, as in Southeast Asia, they were still better in the earlier period. The exceptions to this trend were East Asia and South Asia, which grew faster from 1980 to 1998 than in the previous period.

But the East Asian result is mainly due to the quadrupling of GDP over the last two decades of the twentieth century in China (with 83% of the population of East Asia), which was *outside* the influence of the neoliberals. The South Asian result is due to faster growth in India (which has three-quarters of the population of South Asia)." China, which broke all growth records, was quite protectionist, did not allow free capital flow, and was not a member of the World Trade Association (WTO) during this period of rapid growth. The study points out that, "in both India and China, their opening to trade took place about a decade *after* the increase in growth began." Referring to the IMF and World Bank, CEPR concludes: "The failure to acknowledge this dramatic decline in growth rates has left a gaping hole in the debate over the policies of the world's two most powerful financial institutions."

Similar conclusions are reached by Harvard economist Dani Rodrik in a devastating criticism of the methods used by supporters of the "globalization leads to greater growth" school. For example, he calls the often-cited Dollar/Kraay analysis "extremely misleading," pointing out how they introduce subjective bias to support their a priori conclusions, as they fail to follow their own criteria, arbitrarily including some countries and excluding others in their analysis to bolster their case. Corrected for these manipulations, Rodrik finds "no evidence" for their claims. Rather than liberalization of markets, he concludes that the most important single factor promoting growth is the establishment of quality institutions, citing other studies besides his own to back up his conclusion.[9]

"Growth is good."

The reality? Not true as a general statement. Only ecologically sustainable growth is good. But an economic system that treats ecology as a subordinate rather than the other way around can never be sustainable. Thus neoliberal economics confuses capital depletion and return on capital, treating depletion of natural capital as if it were part of the economic return, an elementary error in basic investment theory. A business administration student that considered part of the invested capital as yield on investment would flunk his exam—yet this is precisely what economists do, not least when arguing the benefits of industrial agriculture as opposed to organic farming. They give no consideration to the depletion of the natural capital in soil quality and water aquifers. Growth has been uneconomical in the industrialized countries since the 1970s, with marginal costs exceeding marginal benefits. This type of growth is analogous to cancer and is doomed to crash the ecosystem eventually. Runaway global warming is just one way this could happen. There are many others.

"Free markets benefit all, including the poor."

The reality? During the "free market" period, the rich have become richer and the poor poorer, continuing the long term global trend toward an increasing gap between rich and poor. Table 5.1, based on figures taken from the UNDP Report for 1999, shows the trend in per capita income differences expressed as a ration of the richest to the poorest countries.

The claim that unrestricted capital flows will enable the developing countries to develop production sectors where they have a comparative advantage is simply false, and ignores Ricardo's basic condition that comparative advantage requires that capital is immobile across borders. The Neoliberal

Year	1820	1913	1950	1973	1992
Ratio	3:1	11.1	35:1	44.1	72:1

Table 5.1. Rich/Poor Income Ratios 1820–1992. From UN Human Development Report 1999, p. 38

Project is intentionally preventing the developing countries from developing. The last thing neoliberals want is competitive developing countries. They want cheap labor and cheap raw materials for the industrialized countries and a market for their industrial products. The current system is rapidly creating greater inequalities in the world—more poverty among the poorest and more wealth among the wealthiest.

"Protectionism impedes growth."

The reality? Economic historian Paul Bairoch states, "It is difficult to find another case where the facts so contradict a dominant theory."[10] Bairoch's statement illustrates precisely why it is so difficult for ordinary people to understand what is going on in the world, and why. The public has been brainwashed by an ideologically driven flawed theory posing as fact.

What the neoliberals are alluding to when they deride protectionism is a particular myth, which evolved around the Great Depression of the 1930s, in which "protectionism" was, they claim, the cause of the Depression. The myth, which "free market" theorists have been very successful in promoting, has been thoroughly refuted by several economists, who point out that the major cause of the Depression was not protectionism, but rather *the failure of self-regulating markets*—in particular, a lack of consumer demand after the market crash of 1929, the return to a gold standard by Germany, France, and Britain between 1924 and 1926, which led to deflation, and the failure of the U.S. administration to inject money into the economy to stimulate demand and counter the deflationary pressures. The U.S. government actually made things worse by drastically cutting the deficit instead of increasing it, while the Fed increased member-bank reserve requirements, tightening money availability instead of relaxing it.[11]

These were the days before the era of Keynes, whose ideas of state intervention in the economy revolutionized economic thinking. Protectionist policies, which were rampant in those days, both before and after the crash, were at most a minor factor. Most of them were, in fact, imposed as a *reaction* to the Depression to prevent further erosion, as pointed out by Lang and Hines.[12] But the myth lives on, and is kept alive by the "free marketers" because it suits their purpose.

We have to distinguish between different *kinds* of protection—three kinds, in fact. The first—protection for key industries, including subsidizing them, as part of a conscious, long-term strategic government plan of nation building—is positive protectionism, and promotes real growth, as the history of mercantilism shows quite clearly.

In many cases, tariffs and subsidies, the second kind of protectionism, have been adopted without any strategic plan, for example, as a new source of revenue (tariffs), or as a sop to regional economic or political interests or special-interest lobbies (subsidies). This kind of protectionism simply leads to inefficiencies and stagnation. This is the kind of protectionism we should get rid of. It is also the kind of protectionism that the United States and the EU insist that others should drop, while refusing to do so themselves, for example, agricultural and fossil fuel subsidies and American "pork barrel" politics.

The third kind is protection of the noneconomic aspects of a society, and is definitely a desirable form of protectionism. This could include, for example, import restrictions as part of a state's environmental protection policy, e.g., a policy to not accept imports from corporations or countries following environmentally damaging policies. Or it might involve a policy of food security to ensure survival in an international crisis, or perhaps incentives for small businesses and penalties for large businesses in order to create a more decentralized, harmonious, and cohesive society that a democratic nation decides it wants for itself, rather than a centralized and inequitable society dominated by foreign commercial interests and large monopolies. Or it might be with a view to creating full employment. From a narrow economic viewpoint, these policies may well represent a net cost to society, like many other government programs, but the very fact that such policies are adopted implies that the trade-off is considered politically acceptable by the populace, and therefore is expected to be positive on balance.

From the viewpoint of foreign commercial interests, policies protecting citizen interests are definitely bad news; for such foreign interests can be kept out of these markets, or in the least be forced to obey the local rules. Therefore, neoliberals consider such policies as "restrictions of trade" and insist that the laws be changed to favor foreign commercial corporation wishes over local citizen wishes. One would think that such a brash, self-serving attitude of foreign commercial interests toward a sovereign nation would evoke ridicule, if not belly laughs, from the natives. And indeed, it should. The shocking thing is that they actually got away with it with the WTO while we innocent citizens were looking the other way in 1994, in what can be considered a bloodless coup. The WTO essentially hijacked a major part of economic policy making from its member states.

What the "free marketers" have done in the WTO is to throw out the baby with the bathwater. To get rid of the negative kind of protectionism (the second type), they managed to ban *all* kinds of protectionist policies in the

WTO trade treaty. This is naturally of great benefit to the corporate promoters as it suppresses competition and creates more profits for them, but it is certainly bad news for the environment and not in the interests of the citizens of the WTO member countries, and particularly not in the developing countries. Essentially, this clause prevents sovereign governments from exercising control over vital aspects of their own countries.

"Globalization is inevitable."

The reality? This statement is not only wrong, but purposely intended to confuse. Neoliberals have promoted "globalization" as an evolutionary process in order to eliminate debate. They like to say things like "Globalization is inevitable," and "There is no alternative" to intimidate the opposition. The cause of the confusion is that the term "globalization" is used with different meanings by different people, for which reason I try to avoid using it at all. For some, the term refers to the gradual "internationalization" of global society, which has evolved in parallel with advances in communication and travel, a phenomenon, which most people would consider positive, and which could well be inevitable. Others, for example, the "antiglobalization" movement, use the term when referring to the dominant *economic* system. Their message would be clearer if they called their movement "anti-neoliberalism." It is absolute rubbish to claim neoliberal economics to be inevitable. If anything is inevitable, it is the opposite, steady-state economics, without which our civilization is unlikely to survive.

Most of the people opposed to neoliberal economics are very much in favor of international collaboration, particularly in terms of solving human rights and environmental problems. They see the need to learn from other cultures, but they also recognize the need for cultural, economic, and political self-determination. Most would like to change the economic system to something more in keeping with the needs of people and nature rather than commercial corporations.

"Markets are self-correcting."

The reality? This is the greatest lie of all in the neoliberal "religion" and yet is the basis of their demands for deregulation. Every economist from Adam Smith to John Maynard Keynes knew that markets require government regulation to function. This is true for *any* economic system. Financial institutions are the first to run for help from the taxpayers when markets fail, as we saw most recently in 2008. Regulation is especially essential for neoliberal economics because this particular system is intrinsically unstable and will lead to recurrent financial crises. This is so important to understand that I will explain why, with several historical examples, in chapter 6.

"The same rules apply to all countries."

The reality? This myth—sometimes promoted as the "level playing field" concept—is demonstrably false. This is perhaps the most certain proof that neoliberalism is a political project and not just about economics. For example, the IMF "structural adjustment programs" forced on developing countries when they start building up unacceptably high trade deficits—high interest rates, currency devaluation, cuts in public spending, and contraction of the economy—do not apply to the United States. When the United States got into precisely the same situation in 2001, the opposite policies were implemented. Interest rates were cuts eleven times that year to stimulate and expand the economy in spite of an enormous foreign debt and an exploding trade deficit. "Structural adjustment" stops at the U.S. and EU borders.

The "level playing field" metaphor, implying fairness, relates to the WTO rules that apply equally to all members. But this is the fairness of putting an 800-pound gorilla in the boxing ring with a 90-pound weakling. It may be that the same rules apply to both parties, but guess who is going to win every time? To win a dispute in the WTO against the United States or the EU is not only costly, but requires educated civil servants, public administration institutions, and legal expertise that many developing countries just do not have. A trading regime like the WTO is only appropriate for relations between equally strong players.

The Neoliberal Project is consciously designed to keep the developing countries in their "proper place" as suppliers of cheap raw materials and labor—a form of financial colonialism. "Colonialism: the principle or practice in which a powerful country rules a weaker one and establishes its own trade and culture there" (Longman Dictionary of Contemporary English, 1995). Note that colonialism does not require military rule. That was eighteenth-century thinking. As former U.S. secretary of state John Foster Dulles is claimed to have said, "There are two ways of taking over a society's economy. One is by armed force, and the other is by financial means."

Subsidies

We see the same colonialism pattern with subsidies. The developing countries are forced to cut subsidies to their domestic production while the

United States and its allies are allowed to give enormous subsidies to theirs, with the result that the rich countries can undercut domestic prices in developing countries, even including local food production. Though estimates vary, the amounts are staggering. For U.S. corporations, *Time* magazine estimated subsidies of $125 billion per year in a major article.[13] The Cato Institute estimated $75 billion per year in testimony before Congress.[14] The *Boston Globe* estimated $150 billion per year in a 1996 article. For comparison, total corporate earnings in the United States in 1997 were $325 billion. So we are talking about "corporate welfare" here of a magnitude corresponding to roughly one-third of total corporate profits and in an amount exceeding the "cost of the core programs of the welfare state of about $145 billion."[15] For comparison, the cost of U.S. foreign aid was $10.9 billion in 2001. This figure is gross. According to the director of the U.S. Aid Agency, 84% of that amount returns to the United States for purchase of U.S. goods and services.[16] Thus the net amount of aid was only about $1.5 billion, which is roughly 1% of U.S. direct corporate subsidies. Even using the gross figure, a cut of direct corporate subsidies by just 10% could finance a doubling of U.S. foreign aid, which is the lowest of all OECD countries as a percentage of GDP (0.11% in 2001).

European and Japanese figures are more difficult to come by, but current WTO rules allow the EU up to $60 billion annually in trade-distorting agricultural subsidies without repercussions, while Japan is allowed $30 billion, both negotiated back in 1994 based on pre-WTO levels.[17] The United States has agricultural subsidies of about $50 billion per year, which includes an 80% hike in May 2002, a move that angered the international community just as world leaders were planning to gather at the Earth Summit in Johannesburg to discuss how to build a sustainable world and reduce poverty in the developing countries. The U.S. hike was a slap in the face to its fellow WTO members, at a time when the *reduction* of subsidies was a major subject for discussion at the WTO meeting in Doha. The same source estimates current EU agricultural subsidies at about EUR 45 billion.[18]

What about the rest of the world? For the entire OECD group of twenty-nine rich countries, total agricultural subsidies were roughly $360 billion in 1999,[19] or roughly 7 times the total of all foreign aid, which amounted to roughly $54 billion. Developing countries themselves subsidize their farmers with about $57 billion.[20] An across-the-board global cut of 15% in OECD agricultural subsidies alone could finance a doubling of foreign aid. A comprehensive study by the Institute for Research on Public Expenditure s estimated total world subsidies to be at least $700 billion per year in just four sectors—agriculture, energy, water, and road transportation. This includes consumption subsidies in developing countries of about $230 billion. Most of these subsidies encourage the use of fossil fuels, benefit the wealthy, and penalize the poor. The indirect environmental and social costs, which are very substantial, are not included in these figures.[21] An economic system with no penalties for destroying the environment and production prices further distorted by enormous subsidies can only lead to inappropriate decisions and wrong resource allocations all through society.

To illustrate how these subsidies often work in practice, it will be instructive to look briefly at the recent subsidy history of three particular industries, which are important to the developing countries—sugar, coffee, and cotton. The following are not the words of some "wild and uninformed antiglobalizer" but none other than the former director-general of the WTO, Mike Moore:

> U.S. producers, which developed their own sugar beet industry and which control vast sugar cane plantations, have benefited hugely from protectionism. The U.S. assists the domestic sugar industry through price supports and import restrictions in the form of a tariff-rate quota, under which sugar-exporting countries are given a tiny quantity that they can sell in the U.S. at the regular tariff, with exports beyond that subject to a tariff rate of nearly 150%. These sugar import restrictions and price supports cost domestic users of sweeteners $1.9bn in 1998, while benefiting domestic sugar beet and sugar cane producers to the tune of $1bn. Moreover, 42% of the total benefits to sugar growers went to just 1% of all farms.
>
> The stories of coffee and cotton are just as tragic as the story of sugar. Ten years ago the industry was worth $30bn and farmers received about $10bn. Now the industry worldwide is worth $60bn and farmers receive about $5.5bn. Prices for farmers are below the prices they received in the Great Depression. A sad and familiar story of the lack of coherence between international agencies, governments interfering with "aid" that distorts the market, and great companies not passing on the lower cost to consumers.
>
> Aid to Vietnam from rich countries lifted that country from nowhere to the world's second biggest exporter of coffee. It is an important crop for poor countries and accounts for 64% of

exports from Ethiopia, 60% of Uganda's exports and 25% of El Salvador's. The theory of competition returning gains to consumers and free trade principles is not working. Rich countries often have no tariffs on coffee beans, but escalate tariffs to keep out the processed higher-value products that return more income to job-starved poor countries. Such policies are short-sighted, particularly given that the climate to grow coffee was exactly the climate necessary for heroin production.

Last year, U.S. farmers harvested a record crop of 4.38bn kilograms of cotton, aided largely by a U.S. government check for $3.4bn. West Africa is the third largest exporter of cotton, and farmers in Mali, the largest grower in the region, posted a record harvest last year as well—200m kilograms. The difference was, that without subsidies, the state cotton company lost money; prices have fallen by 66% since 1995 (to $0.88 per kilo), falling 10% this year alone.

The World Bank and the IMF estimate that removal of U.S. subsidies could lead to a fall in production, a subsequent rise in the global price for cotton, and a revenue increase of $250m annually for the countries of west and central Africa. But in fact, subsidies for U.S. cotton farmers are likely to see their support increase by 16%. This was for a total of 25,000 farmers whose net household worth averages about $800,000.

Agricultural trade policies like those for sugar, coffee and cotton are not just economically and politically inequitable; they prevent desperately poor countries from exporting to rich countries. Alas, a similar story could be told about the rice and fish subsidies of rich countries like Japan and South Korea. Agriculture is a difficult subject in trade negotiations. But without significant reforms in agricultural trade, poverty alleviation efforts will fail.[22]

This quote from the former head of the WTO ought to make an impression on the many sympathizers of "free markets" who tend to marginalize and ridicule opponents of neoliberal economics. These comments from one of their own could just have easily have been said by any antiglobalizer, but would have been ignored or ridiculed by the media.

Social Effects

One of the best-documented effects of neoliberal economics is the increasing gap between rich and poor, both within individual countries and between the rich and poor countries. Given the enormous subsidies to the already wealthy in both developed and developing countries, and the protectionist policies of the rich countries outlined above, the result is entirely predictable, and should not surprise anyone. The most widely used measure of income dispersion in a given country is the Gini coefficient (named after the developer—Italian statistician Corrado Gini), which can range from 0 to 1.

The value is Gini = 1 if all income accrues to one person, and Gini = 0 if all receive the same amount. A Gini coefficient of 0.3 or less indicates substantial equality; 0.3 to 0.4 indicates acceptable normality; and 0.4 or higher suggests an increasing risk of social unrest.

Figure 5.1 shows the unweighted (i.e., not weighted by population) average Gini coefficient for all countries in the period 1950–98. Note how the Gini curve increased rapidly in the neoliberal period, 1980–98. This is a second indicator of general increasing inequality in all countries in the latter period.

Table 5.2 shows the rank (out of 134) of Gini coefficients in 2010 for selected countries.

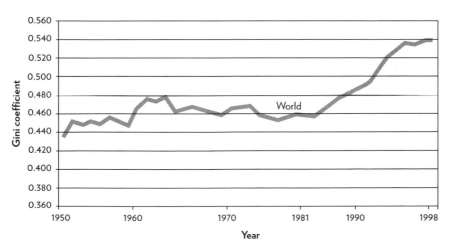

Figure 5.1. Unweighted World Average Gini Coefficient. From Branko Milanovic, "World Income Inequality in the Second Half of the 20th Century," working paper, June 2001; see www.worldbank.org.

Rank	Country	Gini Coefficient
1	Sweden	.230
2	Slovenia	.240
3	Denmark	.240
4	Norway	.250
5	Iceland	.250
6	Czech Rep.	.260
61	Japan	.381
91	USA	.450
99	China	.470
125	Brazil	.567
133	South Africa	.650
134	Namibia	.707

Table 5.2. Gini Coefficients for Selected Countries. From CIA Factbook, (February, 2010); see www.cia.gov.

A Gini coefficient higher than 0.6 is predictive of likely social unrest.[23] Thus a casual look at this list can indicate where we can expect to see violence.

Inequality in America

Income inequalities have been increasing within countries over the last few decades at the same time as they have been increasing between rich and poor countries. The United States is a prime example. Many young American families rightfully feel that they have been left behind economically since the 1970s, and are worse off than their parents, in spite of apparent economic growth. The data confirms why. In the pre-neoliberal era, increases in income tended to follow increases in productivity, and were fairly evenly distributed among income groups as shown in table 5.3.

Group	1950–78
Lowest 20%	138%
Next 20%	98%
Next 20%	106%
Next 20%	111%
Highest 20%	99%

Table 5.3: U.S. Income Growth 1950–78. From U.S. Bureau of Census, Current Population Survey.

Group	Growth
Lowest 20%	1%
Next 20%	9%
Next 20%	15%
Next 20%	22%
Highest 20%	75%
Top 1%	200%

Table 5.4. U.S. Income Growth 1979–2005. From Budget of the United States Government, FY 2009, Historical Tables; see www.econdataus.com.

Table 5.4 illustrates the way income grew for the same groups in the neoliberal period 1979–2005. The pattern shifts significantly, with most benefits accruing to the wealthiest citizens.

A calculation by economist Paul Krugman makes the point even more dramatically, based on a slightly different time period (1979–89). Nobel laureate Krugman points out that, to get the full picture, we have to look in more detail within the highest income group. He calculated that fully 70% of the rise in average family pretax income in this period went to the top 1% of families.[24] Indeed the top 1% received more of the gains than the bottom 90% combined. For the longer period, 1979–2005, the top 1% gained a phenomenal 200%. Krugman adds, "Most economists who study wages and income in the United States agree about the radical increase in inequality—only the hired guns of the right still try to claim it is a statistical illusion."[25]

Several reasons have been suggested by various commentators in way of explanation—increased imports from low-wage countries, the effects of information technology on salaries, and weaker trade unions. But Krugman points out that none of these is sufficient to explain the magnitude of the shift to the top 1%. He suggests instead that it was an attitudinal shift away from the egalitarian ethic to a "greed is good" ethic that was the major factor. During and after the Reagan years, it simply became more acceptable to be superrich. This shift in attitude not only shifted wealth, but also increased the political influence of the wealthiest via campaign contributions, assuring them of favorable legislation that would make them even richer at the expense of the lower and middle classes, for example, via massive tax cuts favoring the wealthy and increased subsidies for the corporations under their control.

Inequality Matters

Increasing inequality is not just a moral issue. The negative effects on well-being are widespread and significant, as shown in the following two studies, thus identifying the trend to greater inequality as a major driver of destruction in the social sphere.

Dr. Paul Stevenson of the University of Winnipeg argues that it is the causal link between capitalism and inequality on the one hand, and between inequality and social problems on the other, that is critical to our understanding of the role of the economic system in social breakdown. Citing dozens of studies on the subject, he identifies the single most important cause of inequalities to be the "private ownership of income-generating property." Unemployment is identified as a second important factor, and has in turn "been linked to increased rates of mental illness, suicide, homicide, divorce, heart attack deaths, stroke deaths, cirrhosis of the liver deaths, aggression, and so on."

In his comprehensive paper, Stevenson refers to a number of other studies, which link income inequalities to longevity and mortality rates, chronic health problems, occupational health and safety, stress, migration, family breakup, mental illness, higher death rates, higher unemployment rates, and higher incarceration rates. Furthermore, income inequalities correlate with a higher percentage of people receiving social assistance, smaller expenditures per person on education, higher rates of homicide, poorer health care, higher infant mortality, political repression, violence, the breakdown of democracy, and the criminal justice system's tendency to "weed out the wealthy." Stevenson also refers to studies indicating that "foreign investment in Third World Nations is consistently related to increased inequality among nations and within nations and generally related to lower economic growth and higher unemployment," contrary to neoliberal economic theory. The importance of these many studies is that they show the direct causal relationship between our current economic system and our social ills.[26]

A recent study by two UK sociologists, Richard Wilkinson and Kate Pickett, comes to similar conclusions.[27] Before presenting their conclusions, consider for a moment the logic that drives the current focus on economic growth. The implicit assumption is that greater economic growth leads to greater average income, which in turn leads to greater happiness and greater health. In foreign aid policy, the similar logic is that the way to eliminate poverty is by increasing average income in developing countries. In a frontal attack on both of these deeply ingrained assumptions regarding economic growth

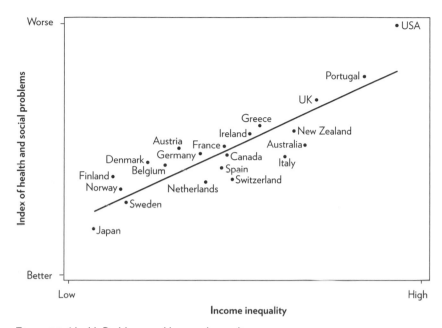

Figure 5.2. Health Problems and Income Inequality. From Richard Wilkinson and Kate Pickett, *The Spirit Level: Why Greater Equality Makes Societies Stronger* (New York, Bloomsbury Press, 2010), p. 20; copyright © 2010 by Richard Wilkinson and Kate Pickett; reprinted by permission of Bloomsbury Press, New York.

and foreign-aid policies, Wilkinson and Pickett show that the facts falsify the prevalent theory. When industrialized countries are compared, it turns out that happiness and longevity are unrelated to average income. Contrary to traditional economic thinking, increasing income does not produce happier or healthier people. What *does* explain differences in health—and with great statistical significance—is the degree of income inequality in a given country. Countries with the greatest income inequality score worst on the authors' "Index of Health and Social Problems," as shown in figure 5.2.

The authors go on to show that increased levels of inequality lead to an intensification of a whole range of social ills that affect everyone in society, including low levels of social trust; mental illness (including drug and alcohol addiction); lower life expectancy and higher infant mortality; obesity; poor educational performance; teenage births; homicides; imprisonment rates; and reduced social mobility.

While the results may seem counterintuitive at first, the explanation seems to be that an individual's perceived sense of self-worth is the most important determinant of both health and social ills. Well-being, in the sense of individual health and social satisfaction, should be understood as being due to relative rather than absolute conditions. In other words, the negative consequences of trying to "keep up with the Joneses" may be far more serious for our quality of lives than we have hitherto imagined. The authors write, "The view that social problems are caused by poor *material* conditions such as bad housing, poor diets, lack of educational opportunities and so on, implies that richer developed societies would do better than others. But this is a long way from the truth; some of the richest countries do worst."[28] It is the perception of low status and low esteem that encourages violence, obesity, teenage pregnancy, drug use, and so on; and it is the fear of it that drives consumerism, stress, longer working hours, and dysfunctional behavior in unequal societies.

As a corollary, "poverty" should be seen not so much a function of material possessions as a matter of perception of one's social status. If so, then the way to reduce "poverty" is not to increase average income, but rather to change perception. Greater equality leads to greater self-esteem and improved quality of life across the whole spectrum.

It also means cost savings! This alternative way of dealing with social ills and health has enormous budgetary consequences, especially in an energy descent world under great financial strain. For example, the United States spends between 40% and 50% of the world's total spending on health care (about $6,000 per person per year), although it represents only 5% of the global population. In spite of spending more per person on health care than any other country, the United States has by far the worst score on the Index of Health and Social Problems. The explanation, according to Wilkinson and Pickett, is that the United States is also the most unequal society in the group by a wide margin, as shown in figure 5.2. More than any other country, the United States stands to benefit from a shift to a more egalitarian society, resulting not only in better average health and fewer social ills, but in tremendous reductions in health care expenses and the costs of treating the symptoms of social dysfunction.

In addition to the above social arguments, the high degree of inequality in the United States has been identified recently by the former chief economist of the IMF as one of the prime causes of financial crises, including the 2007–8 crisis, a point to which I will return in chapter 6.

Free Markets and Democracy

The link between the inequalities created by neoliberal economics and democracy is direct, as pointed out by David Held, professor of political science at the London School of Economics, and a leading scholar of modern democracy, who writes, "Inequality *undermines* or *artificially limits* the pursuit of democratic decision-making." "Democracy," he adds, "is embedded in a socio-economic system that systematically grants a privileged position to business interests." He identifies as a central weakness of neoliberalism its tendency to see markets as "powerless" mechanisms, thus neglecting "the distorting nature of economic power in relation to democracy."[29]

The classical rejoinder of the neoliberals to greater equality is that it will lead to less growth. Ecological economists could point out that further growth is uneconomic, and less of it would be better for society. However, even if we disregard this aspect, there is evidence to refute this claim. A comprehensive study of growth and inequality for several countries during the period 1960–90 showed that the growth rates were higher in low-inequality countries (e.g., East Asia) than in high-inequality countries (e.g., South America). The authors' suggested explanation is that the poor in unequal societies do not have enough income to make what otherwise would be growth-stimulating investments.[30]

The promoters of "free markets" often speak on festive occasions about "spreading democracy" as part of their mission. But this too is just another myth, and a cruel one. "Free markets" and democracy are simply incompatible. The last thing the American elite wants to see is developing countries becoming democracies with their own priorities and own ideas about foreign policy and economic strategies, for example, giving priority to producing their own essential needs, developing their own foreign policy, and refusing foreign loans. The reality is that without the availability of cheap resources and labor from the 100 or so developing countries that are financial colonies of the dominant Western powers, the standard of living in the rich countries could not possibly be sustained, and the Western elite knows it.

John Gray, professor of European Thought at the London School of Economics puts it this way: "Those who seek to design a free market on a worldwide scale have always insisted that the legal framework which defines and entrenches it must be placed beyond the reach of any democratic legislature."[31] The WTO and IMF are both excellent examples of such undemocratic institutions.

In Gray's opinion, it is also a myth that "free markets" embody the so-called universal truths of the founding fathers, and that there once existed an American golden age of "laissez-faire" that is now being revived. Not so, says Gray. The American tradition is one of protectionism, not free markets. Furthermore, a number of studies confirm that there "is no statistical relationship between growth and democratic government."[32] China is the classic counterexample that falsifies *that* dubious theory—an example of enormous growth with neither democracy nor free markets. Gray calls the current free-market euphoria a historical "singularity" with roots in the Enlightenment dream of a homogeneous universal culture, and he is convinced that The Neoliberal Project will fail.

Gray sees neoliberalism as a particularly American project, representing an "archaic worldview . . . a relic of the 17th century Enlightenment," that is built upon the false "premise that they can project American values to the last corner of the earth." He calls the project "a utopia" and "a theology" that is doomed to fail because capitalism has many very different variations, a European, a Japanese, a Chinese, a Russian, an Indian, and so on, steeped in local traditions and cultural values that will never be given up. They have little incentive to do so, observing that countries that have repudiated the American model have demonstrated "superior economic growth, savings rates, educational standards and family stability," facts that are "repressed, denied and resisted" in the United States, while the "human costs of the free market are taboo subjects in American discourse."[33]

One of the central effects of neoliberal economics is the occurrence of periodic financial crises that are an inevitable consequence of the system's "financialization" of the economy. Let us now turn to this very important issue in a period of continuing financial turmoil.

SIX

Financial Crises

In my view, derivatives are financial weapons of mass destruction.
—WARREN BUFFETT

The period from 1945 to 1980 was, in retrospect, a period characterized by relative peace, rapid economic growth, no major financial crises, a general sense of social cohesiveness and a feeling that things were getting better, particularly in Western Europe, where nations that had been engaged in recurrent wars for centuries finally found a way to work together in peace. Keynesian economics dominated, and it looked for a long time like a major economic depression was a thing of the past. Many have called this period a "golden age," particularly when compared to what followed.

1980: The Turning Point

With the coming to power of Reagan and Thatcher and the ascendancy of the neoliberals in 1980, everything changed. The subsequent period from 1980 to the present has been characterized by a deterioration of social cohesiveness, environmental destruction, increasing stress, increasing criminality, a shift from solidarity to individualism, a "greed is good" mentality, a dramatic widening of the gap between rich and poor, and not least, a series of major financial crises resulting from the "financialization" of the world economy. All these phenomena fit together as part of the same pattern, and are more or less a direct consequence of the ideology of The Neoliberal Project, which deviated significantly from the ideology of all previous economics systems.

Recall that 1980 was also the point at which the marginal costs of growth began to exceed the marginal benefits—the point at which a global collapse may well have begun. It is as if the dominant culture entered a final stage of frenzy, denial, absurdity, and fantasy in an attempt to stave off the reality that its way of life was coming to an end. Nowhere was this truer than in the field of finance, which removed itself further and further from any contact with the real world.

I was part of that incredible financial world for twenty-five years, beginning in 1975. I began my research into the exciting new field of foreign-exchange strategies under floating exchange rates in 1980 and was active in that branch until 2000, when I opted out, selling off my company and coming back to Earth. Making money from buying and selling currencies in an era of deregulation using the newly available access to home computers and real-time data was virgin territory and a stimulating intellectual challenge for me. Add to this the newly available opportunities of derivatives like options (the subject of my 1964 PhD thesis), that required advanced mathematical skills, and the temptation to get involved was irresistible for me and many other "rocket scientists" around the world. In 1988 I founded the first hedge fund based exclusively on trading only "over-the counter" currencies (i.e., trading directly with major banks rather than on regulated exchanges). As for social relevance, I saw our activities as contributing to market liquidity and greater efficiency for companies involved with currency-risk management. I did not think of what was going on as a casino initially, but my view gradually shifted as things went to greater and greater extremes, and I began to get concerned about the greater risks to society of all this financial speculation. Perhaps this concern was because my motives were different from the others. I was primarily interested in earning money for a limited period for the benefit of the charitable activities of Gaia Trust, a charity that I cofounded in 1987 with essentially no capital, and which owned 90% of my company. Gaia Trust's mission was and still is to support the transition toward a sustainable, more spiritual civilization.[1] There was good reason for concern. I saw repeated financial crises occur that were a direct result of unnecessary financial speculation. But rather than lead to reforms, the crises led to even greater speculation year after year as the financial industry became the most dominant industry in the world economy, which I considered absurd.

Banks, in particular, mutated from traditional low-risk lenders to local private and corporate customers to high-risk, high-tech international speculators, often through bigger and bigger mergers that gave them political influence and enormous capital resources. They exploited regulatory rules to park many of their activities "off balance sheet," so not even their shareholders, let alone the regulators, were aware of the hidden risks they were taking. Securitization of debt instruments such as subprime loans that could be sold to an unsuspecting public became a new and lucrative source of income, as did trading for their own account in currencies and stocks, an example of conflict of interest with their customers, and almost unheard of in the 1970s. The moral bonds gradually disappeared in a frenzy of greed that became the norm in the industry. The post-1980 financial sector has to be considered another major driver of destruction because of the financial instability that is an unavoidable consequence if its methods.

Figure 6.1 illustrates how financial-sector profits exploded relative to all other sectors in the era of minimum regulatory oversight that characterized the period after 1980, reaching a peak shortly before the subprime loan crisis manifested and set profits back momentarily, until the financial institutions were bailed out by taxpayers.

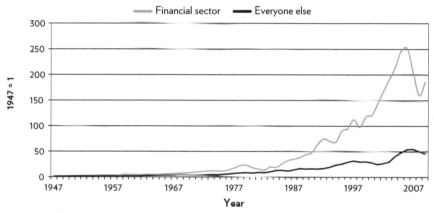

Figure 6.1. Financial Sector Growth Explosion. From Morgan Housel, "Banks Blowing up the Economy," *Motley Fool*, April 13, 2010; see www.fool.com.

Salaries of financial sector employees also ballooned, increasing from a mere 7% premium in 1959 to a 56% premium in 2006, as shown in figure 6.2.

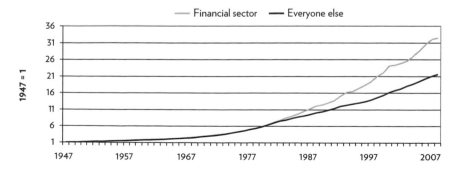

Figure 6.2. Growth in Financial Sector Compensation. From Housel, "Banks Blowing up the Economy," *Motley Fool*, www.fool.com.

In what follows, I will explain why recurrent financial crises are a systemic characteristic of post-1980 economics. I will also outline three simple reforms that would put a stop to the destruction, and explain why these reforms will never be implemented as long as the current political/ economic elite is running things. The three financial-crisis "culprits" are closely interrelated, and all the financial crises can be explained by some combination of these three—deregulation, unrestricted capital flows, and naked derivatives.

Deregulation

The basic problem with removing government regulations from markets was pointed out back in the 1700s by Adam Smith, who did not trust the morality of a merchant class that had no concept of restraint or social responsibility. Since human ingenuity is limitless, any relaxation of the rules will inevitably lead to unintended and unforeseen exploitation by profit-seeking businessmen, typically at the expense of the non-profit-seeking parts of society—local communities, working people, and the environment. History has shown repeatedly that markets are not self-regulating as the neoliberal ideology assumes. On the contrary, unregulated markets tend to go to extremes until they eventually crash.

A clear example demonstrating the shift in ideology is found in one of the very first actions of the neoliberals under Reagan in the early 1980s. Savings and loan (S&L) associations had for as long as Americans could remember been a staple of every local community, receiving federally insured deposits with a ceiling on interest rates and granting home mortgage loans to local citizens. Only 15% of their funds could be used for other purposes, namely 5% in each of land development, construction, and education. They were primarily *social institutions* without a profit motive. To guarantee an anchoring in the local community, and a widely spread ownership, federal regulations required at least 400 shareholders, of which at least 125 had to be from the local community, and no single shareholder could own more than 10%. The local savings and loan institutions tended to keep local savings in the local economy, rather than have them siphoned off to the big city banks. The S&L was a vital part of maintaining viable and thriving local communities, the very backbone of the economy.

But for the neoliberals, everything should have a profit motive. The idea of thriving local communities as something to strive for was completely off their charts. They reasoned: why should savings and loans be an exception to the profit motive? Why should federal regulations limit their profit opportunities (read: *our* profit opportunities)? So, over the next couple of years the neoliberals implemented a massive deregulation of S&Ls, including: allowing one company to own 100% of the shares, thus severing the anchor to local communities; relaxation of minimum equity requirement to just 3% of loans, thus allowing higher gearing and greater risk; relaxation of accounting regulations to a less stringent rule set; reduction of federal regulatory staff overseeing the S&Ls in keeping with Reagan's goal of smaller government.

Federally regulated S&Ls were allowed to eliminate the long-standing deposit interest-rate ceilings in order to attract more depositors; to eliminate the previous statutory limit on loan-to-value ratio; and to have greater flexibility in the kinds of investments they could undertake. California, Texas, and Florida went even further, allowing 100% of their S&L deposits to be invested in any venture whatsoever without restriction.

The entirely predictable result of all this was that it allowed new profit-driven unscrupulous investors to get their hands on the enormous assets built up over several decades from local community savings and engage in an unregulated and irresponsible speculative frenzy as they invested in all kinds of dubious get-rich-quick schemes characterized by conflicts of interests, incompetence, highly speculative investments, and criminal activities using other people's money. The ruling concept was: heads we win, tails the taxpayers pay. When the dust settled in 1990 after a decade of crisis and abuse, S&Ls with assets of $500 billion had failed, wiping out half the industry. Texas, with the most liberal deregulation, was by far the hardest hit. The federal bailout ended up costing taxpayers $129 billion in the biggest financial crash since 1929.

Unrestricted Capital Flows

Of all the ideological pillars of The Neoliberal Project, this is by far the most important. Without it, two of the bastions of the religion would collapse, namely the free flow of goods across borders and the privatization of government monopolies. This is because any country that takes back control of capital flows automatically takes back control of its economy, including who and what is allowed in. Free capital flow is both the source of strength and the Achilles heel of neoliberal economics.

Unrestricted capital flows systemically cause financial crises in two ways.

First, they allow investors of one country to create a financial crisis in another country that would otherwise not have occurred. Second, they act like a virus that allows a crisis in one country to spread to other countries. Thus, they differ from deregulation crises, which are primarily domestic and limited (in the absence of capital flows) to the regulating country, as for example the S&L crisis and the more recent U.S. subprime loan crisis.

To understand the importance of the unrestricted flow of capital across borders to the promoters of neoliberal economics, you must try to see the world through the lenses of the multibillion dollar investment banks, commercial banks, hedge funds, insurance companies, pension funds, mutual funds, corporate treasurers, and so on—whom I will denote collectively as "the players"—who have billions to invest wherever in the world the short-term return is perceived to be highest. They are competing with each other for funds, and short-term performance is the name of the game. There are many investment possibilities, but the most common are equities, bonds, currencies, and commodities. There are many ways to place funds, some of which involve complex "derivative" instruments like options, futures, and credit default swaps. Some specialize in arbitrage, for example, buying and selling government bonds of different maturities or different qualities and "gearing up" forty or more times (i.e., acquiring assets 40 or more times the available capital by borrowing funds). Some of them, for example, the big international banks, not only run their own proprietary trading operations, but also make markets (i.e., will buy or sell with a spread) in all the financial instruments and will also extend credit to the other players.

It is of major importance to "the players" that their investments are liquid, so they can get out quickly if necessary. This is why unrestricted capital flow across borders is so vital to them. But these unrestricted flows are also the reason for the systemic recurrence of financial crises, because the foreign markets in which "the players" invest, even though large enough and liquid enough in normal markets, are extremely illiquid in a crisis. They are simply too small relative to the size of "the players" if and when the mood changes and everybody wants to get out at the same time, which is precisely what happens periodically. There is a saying on Wall Street that nobody ever lost his job for doing the same thing as everybody else. So they think alike, watch what each other is doing, and tend to follow the same strategies. When the mood shifts and they try to make sudden exits, they act like ten bulls in a china shop all trying to get out the only door. They suddenly make the frightening discovery that there are no buyers—*they are the market.* They panic, and the market collapses. It happens repeatedly and systemically.

The irony is that there is no justification for unrestricted capital flow beyond its convenience for international speculators. Joseph Stiglitz, former chief economist at the World Bank, points out that as regards "capital liberalization, there was scant evidence in support, and a massive amount of evidence against," and certainly "no evidence showing it spurs economic growth."[2] Also, as I pointed out earlier, it is unrestricted capital flow that prevents the developing countries from developing the industries where they would otherwise have a comparative advantage. Nevertheless, a return to controls on capital flows, which in my opinion is the only really effective way to curb recurrent international financial crises, is so fatal to The Neoliberal Project that it will never be accepted by the current political /economic elite. They would rather go down with their ship, and will, pulling the rest of us down with them, unless radical reforms are introduced along the lines of my proposals in parts 5 and 6 of this book. For the neoliberals, the ABC of acceptable reforms is: Anything But Controls.

Thailand 1997

By the late 1990s, Thailand, Malaysia, Indonesia, China, and South Korea had all established impressive growth records over the previous three decades by following the tried-and-true historical mercantile formula of all the industrialized countries, in particular, Great Britain and the United States—a government-directed industry policy with high tariffs and other protectionist measures for their most important native industries. They were further helped by traditionally high savings rates. Following Japan's lead, they focused on export-led growth in the areas where they could compete due to low-cost labor (garments, jewelry, footwear, processed foods) and invested heavily in education and research.

While inequalities were increasing, the poor were also participating to some extent in the growth. Savings rates were high, and they did not have a great need for foreign investment. But the Wall Street banks and other "players" were attracted by the high growth rates and diversification offered by these markets. Thus, many of the "Asian tigers" agreed to accept free capital movement, which had been pushed on them by the IMF even though they had no particular need for additional capital. This concession to the IMF proved to be their downfall in every single case, while China and India, with capital restrictions in place, came through the subsequent crisis unscathed.

The first domino to fall in the summer of 1997 was Thailand, whose foreign-exchange rate was "pegged" to the dollar. They had built up far too great a dependence on short-term foreign loans, social tensions were increasing as workers organized for pay hikes, and the trade deficit was increasing. The latter was partly due to the business cycle; partly due to losing market share to China, where labor costs were even lower. Foreign banks became nervous, and with no capital controls on short-term funds, there was a classic run for the exit. This put pressure on the currency as well as the equity market, and in no time Thailand lost most of its currency reserves trying to defend the "pegged" exchange rate, until it finally had to give up and let the Thai baht float. The IMF and Japan, the major creditor nation, put together a £17-billion bailout package to repay foreign investors, with the usual IMF conditions—austerity measures that would contract the economy and allow a buildup of foreign-exchange reserves so they could pay back the IMF and the foreign banks. These conditions included all the usual suspects: holding wages down, keeping interest rates high, reducing protectionist tariffs, cutting public expenses, and dropping subsidies.

The Thailand case was an example of how unrestricted capital flow allows "the players" to destroy a basically healthy economy on the other side of the world, first by investing far more than was needed, then trying to get it all out at once.

Contagion in Asia

We will now look at the second way that the lack of capital controls can destroy healthy economies—the virus effect. The 1997 Thai crisis spread quickly to several other countries not because there was anything fundamentally wrong, but because of the "lemming effect"—"the players" decided it was time to get out of the entire region, and with free capital movements, there were no circuit breakers. The situation was further exacerbated by domestic players who contributed to the panic by the classic "leads and lags phenomenon," i.e., hedge your foreign loans before the local currency is devalued, and delay billing of your foreign customers. The pressure on currency and equity markets was unbearable as everybody wanted liquidity and dollars. Malaysia, Indonesia, the Philippines, Russia, and Korea all went through the same basic pattern with the IMF, each being forced to devaluate its currency as "the players" sold out, and contract its economy in order to repay foreign banks and the IMF, with the usual harsh conditions based on the "one shoe fits all" philosophy of the IMF.

The hardest hit were ordinary working people. Unemployment was soon up 200% in Thailand, 300% in Korea, tenfold in Indonesia. Poverty skyrocketed in all countries, typically doubling or tripling. A year later, total income was down 13% in Indonesia, 11% in Thailand, and 7% in Korea. The one bright spot was the response of the local communities, where traditional social networks were still in place. Citizens worked together at the grassroots level, helping each other out, keeping children's education intact, and sharing food.[3] China and India, with capital controls in place, were untouched.

The One Exception

In tackling the crisis, only one of the Asian nations dared to defy the IMF. The results tell a revealing story about the neoliberal myths. Malaysian prime minister Mahathir Mohamad was furious with the way international financiers, whom he called "ferocious beasts," attacked his currency when the economy was basically sound. Correctly identifying free capital movement as the primary culprit, he imposed capital controls on transfers of capital out of the country in September 1998, pegged the currency at the relatively high level of 3.80 to the dollar, and froze repatriation of foreign investments for one year, except for profits. He also demanded that all foreign holdings of the Malaysian ringgit be repatriated within one month, and cut interest rates to stimulate the economy. Wall Street economists were quick to join the IMF, the U.S. secretary of the treasury, and the WTO in screaming "against the rules" at Malaysia and predicting imminent disaster as a result of Malaysia's capital controls. The very heart of neoliberal ideology had been challenged, and they felt that they had to react forcefully. The neoliberals said foreign investors would lose confidence in Malaysia for years, the stock market would plummet, a black market for the Malaysian ringgit would develop, and that capital outflow could in any case not be stopped. The economy would suffer, they claimed, growth would halt, recovery would be delayed, and, by the way, the controls, once installed, would never be removed.

When the controls *were* relaxed after one year, as promised by Mahathir, the neoliberal critics were shown to have been wrong *on every single prediction* of disaster. Harvard economists Ethan Kaplan and Dani Rodrik, in a comprehensive analysis of the Malaysian decision, concluded: "Compared to IMF programs, we find that the Malaysian policies produced faster economic recovery, smaller declines in employment and real wages, and more rapid turnaround in the stock market."[4] Malaysia recovered more quickly and with a shallower downturn than Thailand, which accepted the IMF program. The lower interest rates meant fewer bankruptcies, less government borrowing, and a smaller national debt than otherwise. The 3.80 exchange rate was maintained for over seven years. The IMF and Wall Street economists were so utterly wrong in their predictions of disaster that we have to conclude that their neoliberal theories are completely out of touch with the real world.

Some observers have suggested that a tax on financial transactions could be a way to reduce financial speculation. Such a tax could raise billions of dollars to support various global initiatives such as climate mitigation, and it would reduce speculation to some extent, and therefore I support this idea.[5] But I doubt that a small transaction tax is sufficient to prevent the kind of currency attacks we saw in Asia in 1998. To do that, capital controls are necessary, in my opinion.

Naked Derivatives

A derivative is a financial instrument whose value is related to an underlying asset, such as a stock, commodity, bond, or currency pair (e.g., dollar/euro). Examples include futures, options, and credit default swaps. The original justification for such instruments was the need for legitimate businesses to reduce the uncertainty in their transactions by paying a small premium for protection. For example, a farmer could sell his wheat crop on a futures market several months before harvest, and thus lock in his income. A pension fund could sell call options on its stocks (giving the buyer the right to purchase the stocks at predetermined prices) to create an income stream to compensate for a possible drop in market prices, at the same time giving up some of its upside potential. A European exporter of industrial goods to the United States could sell his expected dollar income well in advance to lock in the revenue in domestic currency. A European importer could do the opposite, buying dollars futures to lock in the cost of his raw materials. A mutual fund holding corporate or sovereign bonds that was nervous about the credit risk could—rather than selling the bonds—purchase a credit default swap (CDS) to protect against a possible default, in return for a small reduction in his effective interest income on the bonds. (The seller guarantees the buyer the full value of the bond if the issuer defaults.)

And who are the buyers of these instruments? In economic theory they are called "speculators" because they enter into the opposite contract purposely, not because they have any underlying interest. From their perspective, they receive an expected profit on their capital for taking on an unnecessary risk, for example, the seller of a credit default swap to a pension fund receives a constant stream of small premiums for taking on the risk of occasional large losses, much like an insurance company receives a premium for taking on the risk of fire in a large number of homes. These speculators thus serve a useful function in the real world of business.

All of the above are examples of so-called "covered derivatives," which are entered into by normal businessmen and their counterparties—"covered speculators"—as a routine part of their business, when the businessman has an underlying interest to protect. Covered derivatives are primarily defensive, quite useful, have a legitimate business purpose, and create no problem for the broader society. The problem for the broader society arises with so-called "naked derivatives." These are the same instruments entered into by two parties, *neither of whom has an underlying interest.* Naked derivatives are thus pure speculation, analogous to gambling, and have little or no redeeming social virtue. Let us call this activity "uncovered speculation" to distinguish it from "covered speculation."

The traditional justification for allowing uncovered speculation is the notion that it creates liquidity in the market, thus reducing the cost to legitimate businessmen who deal in covered derivatives. This liquidity argument is a truth that requires some modification. In my opinion, it is more like a fig leaf used to justify naked speculation.

A second argument often heard in favor of uncovered speculation is the supposed ability of such speculators to discover price discrepancies in the market, thus leading to more efficient market pricing. The theory is that "the markets" are the best judge of how appropriate the economic policies of a given country are. By selling the country's currency or sovereign bonds, they can express their displeasure with national policies. But the whole premise is nonsense. If they were neutral, qualified observers, it might make some sense. But they are not neutral, and almost never have an underlying business interest in the asset they are judging. For the most part they are biased speculators who are often "talking their book," i.e., trying to push others in the market in a direction that will profit their positions. Is there any good reason why sovereign nations should accept such a state of affairs? No, there is not. And it is time it came to an end.

Furthermore, my own research in the 1980s and 1990s refuted the theory that "the markets" base their actions on fundamental economic data—at least as far as the currency market is concerned. I led a high-powered research team that used state-of-the-art mathematical techniques to study historical currency movements in great detail. Our conclusion was clear: only trend-following models can adequately explain price movements. "The market" does not in general make decisions based on fundamental analysis. It follows trends. Not only do the "players" follow trends, but the largest hedge funds—sometimes working together in a conspiracy against the public—sometimes go one step further and create their own trends—so-called "front running."

By selling a particular currency aggressively—regardless of the fundamentals
—they can create a trend that attracts other speculators; then they cover
their positions at a profit when the small-fry trend followers pile in. In this
way they can create asset bubbles with unrealistic values far from intrinsic
value. Excessive oil and food prices over the past few years have resulted from
front running. Front running in the foreign exchange market was one reason
I got out. It was becoming far more difficult to forecast prices with historical
models of the kind I was using.

The danger to society arises when these "sharks" attack a smaller, less liquid
currency, not because there is any fundamental problem, but because they
see a profit opportunity, especially if they can get others to follow their front
running. And if the worst should happen, the IMF will help them exit with
a minimum of losses. This is basically what happened in the Asian currency
crises of 1997–98 when several basically healthy economies were destroyed
by the currency sharks.

A similar front running situation developed in 2010 with naked credit
default swaps on Greek sovereign debt. And it may well end up destroying
one or more European economies. The total outstanding volume of unregulated credit default swaps in September 2008 exceeded $62 trillion, more
than the GNP of the entire world economy, which is totally absurd. Over
95% of them are naked, nothing but bets between "the players," bets that
could just as easily be on a horse race, while tying up enormous amounts of
capital that is not available for ordinary businessmen, whose applications for
business loans at their local bank are often rejected. These enormous bets are
mostly taken by the largest financial institutions, but even they do not have
enough capital to back up potential losses if something goes wrong. Just five
banks—Goldman Sachs, Morgan Stanley, JPMorgan Chase, Citigroup, and
Bank of America are said to be involved in over 95% of the naked financial
derivatives.[6] And something will go wrong sooner or later.

Furthermore, these bets can become a self-fulfilling prophecy. For example, the Greek sovereign debt crisis of 2010 attracted front running CDS
sharks who claimed that Greece would eventually default on its debt. Their
actions pushed up Greek interest rates far beyond what they would have been
in the absence of the naked CDSs, exacerbating the problem. Regardless of
the final outcome of this particular Greek tragedy, the increasing costs of
protection in this kind of attack on a country's sovereign debt can attract
additional speculators until a panic brings about the very default that was
feared, even when the economic fundamentals do not justify it. It becomes
a self-fulfilling prophecy, just like the currency attacks of 1997–98 in Asia.

The speculators win big time while innocent taxpayers and the unemployed ultimately pay the costs.

In my opinion, all uncovered speculation (i.e., a where neither party has an underlying defensive interest) ought to be banned. First, because speculative buying can artificially push prices up to the point that severe damage is done to the real economy. A recent case is the exploding prices of grain in 2011 that put prices well above where they would have been in the absence of uncovered speculation, with the result that millions of people who could not afford the prices went hungry. Second, such speculation can bring about a financial crisis that would not otherwise have occurred. Third, a ban would free up enormous amounts of capital tied up in speculative products that make no contribution to the real economy. Business people with an underlying interest could still deal in covered derivatives. Granted, it would require them to pay a larger premium due to reduced liquidity. However, relative to the negative consequences of uncovered speculation, this is a small price to pay.

Gearing, or leveraging, is the practice of acquiring a derivative or a marketable asset, such as a stock, bond, currency cross, or commodity future on margin, i.e., with a small "down payment," usually cash, with the balance a debt, and which would typically include interest charges. The smaller the down payment, the higher the gearing. "Down payments" can typically vary from 2% to 10% (corresponding to gearing of 50 to 10 times), depending on the product, the selling financial institution or regulated exchange, and the creditworthiness of the customer. Gearing is quite risky, since both profits and losses are magnified. A less radical solution to the problem of naked derivatives could be to introduce much higher margin requirements on uncovered speculation. On regulated markets, such as stock and commodity exchanges, the minimum margin is normally specified by the regulating authority. In unregulated markets such as interbank currency trading or credit default swaps, it is up to the party exposed to the risk, typically a major bank, to specify minimum margins. Assessing the risk is quite critical to finding the appropriate margin. "Over-gearing" is when the margin is too low relative to the risk, for whatever reason. The crux of the problem is that participants in financial markets are under competitive pressure to underestimate the risk. Offering lower than appropriate margins can be a tempting way to attract business, but it introduces a systemic risk, as reflected in the street saying, "Gear today, gone tomorrow."

Take, for example, the failure of the hedge fund Long Term Capital Management (LTCM) in 1998. This $5-billion fund was allowed by its creditors to gear its speculative positions 25 times (4% margin). Its greatest exposure was in simultaneous long- and short-bond positions with spreads that were historically quite stable. Nevertheless, LTCM underestimated the liquidity risk in its positions. When the "lemmings" got nervous and instigated a "flight to quality," dumping anything the least bit risky—including credit lines to LTCM—and buying highly liquid treasury bills, they left LTCM with illiquid assets and spreads in its hedged position that were not supposed to occur "more than once in a thousand years." They ended up being bailed out by a rescue package organized by the Fed to prevent a chain reaction that could possibly have brought down other "players" and threatened the whole economy.

I had a similar experience on a much smaller scale in the 1990s while overseeing the currency portfolio in our little hedge fund. I was deeply shaken to observe "one hundred year events" occurring more and more frequently in the currency market. Things were happening that were "statistically impossible," just as at LTCM. These observations hastened my retreat from the business, as it became clear to me that my mathematical models (and those of all the other market players) were no longer reflecting the realities of the market. Why? Probably because of front running and the human factor, including the herd reactions of "the players" that takes over from time to time in panics and is not reflected in the historical data. While high margins (I would say at least 50% would be needed) are not quite as good a solution as a total ban, I would venture to say that without over-gearing there would be far fewer financial crises. Next to capital controls, a ban or even 50% margins on naked derivatives is—from the players' perspective—the worst possible reform for the financial elite because it would be like a blow to the solar plexus, and they would rather drag us all down with their ship than accept either of these two reforms.

The Financial Crisis of 2007–8

This most recent crisis had elements of all three "culprits"—deregulation and over-gearing of naked derivatives at the national level in the United States and unrestricted capital movements, which spread it like a virus to the rest of the world.

A major deregulation event that paved the way for the crisis was the repeal of the American Glass-Steagall Act in 1999 under pressure from the financial elite, who wanted more freedom to operate. This act was passed originally back in 1933 to prevent the kind of irresponsible and unregulated speculation that was identified at that time as a major cause of the 1929 stock market crash. The effect of the original act was to separate normal retail banking functions from all other financial activities such as asset management, investment advising, trading on own account, stock brokerage, and insurance, and to introduce a stricter regulative regime in all these sectors. When this act was repealed in 1999, the way was opened for unregulated speculation. By putting all these diverse financial activities under the same hat, effective regulation was neutralized, as these financial institutions could do anything they wanted in the unregulated parts of their dynasties. In effect, even the commercial banks were able to act like unregulated hedge funds, often engaging in complex and risky derivatives that were off the banks' balance sheets and thus hidden from scrutiny.

Washington insiders from the financial community, who had access to Presidents Bill Clinton and George W. Bush, did everything they could to prevent the regulation of derivatives, which are one of the most lucrative income sources for Wall Street.

Brooksley Born, head of the Commodity Futures Trading Commission (CFTC), warned Congress in the mid-1990s that credit default swaps and naked derivatives risked blowing up the global financial system. She was subsequently confronted by Federal Reserve chairman Alan Greenspan, secretary of the treasury Robert Rubin (former head of Goldman Sachs), and deputy treasury secretary Larry Summers, and forced out of her job. Summers even said to her that if she continued to push for regulation on derivatives, "You're going to cause the worst financial crisis since the end of World War II," claiming he had thirteen bankers in his office who informed him of this.[7]

The administration of George W. Bush went even further, cutting market oversight to almost nothing. In testimony under oath, Lynn Turner, chief accountant of the Securities and Exchange Commission (SEC) testified that the SEC Office of Risk Management, which had oversight responsibility for the credit-default-swap market, was cut from a staff of one hundred people down to one person. That is not a typo—a 99% cut![8]

The subprime housing market is often cited as the major cause of the crisis, but this is misleading because the problem is systemic. With Glass-Steagall out of the way, the post-1999 financial world became even more of a casino, unrelated to the underlying economy. Money was not being used productively but for naked speculation. Yet the "casino" is indirectly relevant to the real economy in the sense that the positions of all "the players" are intertwined, so that a failure of one of them could cause a domino effect and bring down the others and hence the whole economy, with only taxpayers left to pick up the bill. A chain reaction almost happened when the investment bank Lehman Brothers in September 2008 crashed in the biggest bankruptcy in U.S. history. At the time, its gearing was over 30; earlier in the year, it was about 40. Gearing 40 times means that if the value of your positions decreases by just 2.5%, you are insolvent. And many of those Lehman assets were high risk and low quality. To get an idea of the size, over $1 trillion in claims have been made against Lehman Brothers. Commercial banks in most countries are not allowed to gear up their capital base more than about 10 times, so Lehman was ultra-speculative by normal standards, but not by "the players'" standards. Lehman did not do anything radically different from the others. It was simply the slowest bull in the china shop.

In a recent study, former chief economist of the IMF, Raghuram G. Rajan, argues that increasing inequality was a deeper cause of the 2007–8 financial crisis. His logic is that lower and middle class incomes were squeezed by neoliberal economics for three decades. In order to maintain their accustomed standard of living, this group thus went into greater debt, far beyond what was prudent. Indeed, they were encouraged to do so by the big banks. At the same time, the wealthy, having increasing incomes, not least due to the Bush tax cuts, saved more and tended to invest wherever they could get the highest short-term return, which in practice meant high-risk products like subprime loans, credit default swaps, and naked derivatives—sold by the same banks that were encouraging their retail customers to acquire more debt. The whole system was unstable and doomed to crash sooner or later. The level of inequality in the United States just before the 2007–8 crash was the highest since just before the stock market crash of 1929.[9]

The statement that "No one saw it coming," prevalent in the mainstream press during the crisis, should be added to the neoliberal myth list. In reality, many economists saw the crisis coming, a fact that is well documented, as anyone who spends a few minutes searching the Internet can confirm. But it is true that little was published in mainstream media because little was heard from their mainstream economist friends, who were more or less silenced by their complicity in the whole Neoliberal Project. It would have been heretical for them to question the religion. The warnings came from independently minded economists on the periphery of the mainstream, and there were actually quite a few of them. They included Steve Keen, Dean Baker, Hazel Henderson, George Soros, David Korten, Nouriel Roubini, and myself. Even in 2000, it seemed clear that the current financial system would melt down unless fundamental reforms were made.[10]

The 2010 Dodd-Frank financial reform bill got a lot of press coverage as a strong response to the financial crisis, but in reality it changes nothing that is vital to "the players." The next crisis is still right around the bend. There were no killer proposals of the kind I recommend. There were a few less radical proposals that would have helped a little, but they were made harmless by the political cronies elected with Wall Street money and the thousands of professional lobbyists that roam the floors of Congress. The financial sector has grown so large in the United States that it has a stranglehold on legislation. The new rules included a little more supervision, a little more transparency, and many more regulations, but nothing that prevented the CEOs of Citigroup and Goldman Sachs from endorsing the changes. Bank shares actually gained ground when the Senate passed the bill, which tells us what Wall Street thought of it. Incidentally, the details of many of the new rules and regulations will not be known for years. In the meantime, regulatory authorities will negotiate the changes with armies of special-interest lobbyists. I am not optimistic about the outcome of that dialogue. Some of the less important financial derivatives will probably have to be exchange-traded (a minor improvement), but the ones that really count—currencies, for example—are covered by exceptions that keep them out of sight of the regulators. Effective changes have been bypassed without even a discussion. No one suggested putting controls on international capital flows. No one suggested a ban on naked derivatives. No one proposed reinstatement of Glass-Steagall or breaking up the big banks. Those kinds of reforms would be effective—too effective for "the players"—and hence their political cronies—to accept.

Threats about effective reforms are what one Wall Street pundit called "using live ammunition," i.e., reforms that could really kill Wall Street's golden goose, as if the financial crisis was just a computer game without human consequences. A similar "player" panic occurred on the occasion of the first potentially effective political response to the financial crisis from Europe, when German chancellor Merkel in May 2010 banned the use of naked credit default swaps on German debt and subsequently, together with France's president Sarkozy, announced that they wished to ban short selling and the use of naked credit default swaps on all EU sovereign debt. When word slipped out, the financial sector was truly frightened that effective action might finally be coming, and financial stocks fell immediately on all stock exchanges across the world. But the global financial lobby acted quickly, calling their political cronies while issuing the usual dire warnings of impending doom if any such action were to be taken. At the time of writing, the situation is still in limbo.

I do not expect any effective action will be taken to prevent recurrent financial crises, certainly not in the United States. The financial mafia is simply too powerful. Therefore, I will go on record again with pretty much the same statement that I made over ten years ago. The current global financial system is systemically unstable and flawed and continues to be an accident waiting to happen. The only unknowns are when and how the next accident will be precipitated. It won't be subprime loans next time. It will be something else, probably the bursting of the growth bubble due to a peak-oil scare, unless something else goes terribly wrong in the meantime, like credit default swaps, a sovereign debt crisis, the breakup of the euro, or a major hedge fund collapse. Take your pick. The whole system is out of control.

At the time of writing, the attention of the financial community is on the sovereign debt crisis in Europe, which could potentially develop into as big a crisis as the 2008/9 subprime loan crisis. However, this is a very different and unique kind of financial crisis, not grounded in the three "culprits"— deregulation, free capital flow and naked derivatives— but rather grounded in a poorly designed European monetary system, which was bound to run into difficulty sooner or later.   I will have more to say about the eurozone crisis in Chapter 13 when I discuss currency regimes. However, whatever the outcome of the ongoing European sovereign debt crisis, it will be nothing like the coming energy descent crisis, which will be far more serious.

Where to Go from Here

We have identified a number of drivers of destruction, all related directly or indirectly to a worldview of separation that considers Nature as a collection of resources to be exploited but with no intrinsic value in itself; and humans as separate both from Nature and other humans. This way of thinking has created a society that is destroying its natural capital, the source of all life; it has created an exploitative economic system that is in direct conflict with the fundamental laws of physics and thus has no concept of limits to growth; it has created increasing inequality, which results in major social and health problems and decreasing well-being; it has created a speculative financial system driven by greed that is destabilizing and out of control; and it has created an explosion of population fueled by the use in a few generations of irreplaceable resources that took millions of years for Nature to produce.

None of the above phenomena are external to humanity. All are man-made; all can be changed. The next obvious step, then, is to examine the human decision making that is allowing these disasters to happen, i.e., the political power structures that define the human factor that is driving the drivers.

PART THREE

The Empire

A house divided against itself cannot stand.

—ABRAHAM LINCOLN

SEVEN

The Kennan Doctrine

The less we are hampered by idealistic slogans, the better.
—George F. Kennan

The guiding doctrine followed by the American political leadership over the past half century, and the reasoning behind it, was formulated in a remarkably clear statement by George F. Kennan, director of the Policy Planning Staff, in his "Top Secret Memo PPS/23" to the secretary of state in February 1948:

> We have about 50% of the world's wealth but only 6.3 of its population. This disparity is particularly great as between ourselves and the peoples of Asia. In this situation, we cannot fail to be the object of envy and resentment. Our real task in the coming period is to devise a pattern of relationships, which will permit us to maintain this position of disparity without positive detriment to our national security. To do so we will have to dispense with all sentimentality and daydreaming; and our attention will have to be concentrated everywhere on our immediate national objectives. We need not deceive ourselves that we can afford today the luxury of altruism and world benefaction. In the face of this situation we would be better off to dispense now with a number of the concepts which have underlined our thinking with regard to the Far East. We should dispense with the aspiration to "be liked" or to be regarded as the repository of a high-minded international altruism. We should stop putting ourselves in the position of being our brothers' keeper and refrain from offering moral and ideological advice. We should cease to talk about vague—and for the Far East—unreal objectives such as human rights, the raising of the living standards, and democratization. The day is not far off when we are going to have to deal in straight power concepts. The less we are hampered by idealistic slogans, the better.[1]

We see here a classic attitude of the worldview of separation. There is no sense of global solidarity or sharing. Kennan's doctrine is a blueprint for empire. There is only the wish to continue to control 50% of the world's resources at the expense of everyone else. Other countries might as well be enemies from outer space. They receive no consideration. They will be dealt with using "straight power concepts." But a dilemma is created by this doctrine, because the proclaimed values of the United States for which it has been widely admired for over 200 years are precisely those values that must be sacrificed, and that in practice *have* been sacrificed: "human rights, the raising of living standards [of the developing countries], and democratization." Therefore the doctrine must not be announced openly to the American people, who would never accept it if they had any choice in the matter. It is a doctrine of the ruling elite. Thus the U.S. leadership has been forced to be hypocritical, cynical, even schizophrenic, saying one thing while doing another. The dilemma facing the political/economic elite is that their citizens truly *believe* in democracy, not only for themselves, but for *everyone*. For the average citizen, democracy is not just a word for political speeches, without consequence for economic and foreign policy. They really *mean* it.

Democracy in America

The Kennan doctrine raises the question of whether or not the United States can still be considered a real democracy of the people, and if not, then what has it become? This question is vital if we are to determine who is really in charge of world affairs and hence the ongoing destruction. Who is really making the top-level decisions in this "Kennanite" world of false flags and double-dealing and why?

Democracy has always been a nebulous term, meaning different things to the rulers and the ruled. For most ordinary people, it means that they are masters of their own fate. It means that they have the right and the power to determine what kind of world they live in. But for democratically elected leaders, things have never been quite this simple. There has always been, and still is, a deep fear of what true democracy might lead to, i.e., giving the people the power to have what they really want rather than what the elected leadership and their financial backers want.

James Madison, the prime drafter of the U.S. Constitution, set the tone very early on, arguing that a major function of government was "to protect the minority of the opulent against the majority." Echoing sentiments similar to those expressed by the aristocracy of Great Britain at the time, he feared that "the property of landed proprietors would be insecure" if elections "were open to all classes of people." Madison scholars are in general agreement that "the Constitution was intrinsically an aristocratic document designed to check the democratic tendencies of the period." For Madison, the solution was to keep political power in the hands of those who "represent the wealth of the nation," i.e., property owners. He called them the "more capable set of men."[2]

In the subsequent 200-plus years, the power struggle between the "opulent minority" and the great majority has continued unabated. For most of this period, the trend has been toward more democracy in the United States, as slavery was abolished, the right to vote was extended to women, the New Deal provided a social safety net, and the civil rights movement of the 1960s extended the voting franchise to blacks. But since the coming of neoliberalism in the 1980s, the trend has been reversed, evolving into the situation, as we know it today, with the minority owners of great private wealth enjoying unprecedented influence while a frustrated majority experiences disempowerment and a constant deterioration in their freedom and quality of life.

Most observers would agree that merely having elections every four years is not sufficient evidence that a nation is democratic. Additional information is required before coming to such a conclusion. This would include answers to the following questions. Do voters have a real choice, or are we looking at what is essentially a one-party system? Do all citizens have reasonably equal voting rights, access to vote, and opportunity to stand for election? Do citizens actually turn out to vote in large numbers? Is the information provided by the media balanced or does it tend to promote a particular political view? Do particular segments of society have undue influence on who is elected through nepotism, financial support, or other means, i.e., are the elected politicians truly representative of the people? Are the candidates for election men and women of the highest integrity and incorruptible? Are there significant obstacles to the formation of new parties? To what degree do citizens have influence on political decisions between elections through some form of participatory democracy? Does the nation in question practice and promote the ideals of democracy in its foreign policy? On all of these points, there are serious questions about the degree of true democracy present in twenty-first-century United States.

Voter Turnout

The lack of real choice in America is reflected in voter turnout. When voters do not feel that their interests are adequately represented by the available candidates or that their vote will have no influence on their daily lives, they simply stay home. If we look at the record since 1946, we see clear evidence of a deterioration of democracy in the United States as measured by voter participation. At the height of the "golden age" in the 1950s and 1960s, U.S. voter turnout (expressed as a percent of voting-age population) peaked at 63.1% (1960) for presidential election years and 48.4% (1966) for non-presidential years. A general decline in voter turnout since the mid-1960s reached an all-time low at 46.6% (2000) for presidential elections and a mere 34.7% (1998) for non-presidential elections. This is not conclusive evidence, but does suggest that it is primarily a sense of lack of real political choice that lies behind the falling voter turnouts in the converging two-party system of the United States. As Noreena Hertz of Cambridge University puts it, voters "feel that in many cases politicians have entered into a covert pact with business. And so, increasingly, they are turning their backs on politics."[3]

Equal Access to Vote

American voting statistics reveal a significant difference from other democracies as regards the percentage of voting-age population that is actually registered to vote. For the United States, the average figure for the years 1968–2008 was only about 70%. In most European countries, for all practical purposes, 100% of those eligible to vote are registered. The difference stems primarily from the American tradition of requiring an active initiative on the part of the voter to get registered thirty days before the election. In Denmark, for example, all eligible voters are automatically sent a voting card by their local community at their place of residence well in advance of the election—everything is computerized and continually updated. This is typical of most modern European democracies. Has the home of the computer fallen behind technologically? Or is it done on purpose?

Award-winning scholars Frances Fox Piven and Richard Cloward, in their comprehensive study of American voting patterns, write, "The United States is the only major democratic nation in which the less well-off are substantially underrepresented in the electorate" and "where government assumes no responsibility for helping citizens cope with voter registration procedures."[4] The American system is thus decidedly biased against the poorer, less-educated citizens, who are the ones most likely not to register, continuing a policy that goes back to the founding fathers. The bias is compounded by the notoriously inefficient American system for registering and counting votes, particularly in poorer precincts, as demonstrated dramatically to the world in the 2000 presidential election.

Is This Representative Democracy?

The single most important factor in getting elected in the United States today is the ability to attract substantial funding from corporations, unions, and wealthy individuals, either directly as donations or indirectly as in "issue advocacy" campaigns and independent advertising in support of the candidate. Noam Chomsky puts it this way: "In U.S. electoral politics, the richest one-quarter of 1 percent of Americans make 80 percent of all individual political contributions, and corporations outspend labor by a margin of ten to one."[5]

Money seldom comes without expecting something in return. The Democratic Party shifted to the right in the 1980s by adjusting positions on defense spending and welfare benefits, thus becoming more attractive to business donors. The campaign-money factor seems to be quite significant in explaining the convergence of the Democrats and Republicans on issues of interest to the corporate sector. Corporations have plain and simply purchased influence. In a series of public opinion polls by *USA Today*/Gallup between 1992 and 2008, a majority of Americans on average (varying from 49% to 61%) thought that "quite a few of the people running the government are a little crooked." In a *CBS News/New York Times* poll in July 2004, 64% agreed that "the government was run by a few big interests rather than for the benefit of all." In another *CBS News/New York Times* poll in January 2006, 48% of those polled thought that "most or about half" of the members of Congress were "financially corrupt."[6]

The control of American corporations over the electoral process was further strengthened recently by a Supreme Court decision in January 2010, which, for the first time allows unlimited and anonymous corporate funding of independent political broadcasts in candidate elections, reversing a long-standing ban. President Obama's comment on the ruling in his weekly radio address was: "This ruling strikes at our democracy itself" and "I can't think of anything more devastating to the public interest."[7]

To illustrate how the mechanics work with a typical case, the following example, described vividly by Dean McSweeney of the University of the West of England, happened to enter the public domain on account of the comprehensive Watergate investigation, and is in all likelihood representative of practices that continue to this day. Election finance laws have changed since, but politicians and wealthy corporations striving for influence continue to find new loopholes in an ongoing struggle to evade the intention of the law. He writes:

> Watergate exposed the futility of existing law in preventing abuses. Companies such as Goodyear, American Airlines and 3M contributed to CRP (The Committee to Re-elect the President), a violation of federal law since 1907. Watergate also exposed the favorable treatment in government toward contributors. Government subsidies of milk prices followed an agreement by Associated Milk Producers, Inc. to donate $2 million to Nixon's campaign. CRP sought company donations accompanied by threats of retaliation for non-payment. Some wealthy backers were rewarded with government appointments despite their dubious credentials. Ambassadorships were allocated by auction. According to testimony at the Watergate hearings, Socialite Ruth Farkas famously complained to President Richard Nixon's lawyer: "Isn't $250,000 an awful lot of money for Costa Rica? "[8]

In 2000, candidates for the Senate spent an average of $5.7 million on their campaigns, a good portion of which was provided by the candidates themselves. Challengers especially tend to spend their own money, on average 20% of the total. But averages tend to blur the extreme cases. For example, Jon Corzine spent $60 million of his own money in his successful bid for the Senate, Mark Dayton spent almost $12 million, and Maria Cantwell $10 million out of her own pocket. Like CEO salaries, money spent to be elected to the U.S. Senate is one of the things that increased most rapidly in the neoliberal period. Adjusted for inflation, total spending for Senate elections increased by 331% in the period 1976–2000. Unadjusted, the increase was 1,203%.[9]

Personal wealth has thus become a major factor determining election to the U.S. Senate. Personal wealth is likely to be even more important in future U.S. elections, as recent finance-reform legislation puts new restrictions on the amounts that can be donated to candidates, while at the same time, the profit windfall to corporate executives in recent years means that more and more people from the business community have the wherewithal to make a Senate challenge using their own funds, following the example of Jon Corzine, who is the former cochairman of investment banking firm Goldman Sachs. Perhaps in the future people may think: wouldn't it be more efficient and cheaper to just ask a committee of the Fortune 500 to appoint 100 senators?

The Culture of Money

A money-based economy skews politics heavily in the direction of those with money—big money. For example, the rejection of the Kyoto agreement by the United States was largely a thank-you to the American multinationals. The corporate members of the Business Roundtable, a lobby organization for the 200 largest U.S. corporations, contribute enormous sums regularly to influence political decisions. The *increase alone* in annual dues was $300,000 per company in 1998. They ran expensive campaigns against not only Kyoto, but also against the "Patients' Bill of Rights" legislation, spending $5 million on issue ads alone in 1998.[10]

It is not just American corporations that influence American politics. According to a report by the Climate Action Network Europe (CANE), in October 2010—based on publicly available records—major European corporate polluters, including Lafarge, GDF-Suez, EON, BP, BASF, Bayer, Solvay, and Arcelor-Mittal, spent $240,000 supporting climate deniers and blockers of effective climate solutions, who were running for the U.S. Senate in 2010. CANE writes: "Their overseas support is all the more galling because the same companies argue that additional emissions reductions in Europe cannot be pursued until the United States takes action," a cynical double-dealing maneuver CANE calls "climate sabotage."[11]

Elizabeth Drew, highly respected American journalist and longtime commentator on the Washington scene, writes the following about the capital of the money-based society. "The culture of money dominates Washington as never before, money now rivals or even exceeds power as the premium goal. It affects the issues raised and their outcome; it has changed employment patterns in Washington; it has transformed politics; and it has subverted values. It has led good people to do things that are morally questionable, if not reprehensible. It has cut a deep gash, if not inflicted a mortal wound, in the concept of public service."[12]

Occasionally the real facts come inadvertently from the mouths of those directly involved. For example, a Congressional lobbyist said to Elizabeth Drew, "I would have to conclude that in a lot of the fights (in Congress) there are no real people involved. It's a battle of corporations. You can get into an abstract discussion about the effects on the economy. Bunk. It's a decision between the very wealthy and the very rich." Another lobbyist educated her about the virtues of "soft" versus "hard" money for politicians. "If you go up to Congressman John Smith and say, 'John. We're going to give you ten thousand dollars,' it's much more valuable to him than if you give an amorphous fifty thousand in soft money to the national committee. The only way you get attention with soft money is it has to be really big: three hundred, four hundred, five hundred thousand, a million—that gets people's attention."[13] In 1998 there were 11,500 registered lobbyists wandering the halls of Congress. Today the number is closer to 25,000.

One of the lobbyists' tasks is to "create the illusion of grassroots support" for a congressman's proposal. One lobbyist confessed to Elizabeth Drew that he had been involved in the mid 1990s with a "completely manufactured" campaign to create a grassroots illusion with a promised budget of fifteen to twenty million dollars. "Sometimes you're trying to convince the Congress that there's a groundswell, but there's nobody behind it. If you have to make it up, you hope you won't be found out. It's like the Wizard of Oz—there's nobody there but you and the smoke and the whistle."[14]

One of the perfectly legal but highly questionable American practices is so-called earmarking, whereby a member of Congress is able to insert a "rider" into an appropriation bill—without any debate—allocation of substantial funds, which are often irrelevant to the bill, for special projects that no one has asked for and are not in the nation's interest, but which are in the member's personal interest. The practice has been exploding in recent years, and reached the amazing level of $32.4 billion in 2004. In 2005 13,998 such earmarks were approved, including $28 billion alone for defense contractors. No one seems to mind, because everyone gets their turn at the spigot. No public record exists to reveal who added the unrequested grants.[15]

Marjorie Kelly, cofounder and publisher of *Business Ethics*, in analyzing the system of governance that has emerged in the United States, identifies as "the core problem of our economy: wealth discrimination." She compares the passive acceptance of the rights of capital to the "divine right of kings" of the European monarchical period, when no one questioned the notion that the king owned the nation and could use it for his private purposes. Thus we now unquestioningly accept that shareholders have all the property rights in a corporation and that it is perfectly all right for a small minority of wealthy individuals to have far greater influence on the political process, the media, and education than the great majority of citizens. She points out that positive wealth discrimination is a direct continuation of the aristocratic tradition that the founding fathers sought to remove and may be an infringement of the "equal protection of the law" provision of the Fourteenth Amendment to the U.S. Constitution. Wealth discrimination must necessarily go the same way that sex and race discrimination have gone before any country can claim to be a truly democratic society.[16]

Corruption in Politics

It is rare that an American politician is caught red-handed actually taking a bribe. Most influence peddling is technically legal—as in the so-called swinging-door phenomenon, where politicians and federal regulators after leaving their public positions are rewarded with high-paying jobs within the industries that they have supported through legislation or regulation. Congressman Randy "Duke" Cunningham was one who was careless, pocketing $2.4 million in return for seeing that contracts worth millions of dollars went to particular defense contractors. He was sentenced to eight years and four months in prison.[17]

A study by Kimberly Ann Elliott for the Institute of International Economics in Washington reports that high levels of correlation are found between corruption and four factors: the presence of monopolies; market dominance by a few firms with lax antitrust enforcement; government subsidies; and the absence of freedom to hold property, earn a living, operate a business, invest one's earnings, and trade internationally. It is noteworthy that three of these four factors—monopolies, market dominance, and large subsidies—are all major characteristics of neoliberal economics, and are all counter to the fundamental principles of Adam Smith's classical economics, which requires small buyers and sellers who cannot influence prices (or politicians!).[18]

The savings and loan crash of the 1980s provides a rare revelation of how the political/economic establishment functions in practice, and in particular the way modern-day merchants influence the political process to get the legislation and regulation they want. Fraud and insider abuse were aggravating factors in the wave of the S&L failures, and the most notorious figure was undoubtedly Charles Keating, CEO of Lincoln Savings in California. Keating was convicted of fraud, racketeering, and conspiracy, and spent four and one-half years in prison.

It turns out that five U.S. Senators, known subsequently as the "Keating Five" (Alan Cranston, Dennis DeConcini, Donald Riegle, John McCain, and John Glenn), were involved in an influence-peddling scheme that put pressure on the Federal Home Loan Bank Board to lay off Charles Keating in their investigation of possible criminal activities at Lincoln. Their apparent motivation became clear during the investigation. Cranston had received $39,000 from Keating and his associates for his 1986 Senate reelection campaign. Furthermore, Keating had donated some $850,000 to assorted groups founded by Cranston or controlled by him, and another $85,000 to the California Democratic Party. DeConcini had received about $48,000 from Keating and his associates for his 1988 Senate reelection campaign. Riegle had received some $76,000 from Keating and his associates for his 1988 Senate reelection campaign. Glenn had received $34,000 in direct contributions from Keating and his associates for his 1984 presidential nomination campaign, and a political action committee tied to Glenn had received an additional $200,000. Between 1982 and 1987, McCain had received $112,000 in political contributions from Keating and his associates. In addition, McCain's wife and her father had invested $359,100 in a Keating shopping center. McCain, his family, and their babysitter had made nine trips at Keating's expense, sometimes aboard Keating's private jet.

Of the five, only Alan Cranston was reprimanded for his actions. Strictly speaking, what the senators did was not illegal under existing law. Jonathan Alter of *Newsweek* called the S&L scandal a classic case of the government trying to investigate itself, labeling the Senate Ethics Committee "shameless" for having "let four of the infamous Keating Five off with a wrist tap." Common Cause, which had initially demanded the investigation, also thought the treatment of the senators far too lenient, and said, "[The] action by the Senate Ethics Committee is a cop-out and a damning indictment of the committee," and "The U.S. Senate remains on the auction block to the Charles Keatings of the world." Joan Claybrook, president of Public Citizen, called it a "whitewash."[19]

In his defense, Cranston was unrepentant, claiming that he did nothing other than what every other senator also did. The only difference was that he got caught. This is the most revealing statement of all, and is consistent with the mild reprimand, and the known facts. This case is just one example out of many, most of which never reach the public domain. If Cranston's claim is true, then the business community has a virtual stranglehold not only on the legislative process, but also on the U.S. government agencies responsible for oversight and regulation of the private sector. We can no longer separate politics from business, which, like Charles Keating, is "paying for the music."

Media Influence

To be considered a truly democratic society, it is necessary to have a media world that permits, and even encourages, diverse points of view in a vibrant public debate, and which allows equal time to views that are counter to the interests of the dominant ruling elite. Noam Chomsky and Edward Herman have developed and tested extensively what they call a "propaganda model" of the American media scene, which shows that the United States currently fails this test of democracy miserably. They show that the structure of the media industry subtly makes sure that the worldview presented is one that confirms and supports the interests of the giant corporations that are the *de facto* political power in the United States.[20]

In David Edwards' words, they achieve a control that is "tighter than anything imagined by Orwell, or practiced by totalitarian governments."[21] The system is subtle in the sense that the vast majority of Americans are not even aware of how one-sided and manipulated their news sources are.

Foreign Policy

The American "propaganda model" tends to present viewpoints that reinforce corporate values and filter out views that represent other values or are critical of U.S. behavior internationally. The result of this is that most Americans have very little awareness of how the rest of the world perceives their society. This was illustrated very dramatically with the Twin Towers attack of September 11, 2001. Most Americans were quite shocked that anyone could think badly of them. The rest of the world, while sympathizing with the victims ("We are all Americans today"), was much less surprised.

Johan Galtung, the highly respected Norwegian peace researcher, calls the U.S. track record for violence since World War II "overwhelming."[22] Quoting a comprehensive study by William Blum—*Rogue State: A Guide to the World's Only Superpower*[23]—Galtung lists 67 "global interventions" initiated by the United States in the period from 1945 to 2001. Many of them, says Galtung, "maybe most, can be characterized as state terrorism."[24]

In his study, William Blum lists 35 cases of attempted or successful assassination attempts by the United States, including democratic heads of state; assistance in torture in 11 countries; 25 cases of bombings; and most disturbing of all, 23 countries where the United States was "perverting elections—interfering with a democratic process." Furthermore, some of the most violent actions were taken against former "clients" who had been supported by the United States financially and with arms, and kept in power as long as they were useful to American foreign policy objectives—Pol Pot (Cambodia), Manuel Noriega (Panama), Mohammed Aideed (Somalia), Saddam Hussein (Iraq), and Osama bin Laden (Afghanistan).

The explanations given to the American public for armed interventions change with the situation—it could be "hindering the spread of communism," the "liberation of suppressed people," "restoring democracy," "removing weapons of mass destruction," or the "war on terrorism," anything but the real agenda, which Galtung describes as reacting to "whatever can be seen as hostile to U.S. business abroad." Referring to the global inequalities brought about by their policies, Galtung notes that most Americans, while benefiting from U.S. policy, are "uncomfortable about it; like the Germans under Nazism." He adds that "When the chips are all down, like slavery and colonialism, massive global injustice is basically . . . a moral problem."[25]

According to longtime CIA career agent Ralph McGehee, misinforming American citizens is a major part of the CIA's mission, writing: "The CIA is not now nor has it ever been a central intelligence agency. It is the covert active arm of the President's foreign policy advisers. In that capacity it overthrows or supports foreign governments, while reporting 'intelligence' justifying those activities. It shapes its intelligence . . . to support presidential policy. Disinformation is a large part of its covert action responsibilities, and the American people are the primary target of its lies."[26] It would seem that the Iraq war is just the latest example in a long-term covert propaganda program, with the underlying purpose of creating domestic support for the control of foreign nations important for American business—actions that would never have been supported if the American people had been fully informed about what was going on and why.

The list of countries that have tried to choose a path different from the United States', with a greater empathy for the poorer segments of society and less for the wealthy elite and their business interests, and with a desire for freedom, democracy, independence, and self-determination, is long, and is basically identical with the cases where the United States has intervened, usually clandestinely. These are not cases of Soviet-style communism by a long shot. They are in most cases broadly supported democratic initiatives, or uprisings against illegitimate and oppressive regimes. Blum's list includes, among others, the following: Italy, 1945–49; Greece, 1947–48; Philippines, 1945–53; Iran, 1953; Indonesia, 1957–58; Guyana, 1953–64; Vietnam, 1950–73; Guatemala, 1954; Cambodia, 1955–73; Zaire, 1960–65; Dominican Republic, 1963–66; Cuba; 1959– ; Brazil, 1964; Indonesia, 1965; Greece, 1964–74; Chile, 1973; East Timor, 1975–2002; Grenada, 1979–84; Nicaragua, 1979–90; Libya, 1981–89; Panama, 1989; Afghanistan, 1979–92; El Salvador, 1980–92; Haiti, 1987–94.[27]

In almost every case, U.S. interference choked off attempts at democratic reform that would have given more power to the people for self-determination and less to the wealthy elite's commercial interests. In almost every case, the result was massive slaughter of freedom-loving people and the installation of U.S.-supported terrorist military regimes that were friendly to American business interests. In almost every case, the real facts were withheld from the American people or grossly manipulated. Sometimes an example can put the message across much more forcefully. Let us look briefly at a few cases.

Iran 1953

One of the pivotal events of the twentieth century—having long-lasting consequences to our day and beyond—was the overthrow of the democratically elected government of Iran in 1953 in a cooperative venture between the CIA and British intelligence. The result was the installation of an oppressive regime under Shah Mohammed Reza Pahlavi, with massive financial and military support from the United States, that held the Iranian population in an iron grip for twenty-five years. Torture, tyranny, suppression of a free press, abolition of democracy and human rights—and, of course, American access to cheap oil and new military bases—characterized this period.

The background was as follows. In the early twentieth century, BP—then known as the Anglo-Persian Oil Company, and later again as the Anglo-Iranian Oil Company—made the first major discovery of Middle East oil in Iran. It was worth an immense fortune. Great Britain then effectively stole Iran's oil resources by paying the corrupt monarchy a pittance for the exclusive rights to *all* the profits from Iranian oil production for all eternity. For almost fifty years, Iranian oil was one of the most important income sources for Great Britain. Therefore, the British were very upset when Prime Minister Mohammed Mossadegh's government decided that enough was enough and decided to return the stolen property to its rightful owner in 1951 when the Iranian parliament unanimously voted to nationalize the Anglo-Iranian Oil

Company. Mossadegh was a pro-Western leader and a nationalist, being very popular at home and highly respected abroad. He was even chosen *Time* magazine's "Man of the Year" in 1951. The British, whose military and financial position had deteriorated severely as a result of World War II, turned to the United States for help. But President Truman did not see any good reason to intervene in the internal affairs of another democratic state and urged the British prime minister Winston Churchill to respect Iranian nationalism. Failure to accommodate Iran's nationalist aspirations, Truman warned, would risk allowing the Soviets to control this strategically important country.

However, when President Eisenhower and his aggressive secretary of state, John Foster Dulles, came to power in 1953, the tune changed. With his military background, Eisenhower could see the importance of having a strong military presence in the Middle East in the developing global competition for influence with the Soviet Union. In addition, access to oil was critical for the military and important for U.S. business interests, who felt left out relative to British and French companies. But he needed a better excuse if he were to get the American people behind him. That was taken care of by postulating the threat of a communist takeover of Iran if no action were to be taken—the very opposite of Truman's warning. The problem with this argument was that there *was* no communist influence to speak of in Iran. Prime Minister Mossadegh was an aristocrat who was both anticommunist and anti-Islam. Thus the CIA was given the task of creating the illusion of a communist uprising by staging various events in Iran while placing false-flag articles in the American media. Then the CIA sent Kermit Roosevelt and his team to Iran to organize a coup under the code name "Operation Ajax," and he was successful. The largest democracy in the Middle East, which could have been a model for the rest of the region if Truman's attitude had prevailed, was thrown on the scrap heap of history, and the first phase of the new U.S. policy of supporting oppressive, but American-friendly dictators in the Middle East was a historic fact. The United States had "crossed its Rubicon" and set out on a new path that ignored the most basic principles of democracy and freedom on which the nation had been founded. In subsequent years, other American-supported oppressive dictatorships followed, with Saudi Arabia, Iraq, and Egypt as the most prominent. We have yet to see the end station of this hypocritical Middle East path.[28]

Guatemala 1954

Guatemala is an interesting case because of the formerly classified material that was released in 1997, more than forty years after the event, after years of persistent Freedom of Information Act requests by human rights activists. The democratic government of Guatemala attracted the interest of the CIA because they had gained the mass support of the previously politically inactive peasantry behind government policies of agrarian reform, labor organization, restrictions on foreign corporations, and other freedoms introduced after the revolution of 1944, which threw out a military dictatorship that had promoted social backwardness and economic colonialism. Among the new government's unforgivable sins was the expropriation of the banana plantations of the politically powerful United Fruit Company, "undoubtedly in retaliation for the fact that none of United Fruit's profits had been reinvested or redistributed in Guatemala itself." CIA boss Allen Dulles was a former member of the company's board of trustees, while the former law firm of his brother, secretary of state John Foster Dulles, represented United Fruit.[29] Thus the die was cast. The CIA argued that the "open political system" of Guatemala might allow communists to gain a foothold, which would threaten American investors' interests.

Therefore, with the authority of President Truman, and collaborating with Nicaraguan dictator Anastacio Somoza, the CIA organized a coup under the code name "Operation PBFORTUNE" that planned to overthrow the democratically elected president Jacobo Arbenz Guzmán and install an American puppet regime under General Carlos Castillo Armas as a military dictator who would be friendly to U.S. business interests. Released documents show that part of the CIA plan was to assassinate fifty-eight key individuals (names deleted). When this plan failed initially, President Eisenhower authorized $2.7 million for the CIA to continue the operation as "Operation PBSUCCESS," a paramilitary "psychological warfare and political action" that included the assassination plan as an option. In 1954, facing execution by the CIA-backed rebels, Arbenz was forced to resign and flee the country in order to save his and his family's lives, and Armas was installed in power by the CIA. The oppressive military regime subsequently massacred over 100,000 civilians during the next three and a half decades in what has been called "the worst human rights record in the Western Hemisphere." American citizens were kept in the dark about U.S. involvement by what the CIA's own review panel called "a brilliant public relations snow job."[30]

Brazil 1964

The military coup in Brazil in 1964 illustrated clearly the American attitude to foreign democracies—they are all right if they support American foreign policy and business interests. Otherwise, the United States prefers, and will actively promote, an oppressive military dictatorship to replace a democracy. Brazil is just one of many examples. The Brazilians' major sin was, as the ambassador to Washington Roberto Campos put it, "a deep urge to assert their personality in world affairs," hardly an unreasonable goal for the world's third largest democracy. President João Goulart insisted, naturally, on Brazil's democratic right to an independent stance on foreign-policy issues consistent with Brazil's interests. Among other things, Brazil refused to support American sanctions against Cuba, just as it had earlier turned down a $300-million American bribe to support the CIA's disastrous Bay of Pigs operation. Brazil was certainly not communist, nor was it anti-American. Brazil supported the United States strongly during the 1962 Cuban missile crisis, even while the CIA was attempting to undermine democracy in Brazil.[31]

Brazil was at this time the country with the world's highest Gini coefficient. For years the poor had been exploited by both the domestic elite and foreign enterprises, and the people demanded reforms. At the same time, rampant inflation and the need for foreign loans resulted in the IMF imposing stringent conditions that would mean more unemployment and lower real wages. Although the United States claimed that Goulart's administration leaned toward communism, this was nothing but smoke and mirrors with no basis in fact. Goulart was no communist. He was a wealthy landowner with close ties to the labor movement—what in the USA would be called a liberal democrat, like John F. Kennedy. In fact, very few with a communist background were to be found anywhere in his administration, and they had no influence.

Furthermore, the Soviet Union had little trade with Brazil and no leverage whatsoever. Trade with the Soviet Union actually increased substantially after the CIA-instigated military coup of 1964. The "fear of communism" was nothing but a poor excuse to justify the official Washington line, while the real agenda—fear of losses on American investments, was suppressed. Thus the CIA began in the early 1960s a covert plan to remove Goulart from power. President Goulart's major challenge at the time was to manage a very difficult balancing act between opposing forces. To gain some support from the left for the harsh IMF conditions, and to ease some of the pressure on the currency, the Goulart administration passed a law limiting the profit that foreign corporations could take out of the country, which infuriated American business interests. The final straw for the American corporations was when he announced in early 1964 his plans to expropriate and redistribute privately owned land and to nationalize private oil refineries.

On April 4, with six American C-135 transports and 110 tons of arms and ammunitions, and a carrier task group in place off the Brazilian coast, the U.S. Air Force was ready to move in if needed when the CIA supported rebels, representing elite business interests, made their move.[32] It wasn't necessary. Goulart was defenseless and fled to Uruguay to save his life. CIA involvement in the period up to the coup has been documented by former CIA officer Philip Agee, who stated that between $12 and $20 million had been allocated to support opposition candidates, to finance demonstrations against the government, to run a propaganda campaign, to support right-wing newspapers, and to promote anticommunism.[33]

The rest is history—a military dictatorship reputed for its political repression and torture ruled for the next two decades with U.S. support—good for the Brazilian elite and good for American business, but a disaster for the Brazilian people. As Peter Gribbin put it in 1979, after observing the 40% fall in real wages in the fifteen years following the coup: "For capitalists, both Brazilian and foreign, the masses are looked upon as costs, not customers: the lower their real wages, the higher the profits from selling to the local upper class and the international market." Brazil attracted more U.S. investment than any other Latin American country during the military junta's regime.[34] As usual, very little of the truth found its way into the American media. Typical of the comments fed to the American public by the "propaganda model" was this one from *Reader's Digest*: "The communist drive for domination marked by propaganda, infiltration, terror—was in high gear. Total surrender seemed imminent—and then the people said No!"[35] And how about U.S. ambassador to Brazil Lincoln Gordon, who called the CIA-supported military coup against the world's third largest democracy a "democratic rebellion" and "the single most decisive victory of freedom in the mid-twentieth century."[36] With that kind of "newspeak" reporting, it is no wonder that most Americans are unaware of the atrocities that the U.S. government has committed abroad.

Chile 1973

Once again, it is recently released classified documents that reveal—many years after the event, yet another U.S. initiative to undermine and overthrow a democratic government in favor of a terrorist, but business-friendly, military regime. Prior to socialist Salvador Allende's election in 1970, Chile—like the rest of Latin America—was being exploited by both domestic and foreign (mostly U.S.) business interests to the detriment of its citizens, who demanded reforms. Allende acted quickly to reverse things, taking over copper mines, banks, and large estates and nationalizing several foreign firms, including U.S. giants Kennecott Copper and Anaconda Mines. Workers and farmers took over many companies and giant farms, and wage levels were increased markedly. The U.S. government was furious.

In a statement, which is quite revealing about his concept of democracy, Secretary of State Henry Kissinger said, "I don't see why we need to stand by and watch a country go communist due to the irresponsibility of its people." President Nixon agreed, and according to CIA director Richard Helms, ordered him to take covert actions to destabilize the Chilean economy. "Make the economy scream," cried Nixon, according to Helms. Subsequently, the United States terminated financial assistance, blocked loans to Chile from the IMF and World Bank (note the prima facie evidence of who controls the IMF and the World Bank, if anyone is still in doubt), and began financially supporting military dissidents in Chile and training their military personnel in the United States and Panama for a coup in a CIA project codenamed "Project FUBELT."[37]

Shortly after the 1973 election, the head of the armed forces, René Schneider, refused to take any action against Allende, as urged upon him by right-wing dissidents, who thereupon assassinated him in a broad-daylight gunfight. According to a recent lawsuit brought against Kissinger and Helms by Schneider's family, based on the released documents, the CIA provided $35,000 to some of those jailed for Schneider's murder.[38]

Allende was killed defending himself in a military coup headed by General Augusto Pinochet on September 11, 1973. Unlike Arbenz and Goulart, he stood his ground and paid the supreme price. In the subsequent round up of Allende supporters, several cabinet ministers were assassinated and thousands of citizens—some estimates are as high as 30,000—were tortured and killed, many fingered by CIA lists as "radicals," i.e., supporters of the democratically elected government.

The repressive regime, which followed, was a disaster for the Chilean people, as the neoliberals from the University of Chicago became economic advisors to the junta. In a foretaste of what would later become the IMF's "structural adjustment program," they demonstrated the recipe: reduce import duties for the convenience of the local elite and foreign multinationals; crush the unions to keep wages down; sell public enterprises to private investors well below book value; cut welfare spending and pensions; deregulate industry; privatize government services like parks, prisons, utilities, schools, and health care; sell off the country's resources as quickly as possible to eager foreigners; and remove any restrictions on foreign investment.

When proponents of these economic policies hailed the result as an "economic miracle," it was just another example of neoliberal newspeak. A miracle it was not, except for the private firms that participated in the rape. Chile's manufacturing base was decimated. The Gini coefficient jumped in twenty years to the second highest in South America as the richest 10% of Chileans increased their share of wealth from 37% to 47% by 1990. Where 20% of the population had been classified as poor in 1970, the figure in 1990 was a whopping 41%. Wage levels actually dropped below the levels of 1970 in the intervening years. Government spending on health care dropped by 60%. Chile's external debt increased from $5 billion to $21 billion in an import orgy. Forest and fishery resources were plundered and nearly destroyed by private capital. But Pinochet, noted worldwide for his regime's human rights violations, did all right personally under U.S. protection, as he grossly enriched himself and his family. Between 1973 and 1989 the economy grew by a measly 1% and first reached 1970 growth rates in 1990. The IMF, the World Bank, and the U.S. government, in another example of Orwellian newspeak, brashly celebrated all this as "a model for the rest of the Third World"— believe it or not.[39]

The Limits of Democracy

The historical record provides strong evidence for the argument that the United States can no longer be considered a democracy, except in the narrow sense of formal elections, nor is there any respect for the democratic rights of foreign states in spite of the lofty rhetoric. What about the United States' closest allies, the UK and the EU?

In 2004, the Power Inquiry—an independent body chaired by Helena Kennedy QC—identified a decline in "formal democracy" in the UK and proposed solutions to reverse the trend. One reason for the concern was the "historically unprecedented" decline in voter turnout in recent decades, which hit a low of 59% in 2001. The study—published in February 2006—concluded that the decline in democratic participation was due to a feeling on the part of citizens that they have little or no impact on political decisions, that there is a lack of difference between the main political parties and an unequal electoral system that leads to wasted votes, and that the UK is facing a situation where "the processes of democracy, including general elections, become empty rituals." The study stated that "the main political parties are widely held in contempt," that they "are seen as offering no real choice to citizens," and that the "main political parties are widely perceived to be too similar and lacking in principle."[40]

The "democratic deficit" in the European Union has long been a subject of much debate in the region. The EU "project" has always been a top-down effort based primarily on the vision of a few European political leaders who saw closer integration of their economies as a way to minimize the likelihood of the kind of wars that had plagued the region for centuries. A second goal was to establish a regional power that could speak with one voice in international affairs, and in particular to the United States. The first of these goals has been a resounding success, the second only moderately so.

One consequence of the approach taken is that many Europeans feel that they are without any influence on the decisions taken in faraway Brussels. This indifference is reflected in the notoriously low turnouts to European Parliament elections compared to turnouts in national elections. The EU is neither an international organization nor a federal state. Therefore a fundamental problem is how to reconcile the principle of equality among nation-states, which would apply to international organizations, and the principle of equality among citizens, which would apply within a single nation-state. For example, the Lisbon Treaty came into effect by the votes of national governments, while it would undoubtedly have been rejected by several countries in national referenda if that option had been made available to all member states.

Both the UK and other EU members are still democracies, but trends in both are disturbingly aligned with what has happened in the United States, where commercial interests have obtained greater and greater influence on decisions. Where is this all heading? And if the United States is no longer a democracy, then what has it become? Let us look more closely at that question.

EIGHT

Who Is in Charge?

Some people call you the elite. I call you my base.

—George W. Bush

How can we reconcile the documented disrespect for democracy, freedom, and human rights in the U.S. leadership, both at home and abroad, with the ideals of the great majority of ordinary American citizens, who truly believe in these principles? The answer, unfortunately, is that a majority of the members of the United States Congress no longer represent the people, but rather their corporate backers, who have a very different set of priorities. This observation is the key to understanding the true power structure in the United States and the world. There are exceptions, high-integrity lawmakers that have avoided the claws of the behind-the-scenes financiers, but they are a disappearing race.

The Corporatocracy

There was a time—a couple of generations ago—when the United States was ruled by a strong democratic middle class. That is no longer the case. Since roughly 1980, financial and political power has shifted dramatically away from the middle class to a conglomerate of large corporations backed by very small group of extremely wealthy Americans—those who successfully launched The Neoliberal Project on the world, with themselves as the planned beneficiaries. The exact boundaries for this elite ruling class are not fixed, and membership is fluid. For some purposes it may be more appropriate to talk about the top 0.1% of wealth holders (about 300,000 people) as the "hard core" and the next 0.9% as the "outer core" for a total of 1%. They have similar values and constitute a broad network of like-thinking individuals.

The inequality in wealth ownership can be documented by publicly available data. Some of the most telling statistics are the following: The top 1% of households own 38.3% of privately held stock, 60.6% of financial securities, and 62.4% of business equity. The top 10% own 98.5% of financial securities and 93.3% of business equity.[1] It follows that they control all the major companies listed on the stock exchanges and even more privately owned corporations. In contrast, the lowest 40% of the population own just 0.3% of the wealth of the United States.

The shift in power is further supported by the systematic disenfranchising of the poorest citizens by voting requirements, by manipulation and censure of vital information by the corporate-controlled media, by the corruption and low moral standards of elected officials, by the enormous and increasing gap between rich and poor, and by the inability of ordinary citizens to influence policy.

Political power is not exercised directly by the superrich, but rather by their allies who run the largest American corporations. This corporate power is grounded in a number of Supreme Court decisions dating back to the early nineteenth century that in essence give corporations many of the same constitutional rights as persons—so-called corporate personhood—and most important of all, the right to make political contributions. This enables them to acquire loyal allies in Congress through campaign contributions and other forms of political support. The Supreme Court also favored corporations when it struck down state laws requiring companies to disclose product origins, thus preventing consumers from knowing what is in their food; prohibited citizens wanting to defend their local businesses and community from corporate-chain encroachment from enacting progressive taxes on chain stores; and struck down state laws restricting corporate spending on ballot initiatives and referenda, enabling corporations to block citizen exercise of local democracy. The basic logic of these court decisions was stated in 1830 by Chief Justice Marshall, who wrote, "The great object of an incorporation is to bestow the character and properties of individuality on a collective and changing body of men."[2] The thinking then was that a corporation was simply a group of individuals acting collectively, and the corporation thus ought to have the same rights as the persons behind it. This logic may have been reasonable in the case of a small, local corporation in 1830 when a few people got together to form one to fulfill some joint objective. In such a case, a hired manager would not dream of taking any major decision without consulting his shareholders. But when the shareholders are numbered in the thousands or even millions as in today's major corporations, the small-town analogy no longer holds. The corporation becomes an entirely new entity with its own "personality" quite distinct from the personalities of the individual shareholders. The CEO in a large modern corporation can no longer know the individual wishes, political preferences, or priorities of his corporate shareholders, which in any case would be quite diverse. So, in practice, his actions must reflect the presumed common denominator of the shareholders: to make as much money as possible.

In effect a mutation has occurred. An unintended "Frankenstein's monster" has been created. The difference between individual personhood and corporate personhood is critical. The individuals who own the corporate shares are flesh and blood humans with families, feelings, and emotions, and they participate to various degrees as social beings in their communities. Profit-seeking corporations, on the other hand, have no feelings, no emotions, and no social dimension. In fact, a large corporation acts very much like a human being suffering from "dissocial personality disorder" as defined by the World Health Organization. Characteristics of this disorder include: "disregard for social norms, rules and obligations; callous unconcern for the feelings of others; incapacity to experience guilt and to profit from experience, particularly punishment; a proneness to blame others, or to offer plausible rationalizations, for the behavior that has brought the patient into conflict with society."[3] Such individuals are known as "sociopaths," also characterized by reckless disregard for safety of self and others, lack of remorse, and indifference to the suffering of others.

What has happened over the past decades is that political power in the United States has been transferred to a sociopathic "corporatocracy"—a word coined by John Perkins in *Confessions of an Economic Hit Man*. The corporatocracy consists of a network of the major American corporations and their willing supporters (more often than not financed by these same corporations or their shareholders) in universities, foundations, the media, think tanks, Congress, and myriad private clubs, where national policies and strategies are discussed and decided without any public debate. This raises an interesting question: would the American people willingly vote a sociopath in as president—or to any other political position for that matter? I think not. And yet, that is effectively who they have put in charge today. The result is entirely predictable and should not surprise anyone: widespread human suffering in the general population while the ruling elite acquires an increasing portion of the national wealth year after year. The corporatocracy controls Congress through political contributions, bribery, campaign finance, lucrative job offers, and whatever else it takes. Politicians that dare to oppose the wishes of the corporatocracy can look forward to massive corporate funding of their opponents in the next election and negative coverage in the corporate-controlled media. The United States has mutated into a type of governance never seen before. Does it have a name?

Perhaps fascism—the merger of state and corporate power? Naomi Wolf, in her book *The End of America*, makes this case, identifying ten typical steps on the way to fascism, and notes that the United States is on course on every one of them: invoke an external and internal threat; establish secret prisons; develop a paramilitary force; put ordinary citizens under surveillance; infiltrate citizens' groups; arbitrarily detain and release citizens; target key individuals; restrict the press; define criticism as "espionage" and dissent as "treason"; subvert the rule of law.[4]

American philosopher and former professor of politics at Princeton University Sheldon Wolin is one of the United States' leading political theorists. He calls the political system that has evolved in America "inverted totalitarianism . . . the political coming of age of corporate power and the political demobilization of the citizenry." Echoing George Orwell's *1984*, Wolin writes, "The new system, inverted totalitarianism, is one that professes the opposite of what, in fact, it is." He calls it "inverted" because it does not require the use of coercion, police power, and a messianic ideology. The genius of the inverted totalitarian system "lies in wielding total power without appearing to. . . . The United States has become the showcase of how democracy can be managed without appearing to be suppressed." The main objectives of managed democracy are to increase the profits of corporations, while dismantling the institutions of social democracy (Social Security, unions, welfare, public health services, public housing, and so forth). Wolin adds: "Through a combination of governmental contracts, corporate and foundation funds, joint projects involving university and corporate researchers, and wealthy individual donors, universities (especially so-called research universities), intellectuals, scholars, and researchers have been seamlessly integrated into the system." According to Wolin, managed democracy aims at the "selective abdication of governmental responsibility for the well-being of the citizenry," which sounds frighteningly like the mission statement of a sociopath.[5] In the same light, political scientist Chalmers Johnson issued this stark warning to the American people in the final book of his *Blowback Trilogy*: "We are on the cusp of losing our democracy for the sake of keeping our empire."[6]

Key members of the corporatocracy are the CEOs of the top 500 or so companies. The record shows that they have not merely been professional managers seeking maximum profits for their shareholders. The name of the game has shifted to seizing as much wealth as possible for themselves.

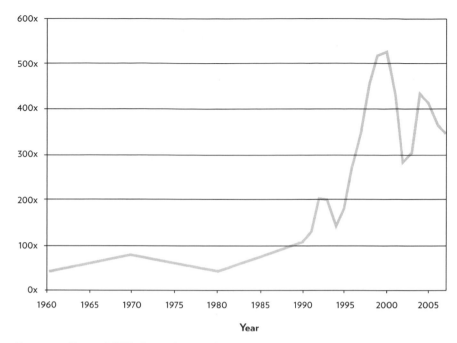

Figure 8.1. Ratio of CEO Pay to Worker Pay, 1960–2007. From G. William Domhoff, "Who Rules America: Wealth, Income, and Power," University of California at Santa Cruz (January, 2011); based on "Executive Excess 2008, the 15th Annual CEO Compensation Survey," Institute for Policy Studies and United for a Fair Economy (www.faireconomy.org).

They have used their positions to grab an ever-increasing share of American wealth and income during the neoliberal period. Figure 8.1 shows how the ratio of CEO remuneration (for companies in the S&P 500 Index) to average worker pay exploded from a level of 42:1 in 1980 to 531:1 in 2000 just before the dot-com crash, and fell to about 344:1 in 2007. The corresponding ratio for Europe is about 25:1, so we are talking about really excessive remuneration here. It is actually quite shocking.[7]

In the period 1990–2005, CEO remuneration increased 300% (adjusted for inflation) while workers gained a mere 4.3%.

Defenders of high CEO remuneration claim that the phenomenon is a consequence of their unique skills and the competition for their services, but this argument is ridiculed by one of their own, Edgar Woolard Jr., retired CEO of DuPont, who says the claim is "bull." He adds that the claim that compensation committees are independent is "double bull," and the argument that high CEO salaries are a reward for creating wealth for shareholders is "a joke."[8]

Perpetual War

War is the most destructive act of the human race, and has become one of the most important tools of the corporatocracy. With modern technology and the ongoing competition for influence among states, the consequences are greater now than ever before. The greatest casualties are always innocent bystanders. While accurate figures are difficult to come by, there is no doubt that the trend is toward a greater percentage of civilian deaths relative to military personnel in wars due to technological developments, for example, the greater use of unmanned drones, air-to-ground missiles, and high-altitude "precision" bombing. One analysis provides the following estimates of the percentage of civilian casualties in war: World War I, 10%; World War II, 50%; Vietnam War, 70%; Gulf War, 90%.[9] In addition to direct casualties, war damage often has long-term intergenerational effects (cancer, deformities, etc.), for example, from nuclear bombs (World War II), Agent Orange (Vietnam), depleted uranium (Gulf War). In addition, environmental and infrastructural damage is enormous. Besides the direct damage caused by war, the expense of building and maintaining a military capability, even if never used, diverts funds from more productive uses. According to Stockholm International Peace Research Institute (SIPRI), global military spending was about $1.5 trillion in 2010, with the United States being the largest spender at $698 billion, six times the second largest spender, China.

With the collapse of the Soviet Union in 1991, there was much talk about the coming "peace dividend." Now that the cold war was over, it was reasoned, defense spending could be reduced and the enormous funds consumed by the military for a whole generation redirected to segments of the U.S. economy that were in desperate need of more funding—public schools, sewer maintenance, public transportation, roads, railways, environmental reparation, and much more that could improve the quality of American life. Military expenses did in fact decrease slightly over the next few years, but increased dramatically again to record highs after "9/11."

Figure 8.2 illustrates the historical levels of U.S. military spending in inflation-adjusted 2009 dollars. Note that the figures are somewhat higher than the SIPRI figures because they include defense spending that is not military in nature, such as the Department of Homeland Security, counterterrorism spending by the FBI, intelligence-gathering spending by NASA, and interest on defense-related debt.

Most people accept that maintaining a strong military is necessary for defense purposes and that the military budget should logically increase

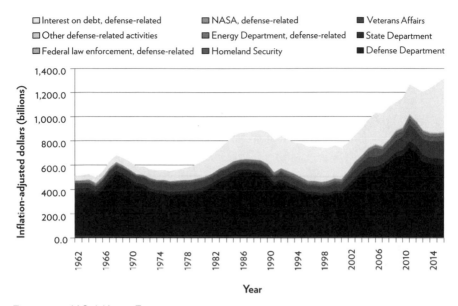

☐ Interest on debt, defense-related   ☐ NASA, defense-related   ■ Veterans Affairs

☐ Other defense-related activities   ■ Energy Department, defense-related   ■ State Department

■ Federal law enforcement, defense-related   ■ Homeland Security   ■ Defense Department

Figure 8.2. U.S. Military Expenses, 1962–2015. With credit to "johnpseudo" http://en.wikipedia.org/wiki/Military_budget_of_the_United_States.

when a potential threat is on the horizon, and decrease in times of peace. But such simplistic thinking ignores the dynamic of military spending that has evolved in the United States since World War II. Budgets seem to increase regularly but rarely decrease. President Eisenhower famously warned in his parting address in 1961 that "we must guard against the acquisition of unwarranted influence, whether sought or unsought, by the military-industrial complex." It has been claimed by some close to Eisenhower that his original phrase was "military-industrial congressional complex," a far more revealing expression, but dropped by the president to avoid insulting his congressional allies. Eisenhower feared that this powerful triangle of mutual interests could "endanger our liberties or democratic processes." Time has shown his concern to have been fully justified. Since Eisenhower's presidency, the triangle has expanded into a pentagon, which we could call the "financial-media-military-industrial-congressional complex," which is just another name for the corporatocracy, with the financial sector taking on the leading role today.

The corporatocracy does not have to look very far to see where the major threat to its power resides. It is found—not abroad as it would have you believe—but with the vast majority of American citizens, who think they are living in a democracy. At some point they may tire of being exploited and decide to exercise their not inconsiderable power, take back control, and reestablish a true democracy. This is the greatest fear of the corporatocracy. Hence the need for the surveillance and control of American citizens legalized in the USA PATRIOT Act and the Department of Homeland Security, as well as the need for a foreign "enemy"—invented if necessary—in order to justify such laws and the permanent flow of enormous funds into their coffers. George Kennan, who probably grasped the essence of the needs of the American elite better than anyone, was prophetic when he wrote in 1987, "Were the Soviet Union to sink tomorrow under the waters of the ocean, the American military-industrial complex would have to remain, substantially unchanged, until some other adversary could be invented."[10]

The so-called "war on terror" was the ideal invention to fulfill the need for an external "enemy" and hence fulfill Kennan's prediction. It also illustrates what Professor Seymour Melman called "perpetual war," which is a necessary and logical consequence of the corporatocracy's plan to maintain power. Johan Galtung has computed the average number of American interventions per year in the period from 1890 to 1945 to be 1.15, increasing to 1.29 per year until the end of the Cold War in 1991, and *increasing* further to 2.2 per year for the period 1991–2001 (22 interventions). "This is compatible," he writes, "with the hypothesis that as empire or hegemony expands more interventions are needed for protection."[11] It also provides further confirmation of Melman's claim that the United States is in fact engaged in a perpetual war. U.S. military expenses increased by 81% from 2001–10, consistent with David Korten's claim that "as empires crumble, the ruling elites become ever more corrupt and ruthless in their drive to secure their own power—a dynamic now playing out in the United States."[12]

The De Facto World Order

In the global context, it is an undeniable fact that nothing major happens in the WTO, the IMF, the World Bank, NATO, or the United Nations Security Council against the wishes of the United States. The United States is always "chairman of the board" in these key international organizations, with a supportive network of close allies that seldom voice any protest. Therefore if we want to answer the question "Who rules the world," we have only to answer the question "Who rules the United States?"

While each sovereign state in principle is independent, in practice there is very little room for exercising any degree of economic policy or foreign policy that is not aligned with the wishes of the United States and hence the

American corporatocracy. More and more authors, journalists, and ordinary citizens are referring to the current World Order as the "American Empire." I am sure many Americans would object to this terminology. Nevertheless—and I find this painful to say, having been brought up in North America at a time when such thoughts would evoke ridicule—I am reluctantly inclined to agree. Things have changed markedly in my lifetime.

Commentators discuss openly today what kind of empire has evolved, and there is no general agreement. A minority even sees some positive aspects. It is certainly unique in many ways. One reasonable definition is a form that some have called "super-imperialism" where U.S. policies are driven not simply by the interests of American businesses, but by the interests of the economic elites of a compliant alliance of industrialized states. In this view, the central conflict is between the industrialized countries and the developing countries rather than between competing industrial powers.

What has evolved is a unique "corporate empire," with the role of the emperor taken on by the corporatocracy. While there is no formal hierarchy, global governance is in effect embedded in an empire, tightly controlled by a broad network of corporations and supporters in the United States and abroad who see an interest in maintaining the status quo. Indeed, a majority of ordinary citizens in the industrialized countries seem quite willing to passively support the system and benefit from it, even though they have no influence on decisions. Furthermore, the "American dream" tells them that they could in principle, become successful enough to join the elite. The role of spokesmen for the collective "emperor" is typically taken on by the most charismatic leaders of the financial and industrial sectors in the United States, who keep in close touch and set the tone for what is acceptable and what is not. Often a member of their inner circle will take on the key job of secretary of the treasury. The president need not be sympathetic with them. George W. Bush clearly was; Barack Obama much less so. Either way, it is very difficult for a U.S. president to push through programs against the corporatocracy's wishes, illustrated, for example by the gentle "rap on the wrist" financial reforms of 2009 and the bitter resistance to President Obama's health-care reform program and debt-ceiling proposals. In the rest of this book, for the sake of reference, I will refer to this world order controlled by the corporatocracy simply as "the Empire."

While the U.S. administration directly or indirectly controls decisions in the key international institutions, it does consult with other states regularly to enable the greatest possible degree of alignment and consensus where possible (e.g., the EU, the G-7, the G-20, NATO, the Council on Foreign

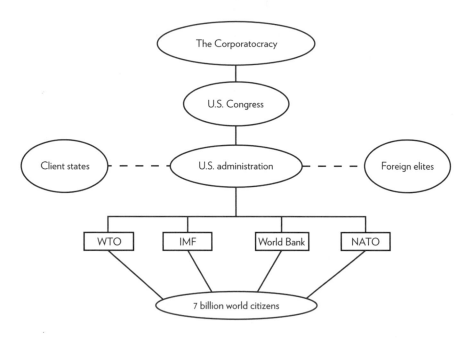

Figure 8.3. The Contemporary World Order.

Relations, the Bilderberg Group, various private clubs and international conferences). This is the "speak softly and carry a big stick" strategy popularized by Theodore Roosevelt. With a military budget as large as all others combined, a nuclear arsenal that could destroy Russia 1,000 times over and upwards of 800 globe-spanning military bases, American arguments tend to be persuasive. Chalmers Johnson writes: "Once upon a time, you could trace the spread of imperialism by counting up colonies. America's version of the colony is the military base; and by following the changing politics of global basing, one can learn much about our ever more all-encompassing imperial 'footprint' and the militarism that grows with it."[13]

It can be argued that the Empire is much broader than the United States, with reference to the many foreign elites in both industrialized and developing countries that are supportive. While this is true, the United States is nonetheless by far the dominant force—the one calling the shots. No other state can be said to be ruled by a corporatocracy, even though corporations are often very influential in their home countries. While the opinions of allies, client states, and foreign corporations are heard, it is the American corporatocracy that is the controlling global leader, and figure 8.3 is a simplified version of the de facto contemporary world order.

Survival in the Contemporary World

Resistance to American wishes, as we saw in chapter 7, is likely to lead to regime change—either by direct invasion or by CIA subterfuge—whether or not resistance is from a democracy or a ruthless dictator. Where direct invasion or subterfuge is problematic or too risky for the time being, the resisting state may be classified as a member of the "axis of evil" or some equivalent, e.g., Iran, North Korea, Iraq, Cuba, and subjected to import sanctions for long periods.

Even foreign domestic policies are to a great extent dictated by the international institutions controlled by the Empire. For example, we saw earlier how WTO rules allow any foreign product into local stores in any member state, often undercutting local produce, while preventing any form of protection of local industries that might lead to real development, environmental protection, or greater competition. We saw also how foreign debt to the IMF and World Bank ensures that the priority of most developing countries is to repay the debt forced upon them by corrupt leaders, while the local elite reaps the benefits of the borrowed funds and the poor get poorer.

The unique status of the U.S. dollar as the most important reserve currency enables the United States to maintain its economic and military dominance while running an enormous trade deficit simply by "printing" as many dollars as are needed, resting assured that other states will hold them in their official foreign-exchange reserves.

The key to survival for other "sovereign" states is in practice acceptance of an economic model that allows the Empire to continue raping the earth without any regard for the wishes of 7 billion world citizens, including 310 million American citizens, and without concern for the long-term environmental consequences, which in the worst case could end human civilization.

Denial, Conspiracy, or Addiction?

Many persons across the globe, particularly in the NGO world, are frustrated over the lack of response of the ruling elite to the global crises facing us, especially in the developing countries, which are the hardest hit. They reason that the decision makers cannot be unaware of the multiple threats facing global society, including unsustainable overconsumption of our natural capital. They must know of the many warnings from scientists and even from the CIA. And yet they do nothing. They all seem more concerned with stimulating even more consumption than with the state of the planet. Critics ask: How can any responsible leadership act this way? They are not stupid, so what is the explanation? Is there a lack of awareness? Is the leadership in a state of denial; engaged in a conspiracy; controlled by sociopathic corporations; ruled by CEOs addicted to power?

For many in the developing countries there is no doubt in their minds that a conspiracy is behind the West's policies. Walden Bello, professor of sociology and public administration at the University of the Philippines, is representative of this school, writing, in connection with the crisis of the late 1990s: "There is a belief going around industrial and government circles throughout Asia that Washington and the IMF conspired with the banks and speculators to bring about the region's meltdown. The alleged reason: to derail Asia from its march to become America's strategic and political rival in the twenty-first century. This is, of course, classic conspiracy theory, but it is a sign of the times that it now has the status of fact among economic and political elites that once served as Washington's staunchest backers in Asia."[14]

An alternative explanation could be that corporate CEOs—while not themselves sociopaths—accept the responsibility of running sociopathic corporations because they are firmly addicted to a lifestyle filled with the rush of power and influence that is as difficult to break as a heroin addiction. Many corporate executives are totally removed from, and insensitive to, the problems of ordinary folks at home and abroad, as they spend money without limits, move only in influential circles, live in guarded compounds, and travel from one five-star hotel to another, often by private plane. If addiction is the case, then perhaps they just don't care what happens to the rest of humanity and the environment as long as they can remain in charge and maintain their lifestyles.

Among NGOs, the implicit assumption of the majority seems to be that the failure of the international community to take decisive action is simply due to a lack of awareness of the problems; hence their widespread efforts to raise awareness of the issues among citizens and their appeals to governments to wake up to the dangers. However, the following story suggests that this assumption may be quite naïve.

Andrew Harvey, a well-known and widely respected spiritual leader in the United States, tells, in a recent publication, of his shocking confrontation with a leading member of the corporatocracy—the CEO of a major agribusiness corporation—shortly after one of Harvey's fiery exhortations to citizens to unite and bring about real reforms. The following is a slightly condensed excerpt from the CEO's message to Andrew Harvey over lunch:

> Most of you that I have met truly believe that if the CEOs—like me, for instance—really knew what harm their corporate policies were doing, they would rend their Armani suits, fling out their Rolex-wreathed arms, burst into tears, and change. This is madness and shows how little you dare to know about what is really going on.
>
> Let me tell you what you are up against. You are up against people like me. I know exactly what my company is doing and what devastation it is causing to thousands of lives. I should know; I am running it and I do not care. I have decided I want a grand gold-plated lifestyle and the perks and jets and houses that go with it and I will do anything—bend the law, have people "removed," bribe local government officials, you name it—to get what I want. I know, too, that none of my shareholders care a rat's ass what I do or how I do it, providing I keep them swimming in cash.
>
> I know too, by the way, that the dark forces I play with are playing with me. I am under no illusion that I will not someday have to pay the price. Don't the French say, "The devil has no friends"? I'm willing to pay that price in return for the pleasure of being able to afford this restaurant, in return for being able to ring up the president of the United States in front of house guests to impress them. Am I getting through to you?[15]

Conspiracy? Power addiction? Sociopathic corporations? Perhaps it doesn't really matter, since the effect is the same as if it were a conspiracy. This is not to say that all persons in the very top brackets of wealth share the views of Harvey's CEO and participate in the dysfunctional game. There are many exceptions—philanthropists using their wealth to support idealistic causes and who are in complete sympathy with the concept of a more equitable and just world. But they are a minority and considered rather suspicious by the hard-liners. I had a personal illustration of this in the 1990s when I was selling my currency hedge fund to high-net-worth individuals as a way to diversify their portfolios of stocks and bonds. After my presentation to a very wealthy Texan, he surprised me with his only question, asking: "If I invest in your fund, will your profits be used to run a 'Save the Whales' campaign or something like that?" We did not mention in our literature the fact that the management company was 90% owned by a charitable entity supporting sustainability projects, but he had apparently gotten wind of that somehow. I answered him honestly. "That is a possibility," I said. Whereupon he replied, "Then I do not wish to participate. I don't mind if you want to buy a Ferrari or a Mediterranean yacht, but I don't want to get involved in politics."

Moving Beyond Corporatocracy

Harvey's lunchtime partner may or may not understand that our global civilization has been undergoing a gradual collapse for about three decades. He may or may not understand that, at its root, is a worldview that sees humans as separate from nature and from each other. And he may or may not care that we are raping irreplaceable resources, exploiting weaker parts of human society, chasing unsustainable economic growth, and disregarding our natural capital on which all life depends. He may simply be part of the corporatocracy, driven by elitist self-interest and indifferent to the dangers like global warming, species extinction, the poisoning of our air, soil, and water, or declining fertility. He is part of an economic system that lacks any concept of limits to growth. That system is driving our planet to ruin, and must be replaced by a new economic system that is more in line with science and the real needs of people.

However, a new economic system can only succeed if completely new international institutions are established to regulate international law, trade, environmental protection, and real development in the developing countries (DCs). The current institutions cannot be reformed as they are undemocratic and designed to fulfill the needs of the Empire rather than the needs of world citizens. We must begin with a clean slate.

We must design new institutions to deal with international finance that respect the needs of all states on a more equal basis. This must include better control of destabilizing international speculation, and a critical review of the role of the U.S. dollar, which is a major pillar supporting the Empire's power structure.

The American experience has shown clearly that a formal democracy is not enough to guarantee the freedom and self-determination of its citizens. Safeguards are required to prevent a takeover by elements—commercial or otherwise—whose interests are not aligned with the vast majority.

Finally, we must accept that the initiative for change will never come from those who are the major beneficiaries of the current system, and certainly not from the Empire. The initiative must come from elsewhere. Radical new thinking is required. It is necessary in the first instance to design a new international political and economic structure that can achieve the desired result, and in the second instance to develop a strategy to bring it about. This is no easy task, and resistance will be formidable. But there are also some bright spots on the horizon that provide grounds for hope.

PART FOUR

New Values, New Beliefs

It is possible to change our world. Another world is not only possible, she is on her way. On a quiet day, I can hear her breathing.

—ARUNDHATI ROY, "Confronting Empire,"
World Social Forum, January, 27, 2003

NINE

The Emergent Worldview

Everything is connected; nothing is separate.
— P. D. Ouspensky, *In Search of the Miraculous*

Thomas Kuhn, originator of the concept of paradigm shifts in science, points out that a shift occurs when it becomes clear that the old paradigm is no longer satisfactory in dealing with relevant problems. A new paradigm does not appear magically out of nowhere, but is rather an adjustment of certain aspects of the previous paradigm, including a rejection of the things that are no longer reflecting the current understanding of reality. It has been clear to a small minority for some time now that the old reductionist worldview, which I have referred to as the Cartesian/Newtonian paradigm, was no longer relevant to the problems facing humankind. I refer to it in the following also as the "dying paradigm" or the "old paradigm" to distinguish it from the new, emerging paradigm. We are now in the middle of a transition period moving toward a new, not yet fully defined, worldview. The transition will first be completed when a larger minority, including key opinion leaders, makes that acknowledgment and the reality of the shift enters the mainstream. I think the shift is inevitable. It is already underway, and it is only a question of time until it reaches a tipping point, when a new way of looking at life on Earth will manifest and become the majority view within most of our lifetimes.

The Dying Paradigm

Cracks were beginning to appear in the mechanical view of the world already in the early twentieth century. Einstein's theory of relativity, confirmed experimentally in 1919, and the emergence of a radically new quantum physics to explain subatomic phenomena, could not be explained by Newtonian mathematics. The fatal blow to the Cartesian/Newtonian paradigm was a strange consequence of quantum physics first realized in the 1920s. Based on the work of Niels Bohr and other physicists, quantum theory suggested that one cannot separate the "observer" from "the observed." Rather, everything in the subatomic world seemed to be "entangled" or interconnected. While even Einstein questioned Bohr's claim, it was experimentally confirmed many years later (1981) in the famous laboratory test of the so-called Einstein-Podolsky-Rosen-Bohm *Gedankenexperiment*.[1] That experiment falsified the validity of a mainstay of the old paradigm, namely, René Descartes' belief that we can separate the observer from the observed, or in other words, that humankind is separate from nature and that humans are separate from each other. We know now from quantum physics that everything is intimately connected, not only on this planet, but across the entire universe. According to the new, emerging paradigm, there is no external reality—only interconnections and relationships. Nothing is separate.

The development of complexity theory and chaos theory later in the twentieth century showed that Newtonian linearity also gave a misleading picture of a world in which the vast majority of physical processes are nonlinear with many complex feedback mechanisms, and thus not at all amenable to the simple linear methods of Newtonian mechanics.

Now, you may say, what has all this obscure talk about science and mathematics got to do with my everyday problems of just getting on with my busy life and making ends meet? And the answer is: *everything*. Perhaps your job has just been outsourced to China. Perhaps your child has contracted salmonella poisoning from eating industrially farmed chicken. Perhaps you lost your life savings due to an unethical bank that sold you a stake in U.S. subprime bonds that were supposed be as safe as treasury bills. Perhaps a mud slide destroyed your village because a property speculator cut down all the trees on the mountainside for a quick profit. Perhaps you have to find a new source of water because the old one has been closed on account of pesticides from industrial agriculture. Perhaps you are a small farmer and cannot afford to buy the seeds that used to be free because they have now been patented by some foreign multinational firm. Perhaps it is impossible to buy any homegrown healthy food because everything in your stores is imported low-quality junk food.

When the paradigm shifts, everything shifts. All of the above problems are more or less direct consequences of an economic system that is based on the old paradigm and is no longer working for the majority of people—an economic system that has no place for environmental protection, human rights to clean air, clean soil, and clean water, no place for the billions of people who are outside of the "market" and cannot afford to purchase the products imported from multinational firms, no respect for anything but money and profits. The point is that changes in worldview eventually permeate every level of society. Not immediately, because it takes time—typically several decades—for the new way of looking at the world to work its way through all of society. All of the above problems will eventually disappear when the emergent worldview becomes dominant.

The Emergent Paradigm

What then characterizes this emergent new worldview and how does it differ from the old one? First, it is not fully defined as yet, and has no universally accepted name. However, I will make a tentative start. I would venture to say that the most fundamental change from the Cartesian/Newtonian worldview is that the earth is seen to be a living organism analogous to a human being. All parts, whether plants, animals, or minerals, are seen as intimately interconnected and interdependent. Humankind is seen to be an integral part of nature. No components of nature are considered superior or inferior to others, all being essential to the total organism. This part of the worldview has much in common with the traditional worldview of all indigenous peoples, who consider nature sacred. The new paradigm will probably not go quite that far, but humankind will definitely demonstrate less hubris and more humility toward nature. As opposed to the dying paradigm, this new worldview is completely consistent with the findings of modern science, where everything is interconnected and nothing is separate. One of the most radical changes will be the prioritizing of long-term survival above all else. Where the dying paradigm promoted material growth while degrading natural capital—even to the extent of endangering human survival—the emergent paradigm will reverse priorities, downgrading economic growth and upgrading environmental protection and the preservation of natural capital.

We are now about eight decades into the transition period from the Cartesian/Newtonian paradigm to the emerging paradigm. The last paradigm shift took about 170 years—from Martin Luther's break with the Catholic Church in 1517 to Isaac Newton's publication of *Principia Mathematica* in 1687. During a transition period between paradigms, science no longer progresses normally—in very small steps—but becomes abnormal, with the potential for quantum leaps forward in understanding. Kuhn points out that when such a shift occurs, new insights are born, as the world is now seen as if through new lenses.

Gaia Theory: Foundation for a New Worldview

One of the first and most important examples of a theory based on new paradigm thinking is Gaia theory, proposed initially by British atmospheric chemist James Lovelock as a hypothesis in the 1970s and later refined as a theory. When consulted by NASA on the question of possible life on Mars in the 1960s, he claimed that it was not necessary to travel there to determine if there were advanced life-forms. For Lovelock, the fact that the composition of the Martian atmosphere was in stable chemical equilibrium (mostly carbon dioxide, very little methane, oxygen, or hydrogen—typical byproducts of life as we know it) suggested strongly to him that there were no life forms of significance on Mars. He argued that the presence of life would have changed the atmospheric composition to something more Earthlike. Subsequent space probes confirmed his view of the lack of life on Mars. His was an entirely new way of thinking. Mainstream science had until then considered the atmosphere as something, though slowly changing, to which life adapts, with influence going one way only.

Lovelock postulated that the atmosphere and life on the planet constituted one large geophysical system in which life could affect the atmosphere and vice versa. Gaia theory sees the earth as a self-regulating complex system, which seeks a physical and chemical environment optimal for life. The earth's atmospheric composition is kept at a dynamically steady state far from chemical equilibrium because of the presence of life. Regulation takes place by many complex feedback loops.[2]

Lovelock's Gaia hypothesis has been called one of the most provocative ideas to have been put forward in the second half of the twentieth century. It was seen as "nonscientific" by mainstream scientists of the reductionist school, particularly because it was not possible to falsify it, nor were there any obvious ways to test the theory experimentally. Lovelock dismissed his critics with reference to their limited understanding of nonlinear complex feedback systems, where simple cause-and-effect experiments are not usually possible. Much of the early criticism was as much emotional as scientific, such as the criticism that the hypothesis was teleological, i.e., purposeful. Lovelock never actually said it was, although his admittedly "poetic" language was very suggestive. Nor were the reductionist scientists happy with Lovelock's breaking of the unwritten code that serious members of the scientific community do not give frivolous titles to their theories, such as the Greek goddess "Gaia," with undertones of religion and purpose.

In spite of the initial criticism, Lovelock received backing from another unorthodox scientist, who was also thinking "outside of the box," micro-biologist Lynn Margulis, an expert in the role that microorganisms play in evolution. Independently, she had developed a theory, which she called "endosymbiosis," to describe the relationship between organisms that live one within another in a mutually beneficial relationship, one as host, the other as a dependent "symbiont."[3] Margulis' main contention was that a major force driving evolution was the concept of symbiotic (mutually beneficial) cooperation between different organisms and their environment, as opposed to competition of like organisms within a particular environment, as proposed by Darwin. This was clearly a red-flag challenge to traditional thinking. It was every bit as provocative as Lovelock's Gaia theory in that it not only advanced the concept of symbiotic cooperation, but also introduced the concept of organisms actually *affecting* the environment. She did not deny the role of competition, but she considered Darwin's theory incomplete. Her ideas were so unconventional that she had difficulty finding a scientific journal at first that would publish her work. But her ideas were gradually accepted. Subsequently, she and Lovelock worked closely together for many years, reinforcing and corroborating each other's work.

As time went on, in the 1990s and 2000s, both Lovelock's and Margulis' ideas went from "completely off the charts" to reluctant mainstream acceptance as legitimate and groundbreaking science. Acceptance of Lovelock's Gaia theory was particularly influenced by a number of unlikely predictions that turned out to be verifiably true, always a good way to strengthen any "unlikely" theory. Today, Gaia theory also goes by the name of "geophysiology" at some of the many universities that teach the subject. Symptomatic of the shift in acceptance is a recent comment by one of the most vocal critics of the Gaia hypothesis in the early days, evolutionary biologist Richard Dawkins, who wrote, "I greatly admire Lynn Margulis's sheer courage and stamina in sticking by the endosymbiosis theory, and carrying it through from being an unorthodoxy to an orthodoxy. . . . This is one of the great achievements of twentieth-century evolutionary biology."[4] Both Lovelock and Margulis have hundreds of colleagues following up on the many new research paths that have now been opened up, typical of the paradigm-shift period according to Kuhn.

Homeostasis (self-regulation of life conditions) is normally considered a characteristic of living systems, which raises an interesting question: is the earth a living system?

Lovelock was criticized for suggesting that the planet might be considered so in his early work. His rejoinder was to point out that there was no universally accepted definition of "life," so it all depends on the definition.

Gaia as Icon

If Lovelock had called his theory "geophysiological homeostasis," his impact on the world would have been far less. Invoking the goddess of Mother Earth not only provoked the scientific community, but, more importantly, it resonated enthusiastically with an entirely different segment—the early adopters of the emergent paradigm, who were tiring of what for them was a dysfunctional reductionist worldview, and were on the lookout for a unifying metaphor for their quest for change. The fact that Lovelock's hypothesis came at about the same time as the publication of the famous Apollo photo of Earth

Figure 9.1. Gaia, the Living Earth. Photo courtesy of NASA; see http://ay.wikipedia.org/wiki/Archivo:Earth_from_Space.jpg

seen from space created a double whammy that firmly established Gaia, the Living Earth, as the icon that would bring home the concept of a single Earth family inhabiting a precious and vulnerable living paradise in a seemingly cold and hostile universe. This ingenious concept instantaneously personified and energized the embryonic environmental movement. Therefore, for the sake of reference, in the rest of this book, I will call the emergent worldview the "Gaian paradigm" and the values that it represents "Gaian." This puts us on firm scientific grounds while at the same time putting us in tune with the worldwide agents of the ongoing transition.

If a paradigm shift to Gaian values is really permeating all of society at this time, then there should be concrete evidence available. There is, in fact, a growing rumbling beneath the superficially smooth "business as usual" stories coming from the major media and the global political/economic elite. These rumblings represent a call for major change from millions of persons representing myriad organizations and the citizens of numerous countries that are no longer satisfied with the status quo. They are becoming more and more difficult to ignore. Let us look at some of them.

The Cultural Creatives

In the 1990s, sociologists Paul Ray and Sherry Ruth Anderson identified a segment of the American population, which holds values characteristic of the new paradigm, and gave them the label "Cultural Creatives."[5] They documented that this group grew enormously over the thirty-year period from roughly 1970 to 2000. Their findings are based on over 100,000 responses to questionnaires and contact with hundreds of focus groups. It is probably no coincidence that the beginnings of this phenomenon can be traced to the approximate time when the quality-of-life indicators (GPI, ISEW, etc.) began to go south in the 1970s. From a level of approximately 4% of the population in the mid-1970s, the Cultural Creatives grew to about 26% of the population in the United States by 1999 as measured by Ray and Anderson. Subsequent research by Paul Ray from 2008 indicates that Cultural Creatives in the United States, Europe, and Japan had grown to 35% of the population. The two sociologists point out that a shift in values of this magnitude in such a short time frame is most unusual and thus an event of historical proportions. There must be something really significant going on below the radar screens of the media, they say. What then distinguishes the Cultural Creatives from the rest of society?

The Cultural Creatives cherish human values, the environment, and community—all things that cannot be measured in monetary terms. They tend to read more than average, watch less TV, and are global in outlook. Cultural Creatives give great weight to being authentic, i.e., what you say is consistent with what you do. They have learned to see through media manipulation, spin doctors, corporate greenwash, hypocrisy, and double morality, while looking for the real and important, preferring to learn by personal experience rather than intellectually. They are as passionate about the global as they are about the local, with no inconsistency.

Counter to the U.S. majority view, 78% of Cultural Creatives believe that "Americans need to consume a much smaller proportion of the world's resources." A great majority is extremely concerned with global warming, the extinction of species, ecological sustainability, and the destruction of the rainforests and the ozone layer. And they tend to do something about it. They are activists. Four times as many as the general population do volunteer work.

Interestingly, Ray and Anderson point out that not only are 60% of them women, but the gender gap seen in the rest of society is not found among Cultural Creatives, whose men embrace "women's issues." They have also identified a "core group" of a little less than one-half that comprises "more educated, leading edge thinkers." The core group—of which two-thirds are women—puts greater emphasis on spirituality and personal growth. The other half tends to be more "secular and extroverted," with emphasis on environmental, social, and economic issues.

Cultural Creatives tend to reject the very things that characterize the dominant group in society, namely, "owning more stuff, materialism, greed, me-firstism, status display, [and] glaring social inequalities." They are also critical of big government, big corporations, and the narrowness of the media. Ray and Anderson observe that members of this group tend to develop "certain qualities—perseverance; an impatience with hype; a capacity for self-reflection and open-mindedness." Cultural Creatives are the avant-garde of the emergent paradigm.

The Moderns

Now, contrast this group with their description of the dominant group in society (about 49% in 1999), which they call the "Moderns." Theirs is the culture that dominates the media, the government, and the courts, as well as the business and university worlds. "The economy dominates what is distinctive about their lives . . . and they have the taken-for-granted perspective of those who belong to the dominant culture." Hence attitudes like "There is no alternative," "This is simply the way it works," and "This is obviously how it is."

Other viewpoints and ways of life are dismissed contemptuously and flippantly. Moderns do not reason philosophically about what is important in life. They are driven not by personal values or ethics, but rather by the need to adapt to the status quo. What is important for them is making a lot of money; being a success; being on top of the latest trends; supporting any technological and economic progress; power shopping; rejecting the values and concerns of indigenous peoples, rural people, and the other 51% of the population as irrelevant and out of tune with the times. Ray and Anderson enumerate a number of unspoken assumptions of the Moderns: the spiritual is flaky; bigger is better; your body is basically a machine; big business and big government know best; and what gets measured gets done. Like the Cultural Creatives, the Moderns also have a hard core. They are the ones who were in power in the United States during the first decade of the twenty-first century, representing "14% of the people, 19% of the vote, and 80% of the money." The Moderns are the entirely predictable end product of Cartesian/ Newtonian thinking.

The Traditionals

The final group in Ray and Anderson's analysis is the "Traditionals" (about 25% in 1999). This group includes quite diverse political and religious groupings with a common set of "beliefs, ways of life, and personal identity." They have a "general lack of interest in politics." Many have "low incomes, a high school education or less, and they don't vote." 70% are religious conservatives, while the hard core tend to be affluent business and social conservatives. Their values and beliefs according to Ray and Anderson tend to include the patriarchal family; feminism is a swearword; family, church, and community are central; customs should be maintained; traditional gender roles are best; sex and "immoral" behavior should be regulated; one should have pride in the military; the Bible and the right to bear arms are very important; foreigners are suspect; and small-town life is more virtuous than big-city life.

It is interesting to note that the Traditionals share some values with each of the other groups. They can identify with the Cultural Creatives' volunteer work, and their preference for community and family life over technology and big government, but they also resonate with the hard-core Moderns' emphasis on patriotism and the use of military force to maintain the status quo. Traditionalists can be thought of as holdovers from the sixteenth century "scholastic paradigm" with its focus on Aristotelian ethics, religion, family life, small-town virtues, and its general mistrust of higher education and science in general.

Civil Society

The explosion in the number of nongovernmental organizations on the world scene since World War II is to a large extent an expression of the dissatisfaction of citizens across the world with the way their governments have operated. Many were motivated by what they saw as the necessity to take on tasks that governments were not giving a sufficiently high priority to, or their goal was to influence political decision making by pushing various single-issue campaigns. While their range of interests is very wide, concern about the environment, human rights, poverty, and people-centered development are among the most frequent advocacy issues. NGOs have been gaining not only in numbers, but in influence over the years. The number of international NGOs is estimated to be 40,000, while national numbers are even higher: for example, Russia has 277,000 NGOs; India has about 3.3 million. Over 1550 NGOs have obtained consultative status with the UN.[6] Many UN agencies now hold periodic consultations with NGOs on substantive policy and program strategies. NGOs are also gaining increasing access to other multilateral organizations like the World Bank, WTO, and the World Economic Forum in Davos.

Gathering under the slogan "Another World is Possible," 10,000 grassroots activists from 123 countries met in Porto Alegre, Brazil, in January 2000 to begin to coordinate the efforts of thousands of NGOs and individuals around the world that are—in one way or another—working for what I would call a more "Gaian" global society. The get-together was an enormous success, as activists inspired and informed each other of their initiatives, networked, attended workshops, heard inspiring talks, and perhaps most of all, felt for the first time that they were part of a single, historical movement with an unstoppable momentum.

This feeling was increased dramatically over the next two years as the word got around and the Porto Alegre gathering increased to 50,000 people in

2002 and 100,000 in 2003. The numbers were so overwhelming that subsequent meetings of even more people risked being unmanageable. So the focus shifted to regional meetings. For example, the European Social Forum in Florence, Italy, in November 2002 attracted 400 organizations and 40,000 people. The latest meeting took place in Dakar, Senegal, in February 2011. At this meeting they modified their slogan to "Another World is Necessary." It is interesting to note that the World Social Forum (WSF) meetings have attracted more people than typically attend UN summit meetings, suggesting that they should be taken very seriously. So far, the media have not done so, purposely ignoring the WSF as its agenda is—to put it mildly—not friendly to the Empire.

The WSF is not a decision-making organization. It is simply a forum where people can meet and exchange information. It was originally conceived as a counter to the annual Davos meeting of the world's business leaders. The latter has been in a crisis in recent years because of corruption scandals and the 2007–8 financial crash, and may be losing momentum just as the WSF is gaining.[7]

Many of the world's international nonprofits have been leading the way for decades on human rights and environmental issues, social reforms, and disaster relief. They've been recognized as a necessary arm of civil society, one that carries out the mission of the people to form a more life-based global society. Their work ranges from issuing wake-up calls, conducting educational campaigns, and stimulating personal action to assessing the world's needs and finding ways to address them. They've put people on the ground around the world to fend off many of the threats we've discussed in prior chapters. Thousands of similar organizations doing comparable work at the national, regional, and local community levels can be found in every country, and among those are groups that focus on the particular needs of a given region, and groups that are springing up around the world to respond to the ever-growing awareness about the coming collapse, the need for new economic structures and worker rights, and the need for resilience in a post-peak-oil future.

The millions of members of civil society, along with the more progressive business units, universities, and foundations, represent an enormous potential for bringing about positive global change, even in a world where the opposition to change is also enormous. Who among these activists has not dreamed of how powerful they could be if they could only work together? But grassroots activist groups are notoriously independent, each group with its own agenda. Perhaps it is best that way. And while most of them are bringing about positive changes every day within their particular focus, yet the dream of working together on a world-changing cooperative initiative persists. In any case, these organizations are slowly but surely laying the foundation for a new civilization even as the old one is crumbling. When energy descent is a fact of life acknowledged by the mainstream, and the ruling economic/political system risks breaking down completely, it will be to these organizations that society will turn for inspiration and new solutions and a place to begin rebuilding.

Can the millions of diverse NGOs of the world be considered to be part of a single "movement"? American environmentalist Paul Hawken argues in *Blessed Unrest* that this is the case even though the "movement" has no name and its members have no common "mission statement" or agenda, as no one owns it and no one controls it. He sees a common thread in their values in the linking of sustainability and human rights issues, writing "concerns about worker health, living wages, equity, education, and basic human rights are inseparable from concerns about water, climate, soil, and biodiversity." Hawken notes that the movement is very broad and diverse, "taking shape in schoolrooms, farms, jungles, villages, companies, deserts, fisheries, slums—and yes, even fancy New York hotels."

An interesting insight is his conjecturing that, "rather than a movement in the conventional sense, could it be an instinctive, collective response to threat?"[8] This is, I think, a good description of what happened when the "Occupy Wall Street" movement went global. More and more people became aware of the dysfunctionality of modern society and felt obligated to take some kind of action. They are uncoordinated but share similar values. If only they could focus all their energies on a single proposal that is doable at the local level! Perhaps *the breakaway strategy*, to be introduced in the final chapter of this work, will be the proposal that can unite them behind a single, simple goal that can achieve their objectives.

Peaceful Rumblings

There have been a number of signs of dissatisfaction with, and resistance to, the current world order in recent years—some peaceful, some violent—that can give some encouragement to the forces that are looking for positive change.

One good example is the recent formation of the Bolivarian Alliance for the Americas (ALBA) in South America (Bolivia, Venezuela, Ecuador, Cuba,

Nicaragua, Antigua and Barbuda, Saint Vincent and the Grenadines, and Dominica). The formation of ALBA is very significant because it is the first example of a group of countries rejecting the neoliberal economic model outright, while promoting instead a more democratic and socially responsible model of regional economic integration based on a vision of social welfare, increased internal trade, and mutual economic aid, rather than trade liberalization and free-trade agreements. They are striving to become independent of the IMF and American influence, and even introduced in 2010 a new currency called the "SUCRE" for internal trade in the region.

It is still relatively early to draw conclusions about ALBA. There is much uncertainty about how this innovative experiment will play out. An interesting initiative is the dialogue regarding the eventual adoption of a cohesive counter-vision of international law known as TWAIL (third world approaches to international law). It is an approach that draws primarily on the history of the encounter between international law and colonized peoples, and is "rooted in notions of complementarity and human solidarity."[9]

The normal response of the Empire to such an initiative would be an attempt by the CIA to arrange a "spontaneous uprising" in Caracas to overthrow the Venezuelan government and install a right-wing regime favorable to American business interests, as they consider Hugo Chavez to be the main architect of ALBA. Why has this not yet happened? There are two possible reasons: first, the CIA tried that in 2002 and it failed when hundreds of thousands of citizens in the streets backed up Chavez; second, with two wars going on abroad, it may be too much of a stretch, even for the United States, to take on a new campaign. But the possibility cannot be ruled out. If ALBA succeeds, it will be admired and probably emulated in other regions looking for an alternative to neoliberalism. ALBA is a major thorn in the side of the Empire.

A second form of peaceful resistance is the growing independence of the major developing countries, the so-called BRICS group (Brazil, Russia, India, China, and South Africa). In meetings of the G-20, they are no longer afraid to push policy positions that are not particularly desired by the United States. Put off by the Empire's tough bargaining position in the WTO Doha round, the BRICS countries are discovering that they are actually quite powerful when cooperating, and they are growing faster than the industrialized countries economically. Thus we see increasing self-confidence and increasing trade among them with a trend toward less dependence on Empire markets. For example, China recently surpassed the United States as Brazil's largest trading partner, and has also become the major trading partner of India and Russia, ahead of Germany and the United States. China now sets the price for many of the world's natural resources by virtue of its enormous demand, and in some cases on account of a near monopoly on supply, as, for example, important rare earth metals—crucial to hybrid cars, wind turbines, and many other green-tech innovations—where China currently controls 97% of global production. Russia is beginning to play a similar price-setting role on the supply side because of its enormous resource base. China has also become a major player in Africa, competing with the Empire for resources to fuel its rapid growth.

Even close U.S. allies like the EU, Germany, Japan, and South Korea are becoming more independent and are speaking up. For example, in 2010–11 the EU and the United States disagreed on the appropriate response to the problem of excessive debt in both regions. The United States favors putting more money into the economy to encourage consumption and economic growth and would like to see greater coordination of policy among the G-20, while the EU favors cutting expenses and running very tight budgets, which will slow down growth and increase unemployment, but should result in a better balance of income and expenses in the longer run.

European members of NATO have a view on the need for military budgets quite different from the United States', a view that has frequently been a source of friction. While the United States pushes for greater contributions from Europe, the Europeans see the external threats as being far less of a problem and have difficulty understanding the American need for such superior forces when no plausible threat exists that could not be handled at a fraction of current costs. These are all signs of greater international democracy, and at the same time signal a weakening at the center of the Empire.

Several members of the G-20 are very concerned about the U.S. trade deficit and budget deficit and the effect these may have on the value of the U.S. dollar. In a concrete reaction to this fear, in November 2010, China and Russia made an agreement to settle their future trade transactions with their own currencies and not via the dollar as they had done previously. This was a psychological blow to the dollar. Coming on top of ALBA's decision to trade internally in SUCRES, it may indicate the beginning of a trend that will spread to other regions. China in particular is concerned about the dollar, being the largest foreign holder of dollars with close to half of its $3 trillion of official foreign-exchange reserves being denominated in U.S. dollars. There is considerable talk in the corridors at international meetings these days about possible alternatives to the U.S. dollar—another potential threat to U.S. domination. I will return to this subject, including my own proposal for an alternative, in chapter 14.

Violent Rumblings

The uprisings in Tunisia, Egypt, Libya, Syria, Yemen, and elsewhere in the Middle East and North Africa in 2011, besides opening up the possibility of a more democratic region, could also have the positive effect of marking the beginning of a change in American foreign policy and a weakening of the Empire. For many ordinary Americans and Europeans it came no doubt as a surprise that their governments had been supplying Middle East dictatorships for decades with the means to keep their citizens oppressed, including the arms used in 2011 to crush the democratic revolts, not to mention contributing to the bloating Swiss bank accounts of the tyrants. For example, while the United States was sending $10 billion a year to Egypt, President Mubarak was apparently depositing as much as $70 billion of these funds in Switzerland for his personal use, while 40% of the population tried to survive on less than $2 per day. The cynical decisions of the United States and the EU to reverse field and back the democratic forces of revolution were a blow to the reigning corporatocracy, but a victory for freedom-loving people everywhere. President Obama was under great pressure from the American public to pull the rug out from under Egyptian president Hosni Mubarak and support democracy, while the corporatocracy was pushing him just as hard to continue to back the despot. This time the corporatocracy was caught unprepared and lost the argument. On a similar note, a few days before the flight of Tunisia's dictator Ben Ali, French foreign secretary Michele Alliot-Marie suggested sending French riot police to help crush the uprising. She also had a stake in one of Ben Ali's companies and wanted to send tear gas to the country to help disperse protesters. Bad timing! A week later she was forced to resign.[10]

Blowback

The north African revolutions in Tunisia and Egypt are to some extent a result of "blowback," a term coined by the CIA to describe the unintended consequences of American foreign policy. In both cases, the surprise was the unforeseen democratic revolts against Empire client states. With prophetic foresight, the first use of the word "blowback" appeared in the CIA report on their Iranian coup of 1953, which later led directly to one of the clearest examples of blowback yet seen—the ayatollah-led revolution of 1979 that threw out the Shah of Iran and installed in power an anti-American anti-British oppressive religious regime that survives to this day. Iranians of all political and religious groupings understandably were, and still are, very angry with the way the United States and Great Britain interfered with their sovereignty and self-determination. If the 1953 CIA coup had not taken place, Iran would quite possibly be a model Middle East democracy today, and a staunch American ally, and "ayatollah" would hardly be the household word that it has become.

A related example of blowback was 9/11, the 2001 attack on the Twin Towers and Pentagon by Middle Eastern youths from Saudi Arabia and Egypt. Americans had great difficulty understanding the background for 9/11 on account of the effectiveness of what Noam Chomsky dubbed the "propaganda model" that systematically suppressed the facts about the widespread anger in the region due to the American policy of supporting oppressive Middle Eastern dictatorships.

In official American discourse, the "enemy" responsible for 9/11 is usually described as "fundamentalist Islam." According to President George W. Bush, they attacked the United States because they resented American democracy and freedom. Few non-Americans find this explanation credible. There are many examples of the United States working with radical Islamists when it suits its foreign policy, for example in Saudi Arabia—the ideological center of radical Islam, in Pakistan under Zia-ul-Haq, and, of course, with Osama bin Laden in his anti-Soviet campaign in Afghanistan. A more plausible explanation for 9/11 would seem to be blowback. The terrorists who organized 9/11 probably yearned for freedom as much as anyone else. Hatred of the American government for its support of the despotic regimes of Saudi Arabia and Egypt would seem to be a more likely explanation. Examples of blowback are quite dangerous for the Empire when the story is big enough to break through the propaganda barrier and reach the American public.

Beyond the Empire

We can see from the above-mentioned examples of a global civil society "movement," the peaceful rumblings of ALBA and the G-20, the "Occupy" protests, and the violent rumblings of the "Arab spring" that a significant shift in attitudes is taking place globally, stimulated no doubt by the realization that the current world order is simply not working for the great majority. More and more people are reaching the limits of their tolerance of a dysfunctional world order and are looking for new solutions. Many are prepared to put their lives on the line to achieve it. This is true not only for the revolting masses in North Africa and the Middle East, but to millions of grassroots activists and leading intellectuals, as well as to a large minority of ordinary citizens—the Cultural Creatives—certainly in the West. The Empire is showing signs of weakness and decay, reminding us that a push in the right direction can tip a wobbly wagon.

So the question arises: if and when the Gaian agents of change succeed in tipping the wagon, what would they put in its place? One of the most significant changes is likely to appear in the social sphere of many countries.

Egalitarianism

In Gaian society, humans will be recognized as social beings—rather than isolated individuals—that thrive best as respected members of local communities. For millennia we have survived only because we learned to live in tribes and cooperate. In the early days of human evolution, there was no way an individual could survive for long on his or her own. Those tribes that best learned to cooperate passed on their genes to us. The rest disappeared in the sands of time. This social characteristic is programmed so deep in our DNA that no amount of man-made changes in the way we are organized, or in our political system, or even in our worldview, can change that fundamental fact. This is the key to understanding how the shift from the separatist paradigm to the holistic paradigm will affect all aspects of our lifestyle—the way we design our communities, the way we educate our children, our attitude toward wealth and income differences, our attitude toward health and social problems, our attitude toward consumption. All of these things will shift dramatically when the consequences of the change in worldview work their way through the entire fabric of our culture and society. The central concept that will characterize the social aspect of Gaian society—the result of three separate forces pushing in the same direction— will be a shift toward a more egalitarian society, i.e., a more equal distribution of wealth, income, and influence—in technical terms, a somewhat lower Gini coefficient than current society.

The first driving force is an ideological one, more or less dictated by the worldview of Gaian society. Imagine for a moment a world in which there is broad agreement that limits must be placed on resource usage and consumption as a necessary consequence of a focus on survival, long-term sustainability and respect for coming generations. The responses of our current society to such restrictions suddenly forced upon it would fall into two quite distinct patterns; one reaction would be for the strong to attempt to maintain their lifestyle and dominant position by exploiting the weak; the other reaction would be for local communities to come together to deal with the crisis by sharing the limited resources available. But in the Gaian worldview, only the latter would make any sense. Thus, the old paradigm practices of exploitation, of accumulating material things for greater enjoyment than others can achieve, or of measuring success by individual wealth, will all be seen as asocial. Success will be measured more by one's contribution to local society, such as proficiency in a trade or profession, hard work, initiative, artistic talent, kindness, inventiveness, community leadership, etc.—all things that cannot be measured by money.

The second egalitarian driver will be economic. Putting aside any shift in worldview for the moment, imagine global society after a peak-oil shock followed by energy descent, or even after adoption of an effective rationing of fossil fuels to combat global warming. We are heading inexorably to one of these two scenarios at this moment. In either case, we are talking about a period of significant downsizing of the global economy accompanied by enormous shifts in production, transportation, and trade patterns, unprecedented business failures, widespread unemployment, and shrinking national budgets. In such an environment, where a great burden will be placed on all sectors of society, there will be great pressure on those with high incomes to contribute more to the common pot. We saw a similar reaction, on a much smaller scale, to the recent financial crisis, with calls for limits on salaries and bonuses to financial sector executives. Too great a disparity in income will be considered socially unacceptable.

The third driver toward egalitarianism will be evidence-based rationality. Based on solid evidence, it will become much clearer to the broad populace what is already clear to a small band of social researchers, namely, that almost all the social ills plaguing modern society are a direct result of too great a disparity in income. It will be acknowledged that those societies with the lowest Gini coefficients (rich/poor ratios) are also those with the happiest citizens, greatest harmony, and fewest social and health problems, as documented in the earlier-cited study by Wilkinson and Pickett. Furthermore, it will be acknowledged that the cause of the high Gini coefficients in the most socially dysfunctional countries is a direct consequence of the currently dominant economic system.

The idea of a more egalitarian civilization may send cold chills down the spines of fundamentalist "Moderns," who associate egalitarianism with socialism or even communism, with associated visions of top-down central planning, lack of freedom, and an inefficient private sector. But these are false images promoted by right-wing propagandists who fear losing their privileges. If we look more closely at the countries that score highest on equality and lowest on the Index of Health and Social Problems in the Wilkinson and Pickett study, we find the Scandinavian countries and Japan. These are the current societies that come closest to the Gaian ideal. None of these can be considered socialist, and none has ever flirted with communism. All are highly regarded, democratic, competitive societies with quite liberal private sectors and a minimum of corruption. What does differentiate them, particularly the Scandinavian countries, is a larger public sector than the more unequal societies. Their citizens are quite pragmatic about it; they are willing to pay higher taxes provided that everyone pays a fair share and that they get good value for their money, such as free education and medical care, and a greater sense of security. According to the Wilkinson and Pickett study, they also get the additional bonus of better health, fewer social problems, and lower health care costs.

One of the most noticeable differences between current society and a fully developed Gaian society will be the flourishing of millions of thriving, healthy, local communities and neighborhoods all over the world, having a high degree of self-determination and a great diversity in cultural profiles. Lifestyle is going to change markedly. In its diversity, Gaian culture will come to resemble the rest of nature. The main drivers of this shift will also be ideological and economic forces.

Ideologically, holders of a Gaian worldview would prefer not to live in isolated apartments in sterile high rises among anonymous neighbors or in an isolated villa in the suburbs. For them, it would be like a prison. Whether they live in big cities, suburbs, towns, or villages, they will organize their living conditions around a local community of like-minded souls, the way human cultures always did in the past, before the separatist worldview changed everything for a few hundred years. They will vary from the most technologically advanced to bare-subsistence communities, but their values will be similar. Rural villages and big city eco-neighborhoods will vary in size, but a critical issue will be the number of people that one can relate to personally, for this is a condition of real community on a human scale. Recognition and acceptance within the community are important components of the glue holding the community together. Because of the sheer magnitude of the diversity, everyone will be able to find a community somewhere that matches his or her needs and aspirations.

Central to the values of Gaians, these communities will be characterized by natural rather than synthetic products, organic food, clean energy, clean water, and close contact with nature. In a fully developed Gaian culture, most citizens will be aware of the importance of ecology and permaculture design from their primary education. They will be tolerant toward those of other races, religions, and cultures. Their housing will be very energy efficient. Many will produce much of their own energy, primarily solar, while others will be linked to a regional CPH (combined heat and power) facility. The availability of local energy production will be a prime driver of decentralization of society, including a high degree of local democracy and local autonomy. Travel is likely to be much more limited than today, and mostly by highly efficient public transportation.

The thing that will distinguish these eco-communities most from the typical neighborhood of today will be that they will not be just living spaces, but much more. Many residents will have their work there as well, offering various services to their local circle and beyond. The permanence of these local communities will be established by law, which will define rights, including a budget from the public purse and a degree of control over their local environment, and responsibilities that will, in many cases, include primary education and care of the elderly. Usually, each ecovillage will be part of a larger eco-town, and each eco-neighborhood a part of an eco-city. The larger units will have administrative responsibility for various functions that are more practically handled on a larger scale, such as public transportation, sewage treatment, higher institutions of learning, and so on.

Many needs that would be fulfilled today at a regional shopping center (normally after travel by car) will be fulfilled within walking distance and often by other community members. Not least of these will be the local food market, the heart of the community. Much of this food will be produced in the community, particularly in the rural communities, but also to some extent in the cities.

Ideology alone will not bring about the shift in lifestyle, as the resistance of the ruling political/economic establishment is just too massive. The current industrialized country infrastructure creates enormous physical and ideological barriers to the evolution of healthy eco-communities. But once we enter the period of energy descent a change in lifestyle will become an existential necessity. When the shift does occur, it will be as much for economic reasons, almost as an explosion, as jobs disappear, food and transportation costs increase dramatically, and welfare benefits are cut. When things start falling apart, the old barriers will fall. A shift from the cities to the countryside into self-sufficient eco-communities will be one consequence. Those remaining in the cities will come together and form cooperative urban eco-neighborhoods.

Gaian society can be expected to be a healthier, happier, more harmonious civilization than the present world civilization, much of this due to the more egalitarian structure. David Korten has eloquently described the coming transition as a shift "from empire to earth community," having two primary elements, "a turning from money to life as our defining value," and "a turning from relations of domination to relations of partnership based on organizing principles discerned from the study of healthy living systems."[11]

What Else Can We Expect?

There will be many other changes. I would like to focus on just two major things that will have to change—two of the major "culprits" of the contemporary world that are driving us relentlessly toward the abyss—our production technologies and our economic system.

We must find new ways to produce things with much less energy, no waste, and no toxics. And we must replace the destructive neoliberal economic system with a new economic system that is protective of the environment. In the next two chapters, we will take a closer look at these two key areas. Together, they will provide a solid foundation for taking the next step—designing a whole new Gaian world order.

TEN

Learning from Nature

Nature, to be commanded, must be obeyed.

—Sir Francis Bacon

A major difference between Gaian society and present society will be the way we produce things. The new paradigm will revolutionize the way we think about product design. While we tend to be proud of the Industrial Revolution with its accompanying human progress and impressive technological achievements, future generations are likely to look upon this period as an exception—a parenthesis in human evolution, and not a particularly positive one. This will be seen as the period when *Homo sapiens sapiens* got completely out of touch with nature, using up in just a few generations resources that took millions of years for nature to produce, while "fouling the nest" of future human and animal habitation for millennia to come with incredible amounts of synthetic toxic materials and nuclear waste, in addition to triggering global warming with excessive CO_2 emissions from fossil fuel burning.

Imitating Nature

Biomimicry (or biomimetics) is a blossoming new scientific discipline that studies nature's best ideas and then imitates these designs and processes to solve human problems. Nature—over billions of years of trial and error—has found optimal solutions for thousands of diverse life-forms so they could survive and thrive within the limits determined by their environments. Those organisms that have survived have learned to live within their means. Those who could not learn this lesson have disappeared in the sands of time. What surround us in nature are the success stories, and we should be paying more attention. Biomimicry is the key to designing a sustainable future for humanity.

Janine Benyus, one of the pioneers of this new discipline, says, "We are learning, for instance, how to harness energy like a leaf, grow food like a prairie, build ceramics like an abalone, self-medicate like a chimp, create color like a peacock, compute like a cell, and run a business like a hickory forest." She adds, "Practicing ethical biomimicry will require a change of heart. We will have to climb down from our pedestal and begin to see ourselves as simply a species among species, as one vote in a parliament of 30 million. When we accept this fact, we start to realize that what is good for the living Earth is good for us as well."[1]

Driving Forces

The driving forces behind the coming design revolution will once again be twofold—ideological and economic. First, the most fundamental premise of the Gaian paradigm is that all life is part of a single living organism. When we injure or abuse a part of that organism, we damage the whole, just as in the human body. If a part of the organism is suffering, all of the other parts suffer as well, not least the most intelligent and self-reflective member, humankind, which should be steward of Earth, but has abused its responsibility. Thus, many of the problems humankind experiences today—from global warming to the divide between rich and poor, to the poisoning of our homes, our soil, our air, and our water—will be recognized as stemming from disregard of this basic principle. This will be the ideological driver.

Secondly, the limits of available resources, both nonrenewable and renewable, in a period of energy descent, cannot fail to increase the prices of such resources and encourage technological innovations, which will drastically reduce energy use and depletion rates, while making far more effective use of our natural capital. The tendency for resource prices to increase will be further exacerbated by the political policy of rationing nonrenewable resources out of respect for the needs of future generations.

Another factor pushing in the same direction is likely to be heavy taxation of, or outright bans on, materials that damage nature, such as toxics, pesticides, endocrine disruptors, and so on. These will be the economic drivers.

Unlimited Abundance

One of the major prophets of the coming revolution is the German environmental chemist, Michael Braungart. His vision of future abundance is nothing less than mind-boggling, his point being that when we produce without waste, there are no limits, no landfills, no pollution. His concept of production using nature's methods eliminates the very concept of waste, as there is no such thing as waste in nature. There are only resources that are useful food to some other part of the ecosystem. Thus, properly designed industrial production has only positive, useful by-products. Braungart challenges us, saying: "What if buildings actually created an abundance of fresh water, fresh air, and power? What if it was possible to take your chair or carpet, cut it up small and eat it with your muesli?" Braungart's optimistic message is that we will no longer have to worry about scarcity if we truly learn from nature. While this may sound incredible at first glance, he has already produced many examples from the real world to back up his claims.

Case Study: Steelcase

In the early 1990s, Braungart and his partner, American architect William McDonough, were asked by American furniture maker Steelcase Inc. to develop an environmentally friendly fabric for them. The team's goal was to develop a material that was not only aesthetically pleasing, but pure enough to eat, while any by-products would be biodegradable. They quickly found a major problem with the textile mill partner, namely, that their synthetic fabric trimmings were classified as hazardous waste. The team decided therefore to go with a natural fabric—wool—combined with pesticide-free plant and animal fibers. A second major problem was the choice of dyes and process chemicals, which in this line of business are often carcinogenic and toxic, with endocrine disruptors and mutagens frequently present as well. They asked over sixty companies for descriptions of their products, but were turned down by all with reference to fears of revealing their corporate secrets to the competition, a phenomenon that Braungart and McDonough were to experience again and again in other cases. Finally, they found one firm that would cooperate. After careful study, they eliminated 8,000 commonly used chemicals that did not measure up to their environmental standards. This elimination had the interesting effect of also eliminating a number of secondary chemical additives and correctives whose only function was to mitigate the toxics. They ended up with 38 acceptable ingredients, which were sufficient to produce the desired fabric.

After the new fabric went into production, the local authorities could not believe their instruments at first. The normally polluted effluent water was now cleaner than the water going in! Besides the environmental benefit, this provided an unanticipated cost-saving opportunity, as the effluent water could now be recycled. There were other benefits. Areas previously used for storage of hazardous materials were freed up for the use of employees. Some regulatory paperwork was eliminated. Workers could cease wearing gloves and masks, thus increasing employee job satisfaction and safety. The new fabric was an instant success with customers and a financial success as well, as it was of higher quality and less costly to make than its predecessor. Nor was there any need to send the used product to a landfill or incinerator. It could be used instead to improve soil quality wherever it happened to decompose.[7]

Holistic Production

Braungart/McDonough design principles are holistic in keeping with the Gaian paradigm. A product cannot be designed in isolation, but must be seen as an element of a larger ecosystem with ecological, social, economic, and cultural dimensions. In their book—*Cradle to Cradle*—they acknowledge that many corporations are moving in the direction of more ecologically friendly products, but very few are radical enough. They may be making products that are "less bad" but they are still operating in the mind-set of harnessing nature to serve human purposes, and still using harsh chemicals, high temperatures and pressure, and simply "driving the first industrial revolution to new extremes." They must take a further step that considers humankind as an integral part of nature. Natural systems take from nature and give back to nature. Nothing is wasted. Waste in nature is just another word for food. We have to learn from nature how to produce natural products under the same conditions that nature uses—at room temperature and pressure, using just a small fraction of the energy and resources used today in industry. This is the essence of the coming second industrial revolution.

A good example of a natural product far superior to anything we can produce using the "heat, beat, and treat" industrial approach, yet produced at normal temperature and pressure, is spider silk. Ounce for ounce, spider silk is five times stronger than steel and tougher than bulletproof Kevlar, which is made from petroleum by-products under high pressure, using concentrated sulfuric acid, boiled at very high temperatures, while producing toxic waste. Spider silk is not only strong, but, unlike steel, can stretch 40% without breaking. It combines these unique qualities with a composite structure of crystallites imbedded in an organic polymer. Nature developed this benign product 380 million years ago, while material scientists just recently declared composite structures to be the latest new idea. Needless to say, we have a lot to learn from nature if we adopt a more humble attitude and just observe more closely the kinds of solutions that are in front of our eyes and potentially available at a small fraction of current cost without any load on the ecosystem.

This last point is one that Michael Braungart likes to emphasize. As long as our production methods are benign with no damage to our natural capital, he says, there is no limit to abundance. We can produce as much as we want, and whenever we throw away the product, it simply improves the soil and water quality.

However, developing commercial processes for natural products like spider silk is no simple task. A great deal of research will be necessary to understand, duplicate, and scale up the complex biological processes and structures involved. But this will happen naturally as we make the shift in mentality from a mechanical, reductionist focus to the biological, holistic focus of the Gaian paradigm. Indeed, an explosion of research in the life sciences will characterize the coming age of oil descent.

Industrial Cooperation

One of the key differences between the old and the emerging paradigm is the shift from competition to cooperation. Both are vital to nature's way. Now, some people might object to this claim, saying: wait a minute—is survival of the fittest not the driving force behind evolution? Competition is part of the story, but without cooperation, there would be no evolution. In fact, Darwin did not use the often cited expression "survival of the fittest" in his study; he called the phenomenon of natural selection a "struggle for existence," which sends a rather different message. Natural selection occurred by mutations, with the most successful variants surviving, but the innovative solutions can just as well involve cooperation as improved competitiveness. In fact, the major evolutionary jumps were all of a cooperative nature. For example, at a momentous time millions of years ago, individual bacteria combined to form one-celled organisms that were one thousand times larger and better suited to survive. Later, one-celled organisms combined to form multicelled organisms for even greater potential. The human being is the hitherto most complex expression of the continued cooperation between millions of organisms on this planet over billions of years.

In Gaian society, cooperation among corporations will become one way to fulfill the "no waste" theme of benign, holistic production, where one company's "waste" is another company's "food." One of the first examples of this phenomenon is found in Kalundborg, Denmark. Kalundborg's Industrial Symbiosis project includes eight companies, interconnected by a

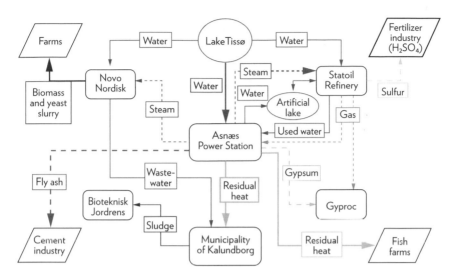

Figure 10.1. Industrial Symbiosis in Kalundborg. From "The Industrial Symbiosis in Kalundborg, Denmark," UNEP: Environmental Management for Industrial Estates: Information and Training Resources; Case Study/Kalundborg–6; www.iisbe.org.

network of material flows: steam, gas, water, gypsum, fly ash, and sludge, as shown in figure 10.1.

Excess steam from Asnaes Power Station is exported to Kalundborg's combined district heat and power supply and to both StatoilHydro and Novo Nordisk, who use it as a heat source before exporting it back to Asnaes in condensed form for cooling the plant. Gyproc A/S receives excess heating gas from the StatoilHydro Refinery and industrial plaster from Asnaes power station. Calcium and recycled treated wastewater are added to the sulfur extracted from the flue gas at Asnaes to form industrial plaster. Insulin production at Novo Nordisk A/S releases material that is exported to surrounding farms as pig fodder. A by-product of the yeast fermentation process is converted into yeast slurry. This replaces approximately 70% of the soy proteins in traditional feed mixes. Novo Nordisk A/S adds sugar, water, and lactic acid bacteria to the yeast in order to make it more a more attractive fodder. This win-win cooperative venture has been running successfully for almost thirty years, saving the companies hundreds of millions of dollars.

A No-Waste Brewery

George Chan, a civil engineer from Mauritius and an expert on Chinese fish farming, was asked to design a no-waste brewery in Namibia by the Chairman of Namibia Breweries in 1996. Less than eighteen months later, one of the first examples of integrated bio-production was a reality, producing no less than six saleable products without any waste. A traditional brewery has to dispose of a number of so-called waste products, mostly spent grain and alkaline wastewater. The spent grain can be used as grain feed, but is not ideal for cattle because of the high fiber content, and the alkaline water typically pollutes nearby streams. Spent grain is about 25% protein, a valuable asset, but the cellulose makes it difficult to digest. What Chan demonstrated out was that you could break down the cellulose component by a special mushroom enzyme, resulting in a substantial production of high quality mushrooms with a high market value—the second product.

That left Chan with the protein component, which he then used to cultivate earthworms, which in turn were used as chicken feed. So chickens became the third product line.

But it did not end there. Namibian pollution laws required that the alkaline water be neutralized at considerable expense. But Chan knew that such water is ideal for cultivating spirulina algae, a high-protein diet supplement, which became the fourth industrial product—indeed, a very high-value product.

But there was still a lot of water left over, and it was heavy in organic nutrients. But George Chan's Chinese background suggested a solution: fish farming, of course, based on ancient and well-tested Chinese techniques. Thus, fish became the fifth industrial product, with an initial production of fifteen tons per hectare.

There was one final "waste" to be taken care of—chicken manure. This Chan put through a digester to produce methane gas, a fuel source that cuts heating bills. So, summing up, what we have here is a company with six products that is extremely efficient with no waste, a higher return on capital than traditional breweries, and with increased employment to boot. While conventional economic thinking says that you increase productivity by decreasing employment, Chan's design increased productivity while *increasing* employment, which I suspect will be typical of many future cases of integrated bio-production, which tends to be labor intensive.[3]

The Service Society

Cheap energy and raw material costs over the last hundred years have led to a business model that maximizes profits by producing shoddy products that fall apart rather quickly only to be replaced by a newer, "sexier" model, reinforced by sophisticated advertising, innovative design, global brands, and wide distribution—sometimes called the "planned obsolescence" of a "throwaway society." The product life cycle follows a "cradle to grave" path— extraction of raw materials from the earth, energy-inefficient production with toxic by-products, short-term use, and termination in an overfilled landfill or polluting incinerator that emits deadly dioxins; or, in the case of many electronic products, toxics are sent to "under-polluted" developing countries to deal with. Old-paradigm companies want their products to burn out fast! That is all going to change, primarily for economic reasons, when the costs of energy, raw materials, and toxic by-products explode. But the change will also be driven by the Gaian ideology of preservation of nonrenewable resources, energy conservation, and benign production technologies.

In the new-business-model, companies will maximize profits by making products that are long-term durable, while leasing a service to customers rather than selling them a physical product. Instead of buying home appliances like refrigerators, vacuum cleaners, freezers, and stoves, the customer will enter a contract with a supplier of services for a fixed annual price. The same will be true for many other products: computers, carpets, automobiles, power tools, furniture, and so on. The supplier will have responsibility for maintenance, upgrading, and replacement when appropriate. In the meantime, he maximizes profits by making products that are long-lasting, easy to maintain, and nonpolluting. And he will have a strong economic incentive to take back the product when its useful life is completed, reusing as many materials as possible.

William McDonough points out that it is not enough in this model just to reuse the materials. One has to redesign the whole product to make reuse optimal. For example, current recycling of metals used in automobile production puts different kinds of metals in the same melting pot, because they were not designed to be separable. In this case, future use of the metals is limited to lower-quality uses, known as "down-cycling." Redesign that takes into account the needs of disassembling and recycling is thus a simple route to substantial cost savings in a service society.

For society as a whole, the shift in the business model will mean that producers will compete to provide the maximum service benefits to customers for a given throughput of natural capital—the bottom line of ecological economics. Business and ecology will be fully aligned for the first time. The most successful businesses will study the way nature works. For example, honey bees build their hives to provide the maximum amount of space with the minimum amount of material use. We see the same phenomenon throughout nature. In fact, every living organism is a near-perfect design for its environment based on millions of years of natural selection. There is so much we can learn by studying nature's solutions. The shift to a service society will have enormous implications for business, for science, and for the way we live.

ELEVEN

Gaian Economics

The economy is a wholly owned subsidiary of the environment,
not the other way around.
—GAYLORD NELSON, former governor of Wisconsin

Economist Nicholas Georgescu-Roegen and former World Bank economist Herman Daly were two notable exceptions in the field of economics when they seriously challenged traditional economic thinking in the early 1970s, but their work has been largely ignored. Daly called his alternative approach "steady-state economics," which takes its starting point with the recognition that all economic activity takes place *within* the ecological space and is limited by it. Daly expresses the principal conflict between classical economics and steady-state economics as the former's failure to recognize that there is such a thing as "absolute scarcity" on a finite planet. He concluded that there is no way around the fact that absolute resource scarcity not only exists but increases as we use up the limited resources of the planet and entropy (dispersion of energy to non-useable forms) increases inescapably, a necessary consequence of the second law of thermodynamics. Absolute scarcity was not a problem for the many millennia when humankind's impact on planetary resources and ecology was minimal, but this is no longer the case. Ultimately, we are limited by the carrying capacity of the biosphere. But neither mainstream economists nor politicians have yet acknowledged this reality.

Sooner or later, humankind will be forced by the realities of the laws of physics to accept Daly's revolutionary approach, and replace traditional economics with steady-state economics, also known today as ecological economics. Of traditional economics, he says, "The abstractions necessary to make mechanistic models always do violence to reality."

When we exceed the limits of the throughput of nature's material that is replaceable by natural processes, we are eating up our limited natural capital rather than living off its income, in the same way that many beneficiaries of inheritances have squandered their fortunes in a single generation. We are currently consuming each year more than nature can replenish. If this continues without a reversal, then humanity is on its way toward certain extinction. Yet rather than a debate on how best to deal with this threat to our very survival, the political/economic establishment encourages *more* consumption, not less, *more* growth, not less. It is difficult to find a more absurd example of counterproductive human behavior. And yet that is the reality of the early twenty-first century.

In terms of Polanyi's "double movement"—the never-ending historical struggle between citizens' interests and commercial interests—Gaian society's attitude toward economics will definitely be closer to citizens' interests. The raw exploitative capitalism characteristic of neoliberalism will be avoided at all costs, as well as the dysfunctional central-planning model of communism. Both of those models will be considered disasters by Gaian society. Gaian economics will be something quite different from any historical precedent, being based on ecological economics—with wide-ranging freedom of the private sector to innovate and develop efficient technologies, but within a framework that is protective of the environment and the social well-being of all world citizens. Such an economic system has never been tried before.

Any economic system will justify the needs of the dominant political class—the economists' "client," e.g., the corporatocracy. That will also be true of Gaian economics, for which the "client" is the mass of 7 billion world citizens. The economic system will reflect their interests. A global economic system cannot be separated from the political/economic institutions that define the relationship among sovereign states. It is all one integrated system. If we want to replace the current economic system, then we have to replace the corresponding institutions as well. They all have to go so we can start with a clean slate.

The task is thus to describe a new economic theory and the corresponding institutional structures that will allow the economic system to function with the overarching goal of achieving ecological sustainability and social justice without sacrificing highly cherished freedoms. This is why I define the term Gaian economics to include *both* the economic system as such *and* the proposed new international institutions that are necessary for it to function properly. I will focus on the economic theory in this chapter, and describe the proposed institutional structures in logical sequence in the following chapters.

Ecological Economics

Fortunately, we do not have to start from scratch with the economic theory, as the basic principles already exist in the work of a small band of ecological economists—including not only Daly and Georgescu-Roegen, but also the pioneers Kenneth Boulding, E. F. Schumacher, Hazel Henderson, and several others—who have carried on for decades on the periphery of mainstream economics without much recognition.[1] The reason is clear. Ecological economists reject some of the most fundamental premises of neoclassical economics, which, they claim, is a set of abstract models divorced from reality and incapable of dealing with the problems facing a world of limited resources. Neoclassical economics, and its successor, neoliberal economics, are based on mathematical abstractions, while ecological economics is based on the laws of physics and biology. Ecological economist Robert Costanza calls mainstream economics "autistic in its deficits in communication and social interaction with other disciplines, preoccupation with mathematical fantasy, language impairment in its limited and specialized vocabulary, and excessive attachment to certain objects (assumptions and models). This intellectual impairment has led to its inability to address many important real-world problems."[2]

In the following sections, we will look at some of the major premises of ecological economics and compare these with the premises of neoliberal economics.

The Issue of Scale

Ecological economics takes as its starting point the fact that the economic system is imbedded in an ecosystem, which is finite, nongrowing, and closed. At any given time in our civilization's evolution, humankind's economic system utilized a certain proportion of the total ecosystem, in the early days very little, later, as population grew, a great deal. This proportion we can call the "scale" of the economic system. As long as the scale was small, the classical approach was quite appropriate, as the amount of resources available was essentially infinite compared to the level of utilization. But after centuries of physical growth, as the economy approached in size the ecosystem itself in the 1970s, that assumption of essentially infinite resources no longer held. Now we must invent a new economic system that can deal with physical and biological limits.

A key question asked by ecological economists is: what is the optimal scale of the economic system, i.e., when should physical growth stop? Mainstream economists do not even ask this question, as they implicitly assume that the economy can grow indefinitely "into The Void," as Herman Daly puts it. As physical growth encroaches more and more upon the finite ecosystem, there are both benefits and costs. These costs arise because the physical economy is sustained by the metabolic flow from the environment and back to the environment. This flow is the natural capital "throughput" of the economic system, which converts low-entropy resources into high-entropy polluting wastes. Resource depletion and pollution are the costs. The result of the economic activity is the stock of "goods" (wealth) and "bads" (or as some have called it, "illth")—the opposite of wealth.

We can define a sustainable economy as one in which the throughput of natural capital is within the natural capacity of the ecosystem to absorb the wastes produced and to regenerate the depleted resources. Small-scale economies are thus sustainable, but as they grow, marginal costs will grow until the economy reaches the point where the marginal costs begin to exceed the marginal benefits. This point defines the optimal scale of the global economy according to ecological economists. Growth beyond this point is no longer economic growth, but uneconomic growth. We saw in chapter 3 that a number of national economies apparently passed their optimal sizes in the 1970s, and since have been producing more "bads" than "goods" in a period of uneconomic growth that continues to this day.

Growth and Development

Traditional economists often use the term "sustainable development" as synonymous with "sustainable growth," a practice criticized by ecological economists because it can create serious misunderstandings. Ecological economists are careful to distinguish between growth, which is physical, and development, which need not be, e.g., quality-of-life improvements. Physical growth on a finite planet is obviously limited, as any biologist will confirm. Development is not. Thus, as Herman Daly likes to point out, the expression "sustainable growth" is an oxymoron (internally inconsistent). In a sustainable economy, growth must cease at some point, but development can go on forever.

Substitutability

Ecological economists point out that a second major error in mainstream economics is the assumption that man-made capital is a good substitute for natural capital—an assumption that allows them to assume away natural resources in their production functions, which consist only of inputs from capital and labor.

Herman Daly illustrates the consequences of this assumption with a touch of humor in the case of baking a cake. All you need is an oven (capital) and a cook (labor). So even if you only have 100 grams of flour, milk, sugar, and yeast to work with, you can make the cake as big as you want with sufficiently vigorous stirring—substituting labor for natural capital.

A real-world example is the fishing industry. In the early days of extensive fishing, the factor limiting total production was fishing boats (man-made capital) since there were more fish (natural capital) than could possibly be caught. The neoclassical model suggests that a lack of fish can be compensated for by building more boats—faulty thinking, which unfortunately has led to major tragedies in many parts of the world, with the Grand Banks of Newfoundland as the most frightening example.

Most mainstream economists today acknowledge a "weak" form of sustainability in that the sum of the two kinds of capital should be maintained. The ecological economists' approach is to recognize that natural capital is complementary to, and not a substitute for, man-made capital. In what is known as "strong sustainability," they require that limits must be placed directly on the natural capital (e.g., fishing quotas) when it becomes the limiting factor.

"Angelization" of Production

Some conventional economists argue that substantial further economic growth is possible in the service industries and through information processing and through "technological progress," activities that do not seem to use physical resources—a logic that Daly calls the "angelization" of production. However, a closer examination reveals that most services (hospitals, insurance, consulting, software development, and so on) require a quite substantial resource base when we look at inputs, inputs to inputs, and so forth. A second problem with this argument, pointed out by Daly, is that there is a limit to how much services can rise in the product mix before the terms of trade shift in favor of goods rather than services. Taking these two counter-arguments together, we can conclude that an increased focus on a "services and information society" can at best delay the time when the growth bubble bursts.

Conventional economists will also argue that economic growth is not the equivalent of physical growth, but includes qualitative changes as well. This is a valid point. However, the qualitative changes that follow with increasing economic growth can be negative as well as positive, and have been so now for many years, as we saw in an earlier chapter.

Valuing Natural Capital

Regarding production functions, I showed in chapter 4 how physicist Robert Ayres was able to significantly improve Solow's one-sector production-model forecast of GNP by adding energy input to capital and labor input in an improved two-sector model. While the Ayres model correctly emphasizes the prime importance of energy in explaining GDP growth, it is still not sufficient as a tool of ecological economics because the GNP measure, which Ayres uses, ignores other forms of natural capital. Mainstream economics treat natural capital as having zero value. The price on commodities is determined only by the cost of extraction, just as the production cost of a man-made product includes only the man-made capital and labor that went into producing it.

Ecological economics takes a different view. Production is viewed as a transformation process, with man-made capital and labor acting on natural capital. Without the natural capital to transform, there could be no production. Furthermore, there will always be less useable natural capital left after the transformation than before on account of the irreversible second law of thermodynamics (low entropy to high entropy). If we continue to operate beyond the optimal scale of the economy, we will find ourselves eventually in a global dilemma analogous to the Grand Banks of Newfoundland, where no amount of man-made capital and labor can compensate for the natural resources that we have squandered.

Managing Consumption, Resources, and Sinks

Gaian economics will differ markedly from current economics in the way in which consumption levels and the use of resources and waste sinks are managed through a combination of limits, quotas, outright bans, tax policy, and subsidies. Such management policies are necessary if the goal is to achieve sustainability.

In the current economic system, there is no attempt at this kind of management at all. Prices of just about everything are terribly wrong and for the most part provide direct barriers to long-term sustainability and encourage overconsumption. There ought to be financial charges to production technologies that damage the environment, deplete nonrenewable resources, or use finite waste sinks. For example, when we exclude the very real environmental costs, such as CO_2 emissions, then fossil fuel prices become far too low and we burn far too much. Low fossil fuel prices have resulted in our culture burning up half the oil available for all human generations in less than 100 years. The same is true about the prices of industrial agriculture products, where artificially low prices have resulted in the destruction of fertile soil and water aquifers all over the world, and the pollution of groundwater with pesticides. A usage charge on fossil fuel burning would encourages development of less polluting energy sources, while charges on industrial agriculture products would encourage greater production of organic foods that are more protective of the environment and healthier as well. An elimination or reduction in the value-added tax (VAT) on organic food would also be a step in the right direction.

Many countries go in the exact opposite direction, offering enormous subsidies, both direct and indirect, which encourage burning fossil fuels even faster. According to a Bloomberg New Energy Finance report in July 2010, the International Energy Agency's chief economist estimated that fossil fuel subsidies that promote consumption, such as below-market gasoline prices, totaled $557 billion worldwide in 2008, ten times the amount of all foreign aid. His figures do not include production subsidies, such as those the United States offers as a form of corporate welfare, essentially a thank-you to Big Oil for their campaign contributions. For comparison, subsidies for renewable energy were a mere $43–$46 billion worldwide.[3] At a time when the most important change needed to combat climate change is a higher price on CO_2 emissions, subsidizing fossil fuels is simply absurd. The current cost structure gives no consideration at all to the needs of future generations and the costs of cleaning up the environmental damage. All of these real costs to society are treated as "externalities," off the corporate balance sheets, resulting in far from optimal resource allocations and enormous inefficiencies in the use of resources.

The same problem arises with the discharge of toxic, polluting chemicals into the ecosystem. The old-paradigm economic system treats the ecosystem as a free dumping ground for unwanted by-products and garbage in general, with the result that water, soil, and air, not to mention human bodies, have all became heavily polluted, thus increasing health problems for both humans and animals, and indeed, for the whole food chain. The same is true of the biosphere and the oceans, which are limited-capacity sinks for CO_2 emissions, and both are under extreme stress.

We see the same pattern in the use of long-term renewable resources such as topsoil, ground water, fisheries, and forest cover. By ignoring the real costs to the ecosystem, and hence to society, the old system encourages the wasting of these resources as if there were no tomorrow.

Management Tools

All of this will change dramatically under Gaian economics, which will use extensively two principally different management tools—physical limits and taxation/subsidies. Both methods are appropriate under the proper circumstances. The ecological economics concept of non-substitutability of natural and man-made capital requires absolute limits as the only effective method of control in some cases, for example, rationing of nonrenewable resources such as fossil fuels, limits on fishing rights, outright bans on the use of the most dangerous toxic chemicals, limits on the use of groundwater, and maintenance standards for soil quality. Some of these will, by their very nature, require international agreements in cases where the entire human civilization has a vested interest, e.g., CO_2 emissions. A major subject for political debate in Gaian society will concern drawing the line between what is in the global interest and what is strictly a national matter. When national policies begin to have repercussions in other states, and no immediate solution seems negotiable, then some form of supranational mediation will be required. An example of this could be fair access to rivers that flow across national boundaries. It is impossible to foresee how this conflict will play out in practice. Each sovereign state in Gaian society will eventually have to accept the long-term goal of becoming sustainable, i.e., with an ecological footprint that is no greater than the sustainable global average.

Taxation policies are normally more appropriate than outright bans in managing consumption, and are in principle a national issue. In Gaian society, many states will probably distinguish between "needs" and "wants" in order to keep their total consumption within the limits that nature can replenish without degrading their environment. Essential needs are actually a small part of total consumption, and include adequate food, shelter, and a well-functioning local community. They can be defined fairly accurately for any given society and have an upper limit. On the other hand, "wants" are in principle limitless. If there are no controls on "wants," then any such society risks consuming more than nature can replenish, and this is precisely what we are currently experiencing in the industrialized countries. The best way to handle this overconsumption is probably a combination of rationing of nonrenewable resources and extra sales taxes on nonessential items. It will require some trial and error to get the prices right such that total consumption is under control.

Pollution taxes can also be appropriate in controlling the by-products released into the ecosystem by any production technology. For example, high charges on toxic effluents will have the effect of encouraging more benign production technologies that are "cradle to cradle" rather than "cradle to grave."

The overriding objective with these natural capital management policies is to establish boundary conditions within which the private sector can use its creative energies, operate freely, and find optimal production technologies without doing damage to the natural capital upon which all life depends. But this approach requires getting the prices right, including the environmental costs. To the extent that corporations find holes in the framework that were not foreseen, then those holes will have to be patched.

The astute reader may be thinking: this will never work as long as some states do not go along with ecological economics. They will be able to produce at lower cost, undercut the competition, and continue to degrade the environment. This is true—based on the way we currently regulate trade in the WTO, but not the way trade will be regulated in Gaian society. This point illustrates why I say that we cannot separate the economic system from the political institutions that regulate intergovernmental relations, in this instance, trade. This is why Gaian economics includes *both* the economic system *and* the political institutions.

Converting to Ecological Economics

The holistic Gaian worldview will completely reverse the roles of ecology and economics. Economics will be seen as a tool to improve efficiency, but always within the framework of the ecosystem. Ecological economics will become the dominant economic theory. The private sector will continue to be an important part of society, and the profit motive will continue to be an important incentive for innovation, but there will be limits on what will be considered acceptable. Some of these limits will be self-imposed by business leaders themselves, for whom corporate responsibility and respect for the interests of all stakeholders will be an important part of any business strategy, but it will also be necessary to have a formal regulative framework to define the playing field for commercial actors. The major focus will be on improving well-being through the effectiveness of resource use. The criterion for measuring success will be the well-being of society using much improved versions of GPI, ISEW, dashboard indicators, and so on, rather than total production or consumption levels.

Conversion to ecological economics is no trivial matter. Research to date

202 PART FOUR: NEW VALUES, NEW BELIEFS

has been grossly underfunded for obvious reasons, and there are many unanswered questions. With a major paradigm shift, a period of what Kuhn called "abnormal science" is usual, where quantum jumps in scientific knowledge are typical. In this period, an explosion of research and development is inspired by the new way of looking at the world. We can anticipate that this will happen in the field of ecological economics, inaugurating an exciting and creative time for economists.

PART FIVE

Toward a Gaian World Order

"To be truly radical is to make hope possible rather than despair convincing."

— Raymond Williams

TWELVE

Designing a Gaian World

Design is the conscious effort to impose meaningful order.
—VICTOR PAPANEK, Design for the Real World

Serious Sustainability

My approach is radical in the original sense of the word—dealing with the root of the problem. The root of the problem is that not a single country on this planet takes ecological sustainability seriously. In chapter 1, I presented documentation for the fact that we are globally consuming about 40% more of our natural capital every year than the ecosystem can replenish. And that figure is increasing every year by about 2%. We are "pulling out the screws of our jumbo jet" one screw at a time. If we want to avoid crashing, if we want to survive as a species, then the first step is to acknowledge the facts. Those who do not make the acknowledgment "don't understand data," as Paul Hawken says. Either we stay in collective denial of the facts and keep pulling out those screws or we start taking ecological sustainability seriously and change our high-consumption lifestyle, especially in the industrialized countries. The good news is that we can do this without sacrificing our well-being. Recall the lesson from the previously cited Wilkinson and Pickett study—happiness, well-being, and health are relative, not absolute concepts, and are not related to the material conditions in your society, but rather to your perception of self-respect and acceptance in your local community, with the greatest physical and mental well-being occurring in the most egalitarian societies.

Serious sustainability is a policy that a country adopts when it puts ecological sustainability at the top of the list of society's goals, ahead of economic growth, ahead of more consumption, ahead of competitiveness, ahead of productivity, ahead of everything else on the agenda. Anything less is not serious. Today, every country is introducing a few ineffective programs to pacify those who are demanding a change, for example, green taxes, the Kyoto Protocol, the EU's carbon emissions trading or the United States'

Environmental Protection Agency or the Clean Air Act, and so on. Let's be completely honest for a moment. None of these programs is making a whit of difference in the big picture. If we want to get serious about survival, we need an entirely different approach. That is what the rest of this book is about.

My ultimate goal in part 5 is to outline the essential contours of a seriously sustainable Gaian world order. My approach is to focus on the international framework that is necessary to regulate intergovernmental relations in a Gaian world in a way that is consistent with the Gaian worldview and Gaian economics. The framework is, in practice, a set of international institutions with rules and guidelines that will allow optimal solutions to gradually unfold in a cooperative effort by governments, the business community, and civil society. In this short introductory chapter to part 5, I will define the necessary institutions and their functions briefly, while the following chapters will describe each in more detail. First, however, I would like to sketch out my assumptions about the general nature of the overall structure.

Human Scale and Global Governance

The overriding objective of effective global governance in a Gaian world will be to ensure survival of the human species—an objective that is beyond ideology. This ought to be the overriding objective of any global civilization. Unfortunately, this is not the case with the contemporary world order, which prioritizes economic growth and more consumption above all else, a populist policy that is putting our very survival at risk. To achieve this objective in practice, it will be necessary to establish enforceable mechanisms that can ensure that global-resource use is kept within the limits that nature can replenish—the very essence of sustainability. This can only be done if all nations cooperate. It takes just one major holdout to sabotage the whole endeavor and put all of humanity at risk. There is just no way to peacefully enforce sustainability policies unless everyone cooperates. In the contemporary world order, such cooperation has never been possible. Only partial and voluntary schemes have been tried, such as the Kyoto Protocol. To date, all such attempts have failed to stem the tide.

There are, in principle, several ways of achieving a global governance structure that can ensure survival of the species, ranging from a ruthless totalitarian regime to a powerful centralized world government of elected representatives, to a more decentralized multipolar regime living under a common protective umbrella. A borderless, homogeneous "free market" world of multinational corporations, global branding, and unrestricted capital movement controlled by a centralized world government—whether totalitarian or formally elected does not make any difference—is the utopian dream of the ruling corporatocracy, as this would allow it to maintain its control, lifestyle, and dominance at the expense of everyone else. Such an undemocratic solution would be unacceptable for a Gaian, whose society is likely to put a high priority on living in decentralized, diverse, human scale communities with a high degree of local democracy. A Gaian society will also insist on the rights of the developing countries, who are considered part of the "family," to real development, including control over their economies and cultures. For a Gaian, "small is beautiful," an expression coined by economist Leopold Kohr, who also wrote, "A small-state world would not only solve the problems of social brutality and war; it would solve the problems of oppression and tyranny. It would solve all problems arising from power."[1] Gaian citizens would likely agree also with Kirkpatrick Sale's claim that "Economic and social misery increases in direct proportion to the size and power of the central government of a nation or state."[2]

Thus, the third governance alternative—a multipolar world of many self-determining, cooperating small sovereign states under a common umbrella of protection of the environment—would be the ideal structure in a Gaian world dominated by Cultural Creatives. However, protecting the environment is not sufficient without specifying the means to do so. Here, the Gaian value system will insist on respect for the human rights of all world citizens, for example, as defined in the UN Universal Declaration of Human Rights.

Thus the international structure in an ideal Gaian world would be a universe of small, independent sovereign states in which a limited degree of sovereignty is delegated to a global governance body, namely, the right of the central authority to issue directives deemed necessary to ensure long-term sustainability of the planet and the observance of human rights in all member states. All other aspects of sovereignty would remain with the individual sovereign states. In this way, a flowering of diverse cultures respecting local preferences and priorities will be allowed to evolve within a structure that guarantees long-term survival and basic human rights. Such an overall structure is independent of ideology, and is rather dictated by the fundamental premises: sustainability, human rights, democracy, and real development. In principle, a sovereign country in Gaian society could be anything from a socialist state to a capitalist state to a religious-based state, anything from a high-tech industrialized state to a low-tech agricultural state, provided only that the ground rules guaranteeing sustainability and human rights are respected.

In the meantime, we do not have an ideal world, so such a world has to be considered a long-term Gaian goal. What we can do in the short run is design the institutions that would allow such a Gaian world order to evolve. Hopefully, some nations will take up the idea and show leadership by making a beginning toward such a world order.[3] This will be the subject of part 6, "Getting There."

The Gaian Institutions

The eight institutions and the primary function of each are summarized in the following paragraphs. These institutions are assumed to be founded by a member association, which I will call the Gaian League for the sake of reference.

The Gaian Trade Organization replaces the WTO for member states. Sovereign control over all trade (e.g., tariff policy, product bans, most favored nation status) is necessary to prevent domestic-member products from being undercut by nonmember imported products of lower environmental standards, as well as for protecting sovereign priorities and preferences.

In addition, controls on capital movement are necessary for the development of comparative-advantage industries in developing countries and to protect small-country equity and currency markets from speculative capital flows, and will in addition free up some currency reserves for more productive purposes.

The Gaian Clearing Union is an institution to regulate and settle international trade without the use of any national currencies, based on a model originally proposed by John Maynard Keynes. The Clearing Union will reduce the likelihood of new financial crises, free up substantial funds now tied up in foreign-exchange reserves, and resolve the financial instabilities that inevitably arise when a national currency (currently the U.S. dollar) is used as the primary source of liquidity and foreign reserves.

The Gaian Development Bank—replacing the functions of the IMF and World Bank, and funded by the above-mentioned freed-up foreign-exchange reserves—will finance real nonexploitative development in the developing countries using local currency loans to revitalize local communities, create employment, and encourage local production of their most essential needs—food, energy, housing, textiles, and so on, as well as value-added products, as they develop into sustainable states.

The Gaian Congress—an assembly of delegates appointed by Gaian League

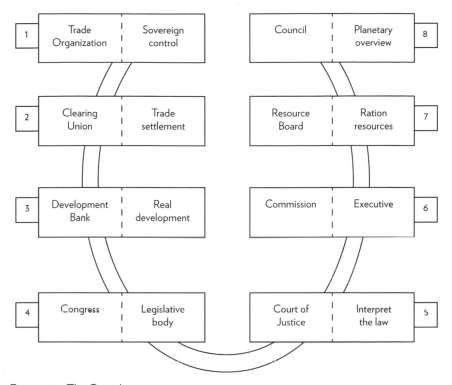

Figure 12.1. The Gaian Institutions.

governments, is the legislative body of the Gaian League, whose resolutions define international law for member states.

The Gaian Commission—headed by a secretary-general—is the executive organ of the Gaian League, carrying out Congress resolutions and administering the Gaian institutions.

The Gaian Court of Justice is the judicial branch of the Gaian League, with the task of interpreting Gaian law.

The Gaian Resource Board is an agency under the commission charged with administering members' use of both nonrenewable and renewable resources. This is a necessary function for long-term sustainability. The first step will be to establish an agency to control global CO_2 emissions.

The Gaian Council is a small elected council of "wise elders" with the power to overrule any Congress resolution or law not deemed to be in the long-term interest of the planet, and to mediate conflicts when requested.

The flow diagram in figure 12.1 illustrates in schematic form the institutions in the order in which they will be described in the following chapters.

THIRTEEN

The Gaian Trade Organization

What we meant by "free trade" was nothing more nor less than, by means of the great advantage we enjoyed, to get a monopoly of all their markets for our manufacturers, and to prevent them, one and all, from ever becoming manufacturing nations.

—CITED BY HENRY CLAY, former American secretary of state

The above quote from Henry Clay, citing a British leader's assertion in an unguarded moment, should put to rest forever cynical propaganda from dominant trading nations concerning the benefits of so-called "free trade" for developing countries.[1]

The WTO Regime

In the WTO regime, sovereign states have in effect given away a portion of their sovereignty to the trade organization, whose trade experts can interpret and enforce the rules in any conflict. These binding rules include no demands on corporations, allow foreign companies to sell their products without disclosing how they were produced, place the burden of proof of health risks on the consumer, and give foreign companies the right to any advantage given to a domestic company.

When the WTO was formed in 1995, the corporate-friendly rules reversed some of the previously most effective protections of the environment. One change was the removal of the right for a state to ban products that were considered unacceptable, e.g., DDT, PCBs, leaded gasoline, etc. In many cases, a ban is the only effective way to control pollution. Second, the WTO shifted the burden of proof of safety from the corporation to the consumer. Third, the WTO outlawed as criteria for introducing tariffs both the method of production (e.g., environmental standards) and the country of origin. The WTO also outlawed the principle of giving a domestic producer any advantage over a foreign producer, thus eliminating the most basic principle of mercantilism (protection of domestic producers), which I have shown is the *only* way to develop into a competitive industrial state, and which *all* industrial states used to get where they are today. WTO rules can be tortuous to interpret for the uninitiated, as the preamble gives lip service to environmental protection and sovereignty. However, sixteen years of rulings make quite clear that the WTO is antienvironmental, antisovereignty and pro-business in the extreme. It should be clear that all these rules have to be reversed if sovereign states are to have any real control over their countries, not least as regards their economies, the environment, and their cultures.

Many proponents of the WTO in the industrialized countries argued back in 1994 and still argue today that we need universally binding rules for the sake of the developing countries. But the actual results after sixteen years' experience with the WTO confirm the assertion about "free trade" from Henry Clay. The prime beneficiaries of the WTO have been the nations and the corporations that were the richest and most powerful already. In the latest breakdown of negotiations in the ongoing Doha round, it was generally agreed that many of the poorest developing countries would actually be worse off under the new proposals from the United States and the EU. Just one example: West Africa is prevented from exporting the only crop that it can produce competitively and that is critical to its economy—cotton. Why? Because the world's richest nation, the United States, gives enormous, price-distorting subsidies to its cotton farmers while keeping African cotton out with high tariffs. The whole purpose of the Doha round was to help the developing countries.

The Gaian League

In chapter 11 I defined Gaian economics to include both ecological economics and a set of necessary institutions. These institutions will in this and the following chapters be described one at a time following the logic of their necessity.

Speaking realistically, not all states are likely to be members of the Gaian League in the near term, and certainly not at the time of the initial founding. One condition for membership must be a commitment to work for a truly sustainable future on behalf of all world citizens. Members must accept the principles of ecological economics as guidelines for managing their economies. In order to maintain a uniform treatment across member states, the

Gaian League must be given the power to interpret what is meant by "sustainability," to issue directives, resolve conflicts, and apply appropriate penalties for noncompliance. Such directives will in general include guidelines for acceptable production technologies, consumer goods, and imports—in general, regulate any activities that are relevant to the goal of long-term planetary sustainability. I envisage the Gaian League as something between a confederation and a loose federation, where membership is voluntary, but each state cedes a specified portion of its sovereignty, namely, as concerns environmental and human rights legislation, to a central authority, while maintaining all other sovereign rights, including defense and foreign policy.

The New Trade Regime

The Gaian society objectives of environmental protection, real development, and comparative advantage require a trade regime quite different from the WTO, which in fact is a barrier to all three objectives. The rules of trade are probably the single most important political decision for a sovereign country that wishes to be master of its own destiny, and not a slave to foreign interests. The WTO is based on the principle that everything is allowed into your country unless it is forbidden. This is the principle of "free trade." In practice, almost nothing can be forbidden. The problem is that protection of the environment is impossible without the mechanism of protective tariffs to prevent foreign products produced with lower environmental standards from undercutting environmentally friendly domestic production. For this reason, "free trade" cannot deliver a sustainable future. The new trade organization will have to be based on the opposite principle, namely, that all imported goods are in principle forbidden unless they are specifically permitted. This we could call the principle of "sovereign trade," and this trade regime is the only one that can deliver a sustainable future.

In other words, we need more protectionism, not less. This statement will strike free-traders as heretical, but is nonetheless true, especially at a time when the environment and local economies are being fatally abused and destroyed by commercial interests with no sense of social or environmental responsibility, and enormous subsidies are being given to the burning of fossil fuels. Someone has to start taking responsibility. Without introducing such protection, we will continue to reward those who trash the environment. This much should be obvious even for fanatical free-traders. Other legitimate national priorities also require protection from artificially cheap imports, for example, the desire for food security, cultural integrity, GMO-free foods, and so on—all important and legitimate political issues.

Therefore the first necessary Gaian institution is a new trade organization. Let us call it the Gaian Trade Organization (GTO) for the sake of reference. In the GTO regime, each sovereign state has a wide degree of control over what it imports and exports, provided it complies with the sustainability directives from the Gaian League. Of course, bilateral and multilateral agreements can and will be entered by GTO members with other members and nonmembers, and these may involve binding rules and binding arbitration on an individual basis provided they do not conflict with Gaian League rules.

The decision of a state to join the Gaian League, and hence the GTO, should be based on a national referendum, recognizing the importance of the decision. Nothing should be forced upon a sovereign state that its citizens do not want, as is the case today. The consequences of trade relations for not only economic stability, but also for social and environmental issues, are just too great to allow implementation without broad citizen backing. We have seen too many examples from the WTO of commercially dominated parliaments and governments voting without real debate to join the WTO and giving away aspects of their sovereignty without citizens realizing what was happening.

The GTO charter will be far simpler than the WTO for one simple reason. The rather complicated and numerous WTO rules are primarily concerned with how to protect the interests of international corporations and how to penalize states that do not comply. The GTO, on the other hand, deals with broad principles and delegates to the member states the freedom to use whatever tariffs and bans they wish and enter whatever trade treaties they wish within broad limits. "Sovereign trade," with its right to ban or put a tariff on any product whatsoever, really levels the playing field, giving even the smallest state a powerful negotiating position based on "something for something," while assuring a sustainable future.

Improved Conflict-Resolution Procedures

Under GATT, conflict resolution was done on a voluntary basis. Under the WTO, it was binding, but with a professionally very narrow committee of trade experts making the decisions. Neither was entirely satisfactory. In practice, conflict resolution will depend on individual trade agreements. In some cases it may well be decided to include provisions for binding arbitration. However, in such cases, the nature of the Gaian paradigm would require a much broader mediation committee than the WTO's three-man committee of trade experts. In addition to trade interests, environmental and social interests will have to be represented in any GTO panel, binding or nonbinding.

Currency Regime

Closely related to the trade regime is the particular currency regime adopted by each state. There are a number of possibilities to consider. While the issues may seem difficult for noneconomists, the choice is absolutely critical for the everyday lives of people in every single country. The decision can determine the exposure to speculative attacks on the domestic currency, control of ownership of domestic companies, the stability of equity and foreign exchange markets, and the control of flight capital and foreign investment.

There is a widely accepted model of possible currency regimes, based mostly on the pioneering work of Canadian economist Robert Mundell.[2] It is based on the so-called impossible trinity of three common policy objectives, which cannot all be met simultaneously. One must choose two and leave one out. They can be designated as:

- independent monetary policy;
- fixed exchange rates;
- free capital movement.

Some readers may note the implicit assumption in the above formulation that there exist several currency regions. However, a number of writers in the past have suggested that a single world currency would be ideal, arguing that we could avoid all the problems associated with having several currencies; this viewpoint deserves a comment. Would a single currency be a good idea? I am afraid not. A currency region works best when the area is relatively homogeneous—the same culture, race, and language, and where the people are mobile, so they can move to where the jobs are. This is not a good description of our planet. A single global currency would be a big advantage for the corporatocracy and the strongest and best educated, who do not have to worry about jobs or moving, but would condemn the weaker regions to a subsistence level of existence. Having different currencies is a necessary condition for the existence of many diverse, self-determining, sovereign nations—a mainstay of Gaian society. Ideally, each state should have its own currency for maximum flexibility of economic policy.

If we combine these three policy objectives two at a time, we get three possible regimes from which we can choose. We can define them by the opposites of each of the above three policy objectives:

- dependent monetary policy (unrestricted capital movement plus fixed exchange rates);
- floating exchange rates (free capital movement plus independent monetary policy);
- capital controls (independent monetary policy plus fixed exchange rates).

Let us look at the advantages and disadvantages of each of these in turn, keeping in mind that no one regime is optimal for all governments at all times. Nor is any given regime necessarily optimal for all the stakeholders in a given country at a given time, i.e., for the corporate sector, the government, and civil society.

Dependent Monetary Policy

A state adopting this regime fixes the exchange rate of its currency to one or more major currencies or gold while allowing foreign capital to enter and leave freely, thus giving up its independence and control over its monetary policy—in particular, control of its interest rate. Historically, this was the most common regime prior to the twentieth century in a period where there was little international capital flow compared to today. So while capital was free to move, there was very little such movement in practice. The gold standard was such a regime, where all the major states agreed to fix their exchange rates relative to gold.

In more recent times, a variant of this regime has been adopted by some smaller countries, who "peg" their currencies to one of the major currencies, typically the U.S. dollar or the euro. In such cases, "pegging" has the advantage of creating a certain stability of the exchange rate vis-à-vis a major trading partner, which can be good for confidence building, particularly for a smaller country. However, if the major currency is "floating"—as is the norm today for the major currencies—then the smaller currency will still float against all currencies that are not "pegged" to the reference currency.

The major disadvantage of this regime is that it almost always ends with a speculative attack on the currency once the exchange rate gets out of line, and this will always happen eventually, because no two economies can run in tandem forever. The historical period of "fixed" currencies under the gold standard was in fact interrupted by occasional large devaluations when the pressures became too great. Today it is typically the small country's currency that gets overvalued and subject to attack because it has less price discipline. When the attack comes, the country typically loses all of its foreign-currency reserves defending the exchange rate before being forced to capitulate and devalue its currency. The hedge funds making the attack are many times larger than most central banks, so there is really no defense when capital flows without restrictions. Particularly in small countries with relatively illiquid markets, this regime is an accident waiting to happen. In fact I would call this regime a time bomb that will always explode sooner or later with a major devaluation or revaluation. This happened many times in the unstable 1970s when the smaller EMS currencies were effectively pegged to the German mark. It happened again in the late 1990s when several Asian countries with currencies pegged to the U.S. dollar felt the consequences of the billions of dollars of "hot money" sloshing through their relatively small equity and currency markets like the proverbial bull in the china shop.

Even in calm markets, this regime presents problems, as the country has no control over its interest rate. It has to follow the lead of "big brother's" interest-rate level, even when the local needs may be quite different. This can be a quite painful and slow way to achieve balance again, for example, by forcing higher unemployment. Another disadvantage is the inability to control incoming foreign investment, just as with the floating rate regime.

In my opinion, a pegged exchange rate is the worst of all regimes, and only justified as a temporary stopgap, for example, to reestablish confidence in the currency. Denmark did precisely this in 1982 by pegging the Danish kroner to the German mark, and later to the euro, to reestablish confidence after a series of devaluations in the 1970s, and it worked. Denmark's currency is considered quite solid today. Denmark is still in this regime after almost thirty years, although it is no longer necessary.

Floating Exchange Rates

This is the regime of choice of the neoliberals for *all* countries, large or small. It has been adopted by most of the major economies and a number of smaller but mature economies (e.g., United States, Eurozone, UK, Japan, Canada, Sweden, Switzerland, Norway, New Zealand, and Australia) since the breakdown of the Bretton Woods agreement in 1971, when the United

States de-linked the U.S. dollar from gold. This system is advantageous for competitive, industrialized countries as it provides maximum liquidity of investments while maintaining control of domestic money-market growth and inflation. It also has the positive characteristic of being self-correcting. For example, a deficit on the balance of trade will weaken the currency, which makes exports more competitive, which tends to correct the balance, with the mirror opposite occurring for a trade surplus. The downside is that there is potential instability in the exchange rate, which can fluctuate widely, and create planning problems for business, and possibly a lack of confidence in the currency by foreign investors. This is not normally a problem for the major economies, but can be for smaller economies, for which confidence in the stability of the currency is very important. A major disadvantage for smaller economies is the lack of control over foreign investment, where large and rapid withdrawals can completely overwhelm currency and equity markets because of the lack of liquidity.

Capital Controls

This third regime differs from the others in its wide range of variability, as there are many possible forms of, and degrees of, control on the capital account (which includes currency speculation, foreign portfolio investments in listed securities, and foreign direct investment). Controls are rarely used on the current account (trade-related payments, interest and dividends). In fact, a condition of IMF membership is that restrictions are not placed on current account transfers. The Bretton Woods agreement that reigned from 1945 to 1971 was such a regime. The period was characterized by rapid growth in trade and few financial crises, but broke down—not because of any inherent weakness in the capital controls regime as such, but because of the gold-linked dollar and the limited amount of gold available to finance the dollar-based international trade model.

The flexibility of this regime can range from an extreme "heavy" version that requires permission on every foreign exchange transaction over a certain minimum to a "light" version that hardly differs from a floating-rate regime. In many cases the focus is on exchange-rate stability in what is sometimes called a "managed float," where rather than formally fixing the exchange rate, the state tries to maintain the exchange rate in a reasonable range without a formal "peg" that will be defended at all costs. If the currency should come under attack, the "aikido" strategy of rolling with the punch (i.e., letting the exchange rate slide a little) is the best way to discourage speculators.

A report from the think tank Global Financial Integrity (GFI) in January 2011 documents that developing countries are losing, every year, close to $800 billion on account of what they call "illicit financial flows," much of which could be stopped by shifting the developing countries' currency regime from unrestricted capital flow to capital controls. This outflow is almost fifteen times the total foreign aid flowing into the developing countries (about $54 billion per year), is increasing in real terms at a rate of 12.7% per annum, and goes a long way toward explaining why so little real development is occurring and why poverty persists. According to GFI, the major sources of illicit financial flows are transfer pricing, tax evasion, bribery, theft, and kickbacks.[3]

A capital-control regime can be quite attractive for smaller states, and particularly developing counties, for two policy reasons. The first is to prevent runs on the currency by not allowing too many bulls into the china shop. In other words, restrictions are put on how much foreign investment (particularly short-term investment) is allowed into the country. In addition, restrictions are imposed that prevent the sudden exit of such funds that could upset relatively illiquid currency and equity markets, as happened with the Asian markets in the late 1990s. The second is to ensure the comparative advantage of the country's production sector by introducing appropriate controls that enable fulfillment of Ricardo's "immobile capital" condition and thus allow competitive trade and real development.

The downside of capital controls usually mentioned by mainstream economists is a decrease in "efficiency." But the "efficiency" they refer to is the efficiency of absolute advantage, where the strongest capital rules everywhere and the benefits are mostly preempted by the already wealthy—an efficiency that rules out the principle of comparative advantage and prevents real development. It is also an efficiency that carries no weight with ecological economists because it does not take into account the throughput of natural capital.

During the period from roughly 1980 to the present, the IMF "structural adjustment program" has been strongly opposed to capital controls. But a slight softening of its position has taken place recently, as the IMF now acknowledges that the lack of capital controls has been a major reason for many of the financial crises of recent years, and that such controls can be justified in some cases.

The Eurozone

The ongoing sovereign debt crisis in Europe at the time of writing is directly related to the adopted currency regime, and therefore demands comment. The eurozone is a unique currency regime that does not fit nicely into any of the above categories. Individual eurozone countries have dependent monetary policies (i.e., no control over interest rates and money supply) in a regime that functions in many ways like a fixed-rate currency regime with all currencies in effect permanently "pegged" to Germany—the largest and strongest member, rather than to an external currency or gold. But normally, a sovereign state with a dependent monetary regime can issue its own currency, and could, in a crisis, devalue the currency relative to the "peg." But eurozone members can do neither of these things. You could say that the members have voluntarily tied their hands behind their backs, giving them very little room to maneuver. They are actually worse off than a sovereign state under the old fixed rate gold standard, where a state could in the least devalue its currency in a crisis.

For eurozone members, the euro is for all practical purposes the equivalent of a foreign currency because there is no federal government that can issue currency and collect taxes. If member governments want to spend money, they have to raise it first through taxes or loans. This is the opposite of a normal sovereign state with its own currency having a central government that can create money and collect taxes, and can always meet all obligations in its own currency, including government debt, with 100% certainty. In other words, if the eurozone had a federal government with a floating euro there would be no debt crisis, and the government would be free to spend the economy into recovery with public works and other spending programs. Of, course, there would be a theoretical risk of inflation if too much money was put into circulation, but in practice there is nothing to worry about as long as unemployment is high and there is industrial overcapacity.

The only way out of a sovereign debt crisis like the current one for Greece—short of leaving the eurozone—is a long, painful period of high unemployment, wage restraint and welfare cuts, far longer than a devaluation strategy would require. Greece can be forced to default on its debt because it cannot issue its own currency. In this sense, its euro debt is similar to foreign currency debt. The optimal solution for Greece would be for it to leave the eurozone—if it could get permission— and float the "new Drachma" freely. Recovery would be much quicker.

A currency zone is always problematic because the same interbank rate of interest holds everywhere. However, the economies of any two regions will always develop differently over time and may require quite different interest rates for optimal development. This problem can be circumvented in theory if labor is willing to move from areas of unemployment to areas where jobs are available. However, if people are attached to place because of culture or language, as in the EU, then they will be far less willing to emigrate. Furthermore, some member countries may follow irresponsible fiscal policies, for example living beyond their means and creating higher inflation and unsustainable government debt. This is what we have seen happen in southern Europe and Ireland.

Generally speaking, a common currency should only be adopted among countries where there is a free flow of labor across borders, a common language, and comparable economies. The American states satisfy this condition, but the EU does not. Furthermore, the smooth functioning of a currency zone requires a central government with the right to issue the currency and to raise taxes as well as the right to spend money on various public programs. The United States satisfies this condition, but the eurozone countries do not. When these conditions are not satisfied, tensions will arise that will eventually bring about a breaking up of the currency zone.

As a general rule a sovereign state with its own floating currency does not have to worry about deficits and national debt (in its domestic currency) as long as inflation is under control. In a crisis, where unemployment is high and industry is no longer competitive due to inflation, such a state can let its currency depreciate, reestablish its competitiveness, and spark a recovery. This is precisely what Sweden did in the 1990s. Today it has a strong and competitive economy once again.

In the absence of a central government that has control over spending and taxes in the eurozone, the European Central Bank is severely limited in what it can do to deal with the crisis.

The basic problem is that the eurozone structure was poorly designed from the beginning for the reasons mentioned above; it is not a long-term viable currency regime. From day one it was only a question of time before a crisis developed. Eventually, the eurozone members are probably going to have to do one of two things; leave the eurozone and revert to their former national currencies, which should be allowed to float freely (a "peg" to the euro would simply invite a new crisis); or form a "United States of Europe" with a central government, with all that implies about surrendering sovereignty. In practice, we will probably see a combination of these two options at some point, with some states leaving the eurozone and some remaining to form a federal government with the euro as its currency.

Why was a central government not formed in the first place? The reason is that there was, and still is, widespread resistance among EU citizens to the idea of a centralized EU government. The political elite in the EU were impatient, hoping that such resistance would gradually disappear, and that the eurozone would prove to be a step along the way toward greater centralization. Unfortunately, they chose a structure that was flawed. The EU leadership should have formed a federal government from the beginning with the few that were willing, and let the remainder float their currencies freely, possibly joining later. As it is now, it is quite likely that the eurozone will break up at some point, which would not necessarily be a bad thing. From a Gaian perspective, a return to several independent nation states, each with its own "managed-float" currency, would be the preferable outcome. The EU can survive without the euro. If a reborn EU shifted focus to the needs of a sustainable planet rather than promoting more uneconomic growth, then everyone would be better off.

The ongoing sovereign debt crisis has the potential to create a global financial crisis every bit as serious as the 2007/9 financial crisis, but, whatever the outcome, it will be relatively mild compared to the coming energy descent crisis, which will be far more serious.

Choosing the Appropriate Regime

In a Gaian world, it would be against all the principles of solidarity to exploit the weaker members of the global society, unlike the current world order, where the developing countries are not only exploited; they are not allowed to develop because having competitors is not in the interest of the Empire. Real development requires that the state concerned has the right to protect its infant domestic industries in the early stages of development until they are competitive. It further demands the right to local ownership and control of domestic resources and key industries. And finally, it demands the right to use its comparative advantage to develop value-added products for export. A state that can only earn foreign exchange by selling its raw materials and cheap labor will never develop. Comparative advantage requires—as pointed out by economist Davis Ricardo long ago—immobile capital. Free capital movement allows powerful foreign interests to take over control of key resources and industries by virtue of a stronger capital base. For this reason, the Gaian states that are not yet developed in the above sense must reject free capital movement, whether based on floating rates or fixed rates.

The choice of regime for some Gaian states will depend on whether or not all states are members of the Gaian League. Certainly in the early days, not all states will be members. In this case, all member states must adopt a sovereign-state regime (i.e., allowing tariffs, product bans, most favored nation status, and so on) to fulfill sustainability goals (protection against unfair competition from nonmember states with lower environmental standards) and to realize their sovereign priorities and preferences. A capital-controls currency regime will be necessary for the developing-country members to enable comparative advantage industries to develop, to control investment and speculative flows, and to protect against capital flight.

In a fully developed Gaian society where all states are members of the Gaian League and sustainability is under control globally, the developing countries would still need a capital-controls currency regime for comparative advantage purposes and a sovereign trade regime for sovereign preference purposes. Industrialized countries would also still need a sovereign-trade regime to the extent desired for sovereign preferences, but their need for capital controls would be much less. They would probably adopt floating rates combined with a "light" version of capital controls in order to maintain an independent monetary policy, but with some control on investment flows.

The reason that unrestricted capital flows have been strongly promoted by the Empire is for the convenience of the financial members of the corporatocracy, who want to be able to get their money out of a foreign country fast. In chapter 6 we reviewed several examples where such flows destroyed healthy economies in the late 1990s. The key change recommended relative to current practice is to reactivate in the GTO the inviolable right of every sovereign state to control capital flows as stated in IMF Article VI, section 3.[4] Since 1980, the IMF has often violated this article by insisting on the removal of capital controls as a condition for IMF loans. This violation of their rights will not be tolerated by GTO member states. Any agreement that nullifies that clause might even be considered "odious" and thus invalid under Gaian law.

GTO members will individually specify the conditions under which capital investment flows are permitted. For example, investors may be required to accept that invested funds can only be repatriated over a suitably long time period that will not upset currency and equity markets. These kinds of rules functioned quite satisfactorily throughout the GATT period. I would consider the best foreign-exchange policy for most Gaian states adopting capital controls to be a "managed float," i.e., an attempt to keep the currency in a reasonable range without locking it too firmly to any other currency. Note that the range must not be publicly announced; to publicize the range limits would be like having a "peg." Speculators would be attracted like sharks to test the will of the country to defend its "peg." A "managed float" policy reduces the likelihood of a speculative attack while maintaining an acceptable degree of flexibility and stability.

Generally speaking, the ideal Gaian world will consist of many small sovereign states, each with its own currency. Having your own currency gives maximum control over your economy, including the ability to avoid the kind of debt crisis the eurozone is currently experiencing. The possibility of controlling domestic interest rates and government spending and taxation, and managing the currency-exchange rate provides a far more flexible range of policy alternatives than is possible within a single currency zone or a "pegged" currency regime.

One of the driving ideas of the EU founders was to create a common currency that could better match the dominant U.S. dollar, thus improving the EU's influence in a very competitive world. However, in Gaian society, "matching the dollar" may no longer be a relevant goal, as the role of the dollar is likely to be reduced considerably—a subject we will now look into more closely as we move on to the second new Gaian institution.

FOURTEEN

The Gaian Clearing Union

There is something a little unseemly about poor countries lending
the United States trillions of dollars, now at an interest rate of close
to zero.

—Joseph Stiglitz, "Farewell to the Dollar as the World's
Currency of Choice," *Washington Post,* August 30, 2009
(also author of *Globalization and Its Discontents*)

A fundamental financial problem is threatening the stability of the international financial system at this time. It has been growing from a minor issue
to major issue over the last thirty years and is now threatening to create a
major disruption in international relations. The true nature of the problem
is not generally recognized, although its effects have moved to the top of the
political agenda, as illustrated in the G-20 meeting in Korea in November
of 2010 when the phrases "currency war" and "protectionism" were circulating in the corridors. From the American point of view, the problem is
the refusal of the Chinese to allow the yuan to appreciate more quickly in
order to stimulate imports and thus help achieve a more balanced trade
between the United States and China. But the real problem is more basic
than that. Fundamentally, this is a design failure, and not something that can
be resolved by a simple adjustment of foreign exchange rates.

The design question that has not been resolved satisfactorily is how to
provide liquidity to finance international trade without creating danger-
ously unstable international imbalances. In the current system, the U.S.
dollar fulfills the role of liquidity provider, and consequently is accepted
as the major reserve currency of foreign central banks. The basic problem
with a financial system where international trade is financed by a particular
national currency is that an artificial demand for the currency is created.
Thus the liquidity provider becomes systemically overvalued in the long run.
The U.S. dollar is not subject to the same negative-feedback mechanism on
trade that affects all other currencies. This makes imports artificially cheaper
for the United States and their exports artificially dearer, which in the long

run leads inevitably to chronic deficits on the American balance of trade, which is precisely what the world has been experiencing for roughly the last four decades since the gold-based Bretton Woods currency regime was terminated. In the current situation, it is very difficult for the United States to achieve balance because its exports are less competitive than they would be if the U.S. dollar were not the major source of international liquidity. The Americans are pressuring the Chinese these days to revalue the yuan to deal with the consequences of this systemic flaw, but the real problem is not that the yuan is too cheap relative to the dollar but that the dollar is too expensive relative to *all* currencies.

It is not in anyone's interest that this system continues for much longer, because sooner or later, trade imbalances will be so great that foreigners may lose confidence in the dollar, and it will collapse, an event that will hurt everyone, including the United States. In this chapter I will present a solution to the problem that will put a stop to the overhanging risk of a dollar collapse, while putting all currencies on an equal footing for the first time. The proposed solution satisfies U.S. treasury secretary Timothy Geithner's expressed wishes in the lead-up to the above G-20 meeting to regulate the allowable magnitude of both trade deficits and surpluses, although it uses a rather different mechanism than the one he suggested, which was to enter a nonbinding agreement to limit the magnitudes of both trade surpluses and trade deficits to a maximum 4% of GDP.

The Role of Central Banks

Central bank reserves consist of holdings of foreign currency assets (typically government bonds and short-term deposits), gold, and SDRs (special drawing rights issued by the IMF), all of which are acceptable in payment of international obligations, the latter two making up a relatively small part of the total reserves. It is necessary for a central bank to have such holdings for several reasons: to provide the necessary liquidity to enable trade with other countries (imports and exports); to provide a pool of funds to use in managing a fairly stable currency in a currency regime that is not freely floating (typical for smaller countries in Gaian society); to provide a buffer for foreign direct investment and portfolio investment, both ingoing and outgoing; to use in some cases to help control the domestic money supply.

Ever since the connection to gold was severed in 1971, the major component of most central bank reserves has been the U.S. dollar, which has de

Currency	2000	2010
U.S. dollar	71	62
Euro	18	27
Yen	6	3
British pound	3	4
Other	2	4

Table 14.1. Central Bank Reserves Distribution in Percent.

facto provided the bulk of the necessary liquidity to carry on trade. The current average composition of foreign reserves in percent, as reported by the IMF for December 2000 and March 2010, is shown in table 14.1 for 33 "advanced economies" and 105 "emerging or developing economies."

The U.S. dollar percentage in the reserves has declined somewhat over the past decade, and continues to decline. More and more countries are shifting their reserves into euros because of concerns about the future value of the U.S. dollar, as the United States continues to pay for foreign imports and foreign wars by "printing" more dollars. Other nations are beginning to show concern about the imbalances and potential for a future crisis due to this dollar glut. In the final quarter of 2009, only 37% of new reserves were put into U.S. dollars.[1] Nevertheless, the dollar remains the dominant currency.

Having a national currency as the international currency for transactions among sovereign states is not ideal. Normally, when a country runs a trade deficit, there is an excess of the deficit country's currency in the hands of exporters around the world. These are sold off in the market, weakening the currency, which results in the deficit country's exports becoming more competitive—a negative-feedback mechanism that tends to correct imbalances and promote stability. But the United States does not feel the same pressure when running a deficit because other countries hold about 62 percent of their excess dollars in their reserves rather than selling them. Thus, the United States does not have the same automatic balancing of its trade as do other countries. Even with a high trade deficit, the dollar does not weaken sufficiently and the United States' exports are therefore not competitive enough to correct the trade imbalance. At the same time, other states, especially China, are accumulating enormous amounts of dollars in their reserves, an imbalance that threatens future stability. This is what has been happening for many years now. The United States has not had a trade surplus since 1975—shortly after the collapse of the gold-linked dollar

Figure 14.1. The U.S. Trade Surplus/Deficit 1960–2009. Courtesy of www.calculatedriskblog.com (/2009/01/ us-trade-deficit- graphs.html).

system in 1971—and the deficit has generally become bigger and bigger since, as shown in figure 14.1.

When the Chinese buy U.S. Treasury bills, they are opening themselves to a potential risk. They and other major holders of U.S. dollars are getting nervous about the situation. The Chinese cannot sell their dollar holdings (say, to buy euros) without substantial losses as the dollar drops in value. Nor would the Europeans be happy to see the euro become so strong that their exports cannot compete. This situation is not tenable indefinitely.

The problem is not that the United States might default on its debt, as some people seem to think. That need never happen. Any country with its own currency can always meet its obligations, *which are denominated in its own currency,* without limit. (Note: This does obviously not apply to debt denominated in foreign currencies!). In other words, the U.S. cannot become insolvent. While it could never be forced to default on dollar debt by outside forces, the U.S. could voluntarily choose to default, for example by falling over obstacles that it puts in its own path, such as the unnecessary debt ceiling, which almost caused a "voluntary" default in the summer of 2011.

The real issue for the Chinese is what they will get for their U.S. dollars when they decide to use them. Their risk is real because the terms of trade are entirely up to the United States and the future is unknown. Then why don't they simply buy U.S. equities and real estate now with all those excess dollars instead of continuing to buy U.S. Treasury Bills and awaiting an uncertain future?

Economist Michael Hudson offers a possible explanation, claiming that "When Saudi Arabia and Iran proposed to use their oil dollars to begin buying out American companies after 1972, U.S. officials let it be known that this would be viewed as an act of war. OPEC was told that it could raise oil prices all it wanted, as long as it used the proceeds to buy U.S. government bonds. That way, Americans could pay for oil in their own currency, not in gold or other 'money of the world.'"[2] Could the United States have sent a similar message to China? Judging by China's reluctance to be more aggressive in purchasing real dollar assets, it would not surprise me.

The world has a dollar glut and it grows larger for every day that the U.S. trade deficit grows larger. In the long run, the dollars accumulating in the foreign reserves of other countries—in particular China—are going to be exchanged for American equities, real estate or trade goods. The only way trade goods can bring balance is for the U.S. to enter a long period of trade surpluses with competitive exports and a cheaper dollar. But if and when that happens, another problem will arise—a lack of international liquidity. This is the so-called "Triffin dilemma" that will always raise its ugly head when a national currency is also the major source of international liquidity.[4] The dilemma is that when the dollar is used for liquidity (i.e., foreigners hold dollars as their primary reserve currency to finance trade), international trade functions well but the U.S. runs a big deficit, which is potentially destabilizing; but if the U.S. does not run a big deficit, then international liquidity dries up (i.e., dollar reserves decrease) and international trade does not function well. And yet the international community needs liquidity to finance trade. If not the dollar, then what? The question arises: Is there any way that this problem could be rectified by changing the way international trade is financed?

A New Reserve Currency?

In October 2009, The United Nations undersecretary-general for economic and social affairs, Sha Zukang, called for a new global reserve currency to end the dollar supremacy, which has allowed the United States to build a huge trade deficit, saying, "Important progress in managing imbalances can be made by reducing the reserve currency countries 'privilege' to run external deficits in order to provide international liquidity. It is timely to emphasize that such a system also creates a more equitable method of sharing the seigniorage derived from providing global liquidity."[4]

Earlier, in March 2009, the head of the People's Bank of China, Zhou Xiaochuan, referring specifically to the Triffin dilemma, suggested that an expanded role for the SDR might provide an alternative to the U.S. dollar.[5] He asked, "What kind of international reserve currency do we need to secure global financial stability and facilitate world economic growth, which was one of the purposes for establishing the IMF?" He then describes the goal as "an international reserve currency that is disconnected from individual nations and is able to remain stable in the long run." He suggested that a currency based on all the major economies, including the Chinese yuan, would be more stable than the current SDR, and that denominating assets and company accounts in the new SDR could make it attractive. Let us look more closely at this idea and see if it can resolve the problem.

SDRs (special drawing rights) are credits allocated by the IMF to member countries, originally in 1969 under the Bretton Woods gold-based regime with the purpose of increasing international liquidity, as there was a shortage of gold. After the collapse of that system in 1971, no alternative monetary system was agreed upon. Instead, the ad hoc role of liquidity provider in a regime of floating rates was taken on de facto by the U.S. dollar, and the SDR faded into the background. The SDR is not a normal currency, nor is it a claim against the IMF. It is a line of credit that is allocated to member countries in proportion to their capital investments in the IMF, which in turn are highly correlated with their GDP and volume of international trade. Member countries can draw upon this line of credit when in liquidity need, in which case they pay interest, or they can earn interest if their holdings with the IMF exceed the credit line. The SDR is used as a part of the reserves of central banks, but can only be realized in exchange for other foreign currencies at other central banks. The SDR is calculated as if it were a basket of the major currencies, with weights of U.S. dollar (44 percent), euro (34 percent), yen (11 percent), and pound sterling (11 percent). As a reserve currency, and as a source of liquidity, the SDR plays a minor role today for central banks, but its role could, in principle, be expanded. Worldwide reserves in 2009 were roughly $9 trillion, while the total SDRs in circulation, even after a recent large IMF allocation, are only about $324 billion, less than 4% of the total.

But there is a fundamental problem with this idea of a new reserve currency. It does not deal with the dollar glut. The SDR cannot replace the dollar. A new reserve currency is neither necessary nor sufficient to do that. The role of the dollar today is to finance international trade. The SDR was never designed for this purpose, and allocating more SDRs or adding more currencies to the basket will make no difference. The SDR does not create liquidity that does not already exist. It simply transfers one kind of central bank asset into another. The dollar would continue to be the major source of liquidity for trade in a world of expanded SDRs. In my opinion, no national currency or basket of national currencies like the SDR can be used to settle international debts without running into the problem of the Triffin dilemma and the continuation of intolerable imbalances. An essential ingredient is missing if we want to replace the dollar as the prime source of trade liquidity and avoid the Triffin dilemma at the same time. To understand what it is, it will help to go back to the Bretton Woods negotiations of 1945.

The United States' chief negotiator at Bretton Woods, Harry Dexter White, wanted a new system to settle international debts based on a new reserve currency—namely, a gold-linked dollar. His British counterpart, John Maynard Keynes, wanted a "multipolar" system that focused on settling international payments in such a way as to give an incentive for both debtor and creditor nations to reduce large imbalances, without giving an advantage to any one country. White won the argument on account of a far stronger negotiating position, but his inferior system subsequently crashed in 1971. Keynes' proposal, which was never implemented, would have worked, and it is not too late to revive it. Keynes' concept was to define a new currency that was decidedly *not* a reserve currency, but would provide the necessary liquidity for international trade. This difference from the SDR is crucial.

The difference becomes clear if we look at the three roles of money, usually described as (1) a store of value; (2) a unit of account; and (3) a medium of exchange. We are used to thinking in terms of our national currencies, which have all three characteristics. But money need not have all three characteristics. The SDR is a unit of account; in fact it is used for the IMF's own accounts and for a few other international organizations. It is also a store of value and used as part of central bank reserves. But it is *not* a medium of exchange. You can't buy anything with it. A central bank can only exchange it for other reserve assets.

Keynes' money unit differed from both national currencies and the SDR by being *only* a unit of account. It was not a store of value, and not a medium of exchange. Its only role was to account for the imports and exports, or more precisely, changes in the current accounts of member countries. The geniality of Keynes' International Clearing Union proposal was to recognize that the liquidity problem could be solved *without* a new reserve currency. His money unit could create exactly the amount of liquidity needed automatically.

Adapting Keynes' Model

Keynes developed his proposal based on a background of fixed exchange rates, the gold standard, and the United States as the world's largest creditor nation.[6] Nevertheless, many of his concepts can be used in a more modern twenty-first-century version of floating rates, fiat currencies, and the United States as the world's largest debtor nation. In what follows I will outline the basic elements of such a modified system that would be ideal for Gaian society's goals for several reasons, not all of which were foreseen by Keynes.

Keynes called his money unit the "bancor"—in some articles the "grammar"—and called his institution the International Clearing Union. For reference purposes, and to distinguish between the two proposals, I will call my corresponding money unit the eco. This name derives from the Ecofund, or reserve fund, that I propose will accumulate the very considerable income generated by the clearing institution, which I will call the Gaian Clearing Union (GCU) for the sake of reference. I envisage the Ecofund as a source of funding for projects that will benefit all nations, for example, climate mitigation, ecosystem maintenance and restoration, disaster help, and so forth. I would further suggest that the eco be defined as the value of a basket of several currencies, for example twenty-five, chosen on the basis of their GDP, liquidity, and volume of international trade. The details would have to be negotiated, but table 14.2 gives an idea of the how such a basket might look weighted by 2008 GDP.

With reference to Timothy Geithner's idea of a 4% limit on trade surplus or deficit relative to GDP, I added two columns with the corresponding figures for 2008 for the twenty-five currencies. Note that much-scolded China is actually not that far above the 4% limit (4.6%), while several smaller states are much more imbalanced by this measure (e.g., Switzerland, Saudi Arabia, Sweden, Malaysia, Australia). To these we could add most of the oil-exporting countries with their large surpluses. In spite of its enormous trade deficit, the United States is not as far off the 4% target as one might suspect (5.3%). Shortly, we will look at a second way of measuring large trade deviations suggested by Keynes.

The exact definition of the eco is not critical, as long as it is fairly stable, and as long as its value can be calculated at any time in every national currency. The eco will be very stable. One thing that is different about currencies as opposed to all other assets is that they cannot all fall at the same time. Some economists may question whether or not the eco is a reserve currency, pointing out that it will appear as an asset on a central bank's balance

Country	GDP $billion	Weight in %	Trade Surplus	As % of GDP
United States	14,204	24.0	–747	5.3
Eurozone	10,900	18.4	–10	0.1
China	7,903	13.3	363	4.6
Japan	4,355	7.4	201	4.6
India	3,388	5.7	–19	0.6
Russia	2,288	3.9	69	3.0
UK	2,176	3.7	–111	5.1
Brazil	1,977	3.4	10	0.5
Mexico	1,542	2.6	–5	0.3
South Korea	1,538	2.6	4	0.3
Canada	1,214	2.1	28	2.3
Turkey	1,029	1.8	–36	3.5
Indonesia	907	1.5	10	1.1
Iran	839	1.4	19	2.3
Australia	763	1.3	–51	6.7
Poland	672	1.1	–18	2.7
Saudi Arabia	492	0.8	89	18.1
Egypt	442	0.7	3	0.7
Pakistan	439	0.7	–6	1.3
Columbia	396	0.7	–5	1.3
Malaysia	384	0.6	26	6.8
Venezuela	358	0.6	17	4.7
Sweden	345	0.6	30	8.7
Ukraine	336	0.6	–4	1.2
Switzerland	325	0.5	68	20.9

Table 14.2. Example Weights for the Eco. GDP data from World Bank, www.worldbank.org; trade surplus data from *The World Factbook 2008*, www.cia.gov; except Eurozone data from European Central Bank.

sheet, alongside other foreign currencies, assuming the country has a trade surplus. If the country has a trade deficit, this same logic would suggest that the ecos owed would constitute a kind of "negative reserve currency." But ecos cannot be converted to other currencies like the SDR can, nor can they be used for capital account flows. Ecos are more like accounts receivable and accounts payable on a corporate balance sheet, rather than capital reserves that can be drawn upon when needed. So I would argue that the eco is not a reserve currency in the usual sense, but rather a unit of account that keeps score on trade.

Keynes suggested calculating his "bancor" as a basket of commodities. However, such a commodity basket would be less stable than a currency basket because commodity prices, as opposed to currencies, *can* all move in the same direction and often do. It would also create even greater imbalances than at present because of the Gaian policy of reducing the use of nonrenewable resources, which will result in systemically increasing commodity prices. Deficit countries would be penalized and surplus countries would benefit from having the currency of settling debts systemically increasing in value relative to domestic currencies, thus exacerbating already established imbalances. A currency basket is a more stable, more equitable, and simpler solution.

A New Clearing Union

The clearing union would be founded by a number of central banks, who would agree to abide by its rules when settling international trade debts. Each central bank would have a "trade account" with the GCU that could be in credit or debit at any one time. Initially, all accounts would be set to zero. The mechanism is that whenever a current account transaction (primarily import/export) takes place between two countries, the two central banks clear the local currency with the local buyers/sellers and then debit or credit the amount in ecos with the central bank's GCU trade account. So, for example, if the deal was for a Mexican firm to import $1 billion worth of Chinese cars, the Mexican central bank's trade account at the GCU would be debited in ecos for the equivalent of $1 billion, and the Chinese trade account with the GCU credited for the same amount in ecos. The Chinese exporter would receive $1 billion equivalent in yuan from its central bank, while the Mexican importer would deliver $1 billion worth of pesos to the Mexican central bank. Note that no actual foreign currency transaction would take place. And no dollars are involved. Compare that with the procedure today, where the transaction would most likely be denominated in dollars, which the United States would create out of nothing, the Mexican firm would buy on the market, and the Chinese would receive and probably keep about 60% of them in its reserves and sell the rest on the open market. By granting the "loan" to Mexico based on the "deposit" from China, the GCU has in effect created $1 billion of liquidity (new money) and circumvented the need for liquidity from the U.S. dollar. Stated in other words, the GCU system creates precisely the amount of liquidity that is needed at any time without any help from elsewhere. Similarly, when a debtor nation's balance is reduced and a creditor nation's balance decreased (e.g., if China subsequently imports $1 billion worth of goods from Mexico), money is destroyed (the "loan" is paid back). As time goes on, the credits and debits will build up for member countries but total debits will always be equal to total credits in a necessary mathematical identity. Of course, a problem could arise if a country's debit balance (debt) became too large for comfort. Too large a credit balance could also be problematic and unstable.

Therefore, the scheme must encourage member countries to keep their trade deficits or surpluses within reasonable bounds and in long-term balance. Limits are required for how big the debit and credit balances can become before penalties for excessive deviations on either side of the ledger kick in. Following Keynes' suggestion, we can do this by defining the normal volume of trade for each country in any year as one-half of its average imports plus average exports over the past five years. A member's account is then allowed to be in debit or credit up to a maximum of its normal trade volume, while the increase in any one year must not exceed one-fourth of the normal volume. A trade deficit of one-fourth of the volume corresponds to exports being 62.5% of volume and imports 37.5%, with the reverse for a trade surplus, so one-fourth of volume is a relatively large imbalance. Interest would be charged on debit balances but *no interest paid on credit balances*. This key rule creates an income stream to finance climate mitigation, ecosystem restoration, and so forth.

Penalty Charges

Annual penalty charges on balances, also suggested by Keynes, are triggered at three thresholds:

> • If the debit balance exceeds one-fourth of the volume for over a year, the bank would be designated a "deficiency bank" and charged an agreed percentage of the excess (the "one-fourth charge," which Keynes suggested be 5%), and any restrictions on capital inflow must be relaxed. If the credit balance exceeded one-fourth of volume for over a year the bank would be designated a "surplus bank" and charged the same percent-

age on the excess, and any restrictions on outward capital flow must be relaxed.

- If the debit balance exceeds one-half of volume, the bank would be designated a "supervised bank" and charged an additional percentage of the excess (the "one-half charge," which Keynes suggested be 5% also), and would be required to let its currency weaken versus the eco, or alternatively deposit sufficient reserve currencies (other than the nation's domestic currency) with the GCU to bring the balance owed back to maximum one-fourth of volume (my suggestion, not Keynes'). A supervised bank could be asked to withdraw from the system, in which case its debit balance would be absorbed by any reserve funds, and if necessary, by the founding equity. Similarly, a central bank with a credit balance of over one-half of its trade volume would be charged the same additional percentage on the excess, and required to allow its currency to strengthen relative to the eco, such adjustment to be repeated in any subsequent year if the credit balance should continue to increase. If a central bank that is in credit withdraws from the union, its credit would accrue to the GCU.

Capital Account Movements

An integral part of Keynes' proposal was the implementation of capital controls on cross-border capital flows, in complete agreement with our analysis of the needs of Gaian society. Keynes considered trade policy as a tool for the betterment of the citizens of a society, much like the classical economists. He was opposed to unrestricted capital flows, and saw strong local communities as the real backbone of any economy. He was both an internationalist and a cultural nationalist—a true Cultural Creative. For example, he said, "Ideas, knowledge, art, hospitality, travel—these are things which should of their nature be international. But let goods be homespun whenever it is reasonably and conveniently possible; and above all, let finance be primarily national."[7] Keynes' thinking was, in fact, very Gaian.

Keynes considered the rights of governments to control capital movements one of the most positive results of the Bretton Woods negotiations. In his proposal he wrote, "I share the view that central control of capital movements, both inward and outward, should be a permanent feature of the post-war system. If this is to be effective, it involves the machinery of exchange control for *all* transactions," i.e., both capital account transactions and current account transactions, the latter being handled by the clearing union. A condition for this was that "capital can be controlled at both ends." Therefore he proposed that "all remittances must be canalized through central banks."

Nonmember Accounts

All foreign exchange transactions of nonmembers with GCU members would have to comply with the rules of the GCU and its central banks if nonmembers wished to trade with GCU members. In particular, all nonmember transactions with members must be cleared in ecos through the GCU. Therefore, a country wishing to import from or export to a GCU member country would have to open an eco trade account by depositing gold or acceptable hard currency assets, *other than its domestic currency*, with the GCU. For example, if the United States were not a member initially, but wanted to buy oil from a member country, it would first have to deposit foreign currencies (anything but dollars!) in a GCU trade account to pay for the oil. This is the key to leveling the playing field among all countries, and creating the conditions under which the U.S. dollar can eventually take its place as one currency among many subject to the same conditions as every other country. Exports sold to GCU members by nonmembers would be credited to this trade account and imports from members paid out of the same account, which would always be in credit, as a nonmember has no access to a debit account. Penalties would not apply to nonmembers, but, like members, they would not receive interest on their deposit, and thus they would contribute to the Ecofund. Unlike members, nonmembers could draw down the funds in their trade account at any time, and even close it down if they wished.

An Illustrative Exercise

To get a rough idea of how much profit might be generated for the Ecofund from trade balances, assuming all nations were members of the Clearing Union, I have looked at the trade figures for the countries with the largest trade deficits and surpluses in recent years. In calculating penalties, I have

Country	Credit balance	Trade volume	1/4 charge	1/2 charge	Total charge	Official reserves
China	1,306*	1,280	19.2	12.8	32.0	2,426
Russia	766*	368	5.5	3.7	9.2	439
Saudi Arabia	678*	185	2.8	1.9	4.7	410
Japan	368	772	3.5	0.0	3.5	1,024
Norway	279*	136	2.0	1.4	3.4	49
Canada	215	432	2.1	0.0	2.1	54
Kuwait	213*	45	0.7	0.5	1.2	20
Brazil	190*	186	2.8	1.9	4.7	239
Nigeria	170*	54	0.8	0.5	1.3	45
Venezuela	160*	64	1.0	0.6	1.6	35
South Korea	157	355	1.4	0.0	1.4	270
Malaysia	150	178	2.1	1.2	3.3	97
Libya	142*	37	0.6	0.4	1.0	104
Algeria	131*	48	0.7	0.5	1.2	149
Iran	123*	73	1.1	0.7	1.8	81
Angola	115*	41	0.6	0.4	1.0	14
Kazakhstan	111*	55	0.8	0.6	1.4	23
Qatar	92*	41	0.6	0.4	1.0	19
Iraq	91*	35	0.5	0.3	0.8	44
TOTAL					76.6	

Table 14.3. Major Trade Surplus States ($ billions). Trade statistics from International Trade Center, www.trademap.org; reserves data from *The World Factbook*, December 2009, www.cia.gov.

assumed 2% as opposed to Keynes' suggested 5%, which strikes me as excessive under current conditions.

Table 14.3 gives a rough indication of how the accounts with the Gaian Clearing Union (GCU) might have looked at the end of 2008 for some of the countries with the largest credit balances, assuming the GCU had begun January 1, 2004. The countries with a credit balance greater than trade volume are noted with an asterisk, and would have had to hand over that excess to the GCU. Note that the credit balance is simply five times the average surplus over the last five years. In practice, things would hopefully never have been allowed to get that far out of balance, as these countries would have been pressured to revalue their currencies during the preceding five years.

Note that in this exercise the credit lines for a number of central banks were greater than trade volume in 2008. According to the GCU rules, this cannot happen. The currencies of these countries should have been revalued during the five-year period and any excess credit above the trade volume transferred to the GCU. Therefore these figures are only indicative of the situation had this revaluation rule not been followed for some reason and a larger credit allowed to accumulate. Penalty charges have been conservatively calculated based only on the trade volume in these cases (i.e., no confiscation of excess balances). The amount accrued to the GCU for 2008 from these nineteen countries would have been a very substantial $76.6 billion. If we included all countries in the exercise, this figure would be larger by several billion dollars. Income figures for the previous four years have not been estimated, as this exercise is just to illustrate the general situation, which must be characterized as unbalanced. Note that fifteen of the nineteen countries with excess credits above trade volume are oil-exporting countries. A second observation is that an implementation of the GCU will in practice require a transition period because of the enormous imbalances. The final column with the official reserves indicates how much of a hardship the charges from reserves might be for each country. In most cases, it would not be a problem. The reserves are inactive passive holdings that are not part of any country's money supply. By paying these charges to the GCU, they are benefiting all countries by creating jobs and a healthier ecosystem. Furthermore, founding the GCU will free up considerable funds from the reserves that are no longer needed to finance trade. These additional funds can also be used constructively to finance real development in the developing countries, a point I will return to in the next chapter. The amounts of the penalty charges and the way they are calculated are a subject for negotiation among the founding members, and the numbers from my example are only illustrative.

Table 14.4 illustrates as a second exercise the mirror situation for the largest deficit countries as of 2008 after an assumed five years of GCU since 2004.

Once again we see major imbalances with several countries in debit well above their normal trade volumes. As with the surplus nations, I have conservatively calculated the interest and penalty charges on the assumption that the excesses have been eliminated earlier by some combination of currency depreciation and deposit of reserve currencies with the GCU during the five years that have passed since the assumed founding. Many countries owe the GCU more than their entire reserves. The United States in particular is way out of balance by this measure. Even though there would be considerable

Country	Debit balance	Trade volume	Interest charge	1/4 charge	1/2 charge	Total charges	Official reserves
United States	4,137*	1,732	34.6	26.0	17.3	77.9	131
UK	723*	544	10.9	8.2	5.4	24.5	67
India	41*	249	5.0	3.7	2.5	11.2	275
Turkey	265*	167	3.3	2.5	1.7	7.5	75
Poland	123	169	2.5	1.6	0.8	4.9	80
Romania	104*	66	1.3	1.0	0.6	2.9	44
Egypt	72*	36	0.7	0.5	0.4	1.6	34
Hong Kong	72	382	1.4	0.0	0.0	1.4	256
Pakistan	63*	31	0.6	0.3	0.2	1.1	14
South Africa	61	81	1.2	0.8	0.4	2.4	40
Croatia	60*	22	0.4	0.3	0.2	0.9	15
Mexico	50	300	1.0	0.0	0.0	1.0	100
Bulgaria	42*	28	0.6	0.4	0.3	1.3	19
Serbia	40*	17	0.3	0.3	0.2	0.8	15
Philippines	40	55	0.8	0.5	0.2	1.5	44
Ukraine	27	76	0.5	0.2	0.1	0.8	27
Total Charges						141.7	

Table 14.4. Major Trade Deficit States ($ billions). Trade statistics from International Trade Center, www.trademap.org; reserves data from *The World Factbook*, December 2009, www.cia.gov.

reserves freed up by the founding of the GCU, these countries would have to borrow hard currency elsewhere if their balance of trade had not improved considerably over the five-year period. The United States would have had to raise about $2.4 trillion, presumably in foreign-denominated government bonds in euros and yen, assuming no devaluation and no subsequent improvement in the balance of trade over the five-year period.

The total profit contribution from trade balances in the exercise was $219 billion for 2008 ($77 billion from surplus nations and $142 billion from deficit nations). Of course, the intention is to reduce the imbalances, so in the long term, the income can be expected to be much less, as all nations move in the direction of a better balance between imports and exports. This should be easier to achieve in a capital-control and sovereign-trade regime than in the present neoliberal regime. The longer-term perspective is thus for a somewhat smaller profit contribution, but a still substantial one. Even in an ideal world there will always be interest earned on deficits. With an average deficit of one-fourth of trade volume for half the world, and no credit nations in the other half above one-fourth of trade volume, there would still be generated an order of magnitude $80 billion per annum in income for GCU if all countries were members. Realistically speaking, not all countries are going to be members from day one, so the numbers will be much less in the early days, and hopefully increase as more countries join up.

The United States' situation is quite unique because of its role as hitherto provider of international liquidity, which now must be unwound. This is going to require some combination of dollar weakening, increased American savings, restrictions on American capital exports, reduced imports and increased exports, and issue of foreign-denominated debt by the United States. In the long run, the dollar glut can only be eliminated by the United States once again becoming a trade surplus nation and continuing there for many years.

Note that the composition of central bank reserves would not change dramatically and suddenly. What would change is that the artificial demand for the dollar, and to a lesser extent for the euro, would be less, while exchange rates and central bank reserves would gradually migrate to levels more consistent with long-term balance.

Keynes' idea of systematically limiting the magnitudes of *both* trade deficits and surpluses has lain dormant for sixty-five years, but the concept was put back on the international agenda at the G-20 Korean meeting in November 2010 by the United States. While the Chinese rejected the U.S. proposal in this instance, the very fact that the concept is back may make it easier for the United States to support the Gaian Clearing Union proposal in the future, as it has an objective similar to the U.S. proposal.

The founding of a new Gaian Clearing Union, inspired by Keynes' International Clearing Union, can put all currencies on an equal footing for the first time, while removing the threat of a new international crisis due to a loss of confidence in the U.S. dollar. The GCU will provide an incentive for all member nations to keep their imports and exports more in balance, also reducing the risk of future international crises. An Ecofund can be established to finance environmental restoration, climate mitigation, disaster help, and so forth, for the benefit of all humankind, with a budget of order of magnitude $80 billion per year if all states participate.

Finally, the very substantial "dead" assets in official central bank reserves that are no longer necessary to finance trade, combined with the additional central bank reserves freed up by the Gaian countries that adopt a capital-controls currency regime, can together be used to found the third Gaian institution, with the objective of financing real development in the developing countries for the first time.

FIFTEEN

The Gaian Development Bank

A rich man is one who knows that he has enough.

Lao-Tzu

A sustainable and equitable Gaian society will require an entirely different approach to "development." In the old paradigm, "development" was synonymous with economic growth, which ecological economists have shown to be both unsustainable and uneconomic. The adoption of ecological economics demands making a distinction between "growth" and "development." Physical growth is limited on a finite planet, while we can continue to "develop" in the sense of increasing the global average standard of living, or "well-being," even when the limits to physical growth have been reached. We can do this in two ways, either by decreasing the population or by increasing the net "well-being" achievable for a given throughput of natural capital by inventing new technologies that allow a more effective use of the available natural capital.

The modern concept of foreign aid and foreign-currency loans to the developing countries (DCs) evolved as a strategy of containment during the Cold War competition for influence between the United States and the Soviet Union. It was always intended (at the highest political levels) primarily to benefit the rich, industrialized countries (ICs) and to keep the poorer countries locked into a role of suppliers of cheap raw materials and labor, and political pawns of the Empire. In addition, the middle and upper classes in DCs were seen as excellent markets for Western manufactured products. This was, of course, never the way it was presented to the public, and there are undoubtedly many well-intentioned people, who never realized the real dynamics of foreign aid and development loans. Historical economist Paul Bairoch put it this way, "It is no exaggeration to say that opening up of those (colonial) economies was one of the major reasons for their lack of development."[1] I suggest that doubters read the works of the whistle-blower John Perkins.[2]

Foreign loans create a treacherous "debt trap"—where the first priority is to repay the loans to the Empire by establishing an IC-dependent export-oriented economy to satisfy the lenders' needs, thus hindering real development. There is considerable evidence that even direct foreign aid (i.e., not including loans) to DCs has also had an overall negative effect. Not only has most of the money historically gone to IC consultant companies, Swiss bank accounts, the local elite, and arms purchases, but the projects supported are typically ones that fit with the Empire's need to extract raw materials or sell its industrial products. The logic behind this exploitative foreign-aid model is impeccable from the IC's point of view—they do not want to develop competitors. This is the prime reason why the DCs have remained underdeveloped in the sense of becoming self-determining nations with control over their own societies.

Real Development

The most important premise for real development is control over the economy. No developing country today—with the exception of China, which has shown that it is exceptionally clever—can fulfill this requirement on account of the long tradition of military colonialism followed by twentieth-century financial colonialism. A necessary condition for taking back control is implementation of the capital-controls/sovereign-trade regime and founding of the Gaian Clearing Union as described in chapter 14.

Gaian society will recognize that DCs achieving a level of consumption comparable with the current IC levels is not going to be possible in a sustainable world. Instead the goal will be to achieve a more modest ecological impact in a happier society under the full control of its citizens. It will also be clear that the ICs level of consumption is unsustainable and must be reduced. Real development will require an initial focus on domestic production of basic necessities like organic food, clean energy, clothing, shelter and infrastructure, strengthening of local communities through job creation, entrepreneurial incentives, and local democracy. A shift from export-oriented trade to import substitution will be necessary, as will high tariffs on imported luxury goods and protection of industries producing basic necessities. A strategic priority will be to develop value-added production using domestic mineral and other resources in industries that are appropriate and where there is a comparative advantage. Dependence on foreign aid and foreign trade in general will be minimized in most DCs.

New institutions will be necessary in many countries in order to carry out effective taxation, legal justice, and environmental protection. Foreign-currency debt will be reduced or even eliminated if it can be shown to be odious.

Foreign Loans

It is quite likely that a great deal of existing DC debt will be legally recognized as "odious" by Gaian society courts and thus not repayable. Odious debt is debt incurred without the permission of a country's citizens in a conspiracy between a corrupt leadership and willing foreign investors, and is currently the subject of various initiatives to establish formal legal criteria under international law.[3] The United States set the first precedent of odious debt when it seized control of Cuba from Spain in 1898. Spain insisted that Cuba repay the loans made to them by Spain. The United States refused to pay that debt, arguing that the debt was imposed on Cuba by force of arms and served Spain's interest rather than Cuba's. The principle argued by the United States was upheld by international law in *Great Britain v. Costa Rica* (1923).

A second concept that could well be invoked to nullify current debt is "fraudulent conveyance" in cases where there was no realistic plan for repayment, and the creditor bank or nation should have known that there was no chance of repayment. Many economists have stated publicly that there is no chance of DCs ever repaying their foreign loans, and the ICs know it. There are thus good solid arguments for DCs in Gaian society achieving court approval of their refusal to service or repay such loans.

In Gaian society, bilateral foreign loans and aid programs from ICs to DCs should no longer be necessary, or even desirable. The opening up of IC markets for competitive DC products should be quite sufficient to achieve the goal, i.e., "trade not aid." The establishment of the Gaian Clearing Union and a capital-controls regime will free up at least half of the foreign currency reserves of all DC member nations, who will no longer have to use their reserves for trade financing or for defending their currency against speculators.

Financing a Development Bank

The freed-up funds can be put to use by founding a new banking institution, which I will call Gaian Development Bank for the sake of reference.

	$ trillions	Percent
Advanced Economies	2.824	34
Developing Economies	5.471	66
Total	8.295	100

Table 15.1. Foreign Currency Reserves, 2010. From IMF COFER Database, www.imf.org.

The Gaian Development Bank will take on the functions now carried out by the IMF and World Bank but with very different policies and with a democratic structure. Functions will include providing temporary liquid funds to members in emergency situations as envisaged by the original IMF, and financing of real development and poverty alleviation in the DCs as envisaged by the original World Bank. ICs can continue to provide multilateral aid to DC members through the Gaian Development Bank, but any bilateral aid would have to be approved by the Gaian Development Bank and consistent with its development policies. Otherwise, ICs will continue to be part of the problem, and not part of the solution.

Most foreign-currency reserves, like most of the remaining nonrenewable resources, are in the developing countries. So they are actually in a strong negotiating position. In fact, the DCs can finance their real development with their own resources without any participation from the Empire should that be necessary. Table 15.1 shows the approximate foreign currency reserves as of June 2010 for a number of "advanced economies" and "emerging and developing economies" (DCs).

While these IMF statistics do not represent all countries, the percent of distribution is a good indicator of the strength of the developing countries. If they all participated, the developing countries could transfer roughly one-half of their foreign-currency reserves to a newly founded Gaian Development Bank, partly as equity (e.g., $100 billion with contributions proportional to the size of their economies), and partly as loan capital (e.g., $2.635 trillion based on the above figures). Even without the participation of China ($2.454 trillion in reserves), the remaining DCs could muster loan capital of over $1.4 trillion, assuming an allocation of one-half. I would suggest that members waive income on their capital deposits. A 3% return on assets, for example, will enable the bank to earn an extra income of about $72 billion per annum (if all DCs participated)—an amount greater than all foreign aid today—to be used for development, and also serve as a buffer to cover losses on bad loans.

A member country could apply to the Gaian Development Bank for a temporary loan if circumstances required it. By pooling reserves, it should be possible to service the needs of all members, as not all are likely to need assistance at the same time. When one country loses reserves another gains, so the total is quite stable. This is the same pooling principle used in fractional banking, electricity power sharing, and the insurance industry.

I would recommend that the main thrust of the Gaian Development Bank be to establish daughter companies in each DC that would perform traditional banking business with a focus on local loans in local currency for local development, particularly in rural areas. By using the principle of fractional banking, the Gaian Development Bank can have an impact ten times its capital base. Financing can be done either by traditional loans, including micro-finance, or by equity participation, the latter as part of a program to encourage entrepreneurship.

Gaian Development Bank branches would have a social rather than profit-making function, being the lifeblood of the local economies where they operate. Moneys deposited in the local bank would be used mostly for local projects, much like the original savings and loan concept in the United States. At least some local ownership would normally be a prerequisite for approval of business loans, and local suppliers should receive preferential treatment, in order to keep the wealth that is being created in the local area. It is important that loans are in local currency rather than foreign currency, if we are to avoid a repetition of the "debt trap" of financial colonialism. Of course, there is a risk to the Gaian Development Bank if irresponsible economic policy erodes the value of the domestic currency. Therefore Gaian Development Bank branches will only be established where acceptable conditions can be negotiated, a point to which I will return.

Equity participation could be important in Muslim countries where sharia banking does not allow *riba*—interest charges. Partnership and community are central to Muslin economics, which should make the Gaian Development Bank concept attractive in such countries. Islamic finance also prohibits *garar* (speculation) and investments in pornography, gambling, prostitution, narcotics, and tobacco. The Gaian Development Bank should adopt all of these Islamic principles, and add a ban on investments in weapons and any kind of environmentally damaging production, including chemical agriculture.

Many of the above principles used to be standard in local communities in the ICs, even in the United States, before the local savings and loan banks were taken over by large multinational banks that were primarily interested in grabbing the local savings and sending them to the nearest financial center to fuel their international financial speculations. Many Gaian ICs will probably reestablish such local banks once again. The IC members of the Gaian Development Bank will be encouraged to reorganize their banking systems according to Gaian principles, including the kind of reforms I put forward to deal with the recent financial crisis in chapter 6. An international agency to oversee financial institutions—as many commentators have recommended as a response to the 2007–9 financial crisis—will not be necessary or even desirable in a regime of capital controls/sovereign trade. Banks that are "too big to fail" should be broken up into smaller regional and local banks with a "back to basics" focus on real production rather than "financialization" of the economy. There is no need for oversized banks that perform no useful social function and are simply an unnecessary risk for taxpayers. Even former federal reserve chairman Alan Greenspan admits that "Federal Reserve research had been unable to find economies of scale in banking beyond a modest-sized institution."[4] Projects that are too large for one bank can always be handled through cooperation among several banks. In any case, it should be up to each sovereign nation to regulate its financial sector as it sees fit.

Food Production

The key to real development is local production of basic necessities, in particular, food. Once a local food market, a local dairy, and a local slaughterhouse are established in a community, secondary support industries will appear naturally, creating local jobs and a thriving local economy. Small-scale textile and housing comes next, each of them spawning even more supporting industries. If food is imported, as is the case in many DCs, who put all their agricultural resources into supplying the Empire with cash crops to earn foreign exchange to pay off their foreign debt, it is impossible to achieve real development. The same goes for importing clothes, building materials, and other low-tech products that can just as easily be produced locally. This vicious circle has to be broken before real development can begin. Of course, not everything can be produced domestically, especially items that require a larger scale to be economic. But what can be produced locally should be produced locally as a matter of policy.

In Gaian society, food production will have to be 100% organic in order to eliminate pollution and maintain soil fertility and the integrity of aquifers. Besides which, organic farming will be recognized as the most economical alternative. But can organic food feed the world? Evolutionary biologist Elisabet Sahtouris has long claimed it is a myth that we cannot produce enough food organically. Traditional agriculture analysts tend to measure the difference in the two systems in terms of financial gain based on grossly distorted prices, rather than in energy terms, which are far more relevant. Sahtouris writes, "In fact, the natural farmer at the turn of the [twentieth] century produced ten calories of food energy for every one calorie of energy input and kept his soil and water table healthy, while the present-day industrial farmer puts at least ten calories of energy into his farm for every one calorie of food he gets out. Meanwhile his land is increasingly impoverished, thus destroying the very basis of his livelihood. Hi-tech agriculture must be counted enormously inefficient and energy wasteful."[5]

A major study in 2007 at the University of Michigan confirms this view, concluding that organic farming can indeed feed the world, and with considerably less environmental damage than conventional farming. The report, based on a survey of 293 studies, estimates that in developed countries, organic systems on average produce 92% of the yield produced by conventional agriculture (at lower cost), while in developing countries, organic farming techniques can produce 80% more than conventional farming techniques (i.e., without synthetic fertilizers and pesticides, which they cannot afford). Organic production even has the potential to support a substantially larger human population than currently exists, although that is not a path that Gaians will follow. A supposed limiting factor with organic farming claimed by critics is the lack of sufficient nitrogen in natural fertilizer. However, the Michigan study points out that there is sufficient nitrogen potentially available from nitrogen fixation by legumes as winter cover crops used in connection with normal crop rotation. Data from temperate and tropical agroecosystems suggest that they could fix enough nitrogen to replace *all* of the synthetic fertilizer currently in use.[6] Synthetic fertilizer production is a major source of CO_2 emissions. But the commercial forces behind chemical agriculture and their political allies will probably not budge until they are forced to by the coming economic tsunami.

Food security is going to become the number-one issue for many countries once we enter the energy descent era, as many countries turn to protectionism. In practice, a much greater proportion of food needs will have to be produced locally. While many innovative solutions are likely to emerge, I will mention just one that could be very important for the many people continuing to live in cities, both in the industrialized and developing countries.

In recent years, the concept of "community supported agriculture" (CSA) has evolved, which is supportive of the Gaian concept of strengthening the vitality of local communities. It is likely to become quite important when industrial agriculture is no longer competitive, and local food production becomes the norm. There are various models, but the basic idea is that the citizens in a local community or neighborhood enter an agreement with an organic farmer in the region to supply them with a share of his produce in return for participation in his costs and risks. Farmers get a better price and greater security than otherwise, citizens get fresher, cheaper food than otherwise, and CO_2 emissions are greatly reduced, in a win-win-win scenario for everyone.[7]

Every country, even the poorest, can be self-sufficient in organic food production with proper agricultural policies. But it may require entirely new thinking and unorthodox approaches, using organic farming and permaculture principles—and some help from outside initially.

Permaculture

Permaculture is a design philosophy that will be absolutely central to Gaian society. The underlying principle, as stated in the 1970s by its cofounder, Australian Bill Mollison, is: "Work with nature, rather than against it." He goes on to define it as follows: "Perm(anent) A(gri)culture is the conscious design and maintenance of agriculturally productive ecosystems, which have the diversity, stability and resilience of natural ecosystems. It is the harmonious integration of landscape and people, providing their food, energy, shelter and other material and non-material needs in a sustainable way. Without permaculture there is no possibility of a stable social order."[8]

Permaculture is about designing human habitats as an integral part of nature, precisely in line with the fundamental premise of the Gaian paradigm. Herein lies its significance. During the fossil fuel era of chemical agribusiness, permaculture has evolved on the periphery of the mainstream beneath the radar of the dominant culture. Nevertheless, the concept today is known throughout the world, and permaculture teachers and designers are found in every country, just waiting for the chance to show the world what they can do. They will be in great demand when we enter the era of energy descent and local food production becomes a matter of survival.

There are many good examples of permaculture design, particularly in ecovillages around the world, for example, Crystal Waters in Australia and Earthhaven in the United States, which are both highly respected teaching, research, and demonstration centers for their regions. A widespread network of intentional communities, Web sites, magazines, and courses characterize the international nature of the movement.[9]

Permaculture principles, when properly applied, can lead to greater productivity than traditional chemical agriculture. A well-known example of this has been provided by the Japanese pioneer Masanobu Fukuoka, who independently developed growing techniques—which he calls "natural farming"—every bit as productive as industrial methods, through experimenting and carefully observing the effect of various plants growing in the same space, as can be found in nature. One result is a highly efficient no-tillage production of wheat, combined with white clover to improve the soil. Fukuoka regards natural farming as a deeply spiritual path that is "for the cultivation and perfection of human beings."[10]

A third pioneer, who independently developed a multitude of similar techniques is Austrian farmer Sepp Holzer, whose farm is on mountainous terrain at an altitude of 1000–1500 meters (3,200–4,900 feet) with an average temperature of 4°C (39°F). In spite of the relatively hostile environment, Holzer has demonstrated that his "wilderness culture" techniques enable an enormous diversity of plants, including many never seen before in his region, an extremely high productivity per unit area, and a minimum of effort. Holzer uses pigs intelligently as his helpers to fertilize, plough, and harrow his land. He creates "edible" forests, where fruit trees and bushes grow in symbiosis with coniferous, deciduous, and decorative plants, including some poisonous ones, which also perform useful pest-control functions. He has imported an army of ants, which he considers to be the "healers of the forest." He states his guiding principle thus: "Man cannot perfect that which is already perfect; we must simply learn to manage nature wisely."[11]

Greening the Desert

Corporate agribusiness has been very successful in propagating the myth that only industrial agriculture with its intensive use of synthetic fertilizers, herbicides, and pesticides can feed the world. Once we enter the energy-descent period, these industrial methods will no longer be economic. In fact, the Empire is going to be hit quite hard. Therefore, the following example not only falsifies that myth, but gives a clear indication of the kind of food production that must be developed in the near future all over the planet.

Permaculture teacher Geoff Lawton and his team received a small grant in 2009 to see what they could do with organic methods in Jordan on just ten acres of some of the most hostile agricultural land anywhere. Rainfall was almost nonexistent; the soil—400 meters (1,300 feet) below sea level—was salinized desert, the microorganisms in the soil had been destroyed long ago by abusive practices, and temperatures were often over 50°C (122°F) in the summer.[12]

Within a few months—to the utter amazement of the locals, who farmed under plastic strips with intensive use of synthetic chemicals and fertilizers— Geoff Lawton used classic nonchemical permaculture principles to turn this inhospitable piece of land into a lush green paradise, with several varieties of fruit trees, including date palms, pomegranate, guava, mulberry, and notably, figs—bearing fruits after just four months, which the local farmers had said would be impossible on account of the salty soil. The system was designed to collect as much of the sparse rainwater as possible into swales (water-harvesting ditches) to power a drip-style mini-irrigation system. On the upside of the swales, nitrogen-fixing trees helped to improve soil quality while shading the water and slowing evaporation, while the downhill side featured fruit trees mixed in with non-fruit trees and lots of mulch (decomposable organic material).

The local farmers were shocked to find mushrooms growing underneath the mulch in the swales, something they had never seen because of the extreme dryness in the area. They were also amazed that the saltiness of the soil had *decreased*, normally only possible by extensive washing with scarce water. It turns out the two surprises were connected. The mushrooms produced a white substance that seemed to repel and neutralize the salt, and the soil was now quite fertile.

"We can green the desert," says Geoff Lawton, and he has proved it. The moral to this story is that if it can be done under these conditions, it can be done anywhere. Another interesting aspect of this project is that the standard techniques of permaculture were not known to the local farmers, or perhaps forgotten after decades of chemical farming. If this is a more general phenomenon, and I think it is, then one can become quite optimistic about the potential to improve food productivity in even the most inhospitable parts of the world—and do it sustainably—by teaching permaculture principles as the foundation stone of Gaian society agriculture.

Ecovillages as the New Development Model

With the increasing awareness of mounting ecological problems in the late 1980s, the ecovillage movement was born as a response to the growing global crisis that was correctly perceived as due to the deficiencies of the separatist, reductionist worldview. The ecovillage concept presented a positive vision of a sustainable lifestyle that combined social, ecological, and spiritual components in a small community that ideally encompassed local organic food production, renewable energy, local jobs, conflict resolution, and more satisfying human relations. Inspiration came from a small number of existing communities that had successfully established themselves using similar principles. These included Findhorn in Scotland, Aurovillle in India, and Solheimer in Iceland. All of these early models had, in fact, a spiritual base. More recent models include Crystal Waters in Australia, Sieben Linden in Germany, Dyssekilde, Hjortshøj, Hertha, and Munksøgaard in Denmark, Damanhur in Italy, Tamera in Portugal, and Ecovillage at Ithaca (NY) in the United States, to mention just a few. It was realized that, in spite of the great diversity of these projects across race, culture, religion, geography, and climate, the common denominator was a value system that was consistent with what Ray and Anderson identified with the Cultural Creatives and what I have called the Gaian paradigm.[13]

At the UN Habitat Conference on Human Settlements in 1996, a global network of ecovillage projects was formally founded as the Global Ecovillage Network (GEN), with financial support from Gaia Trust of Denmark. Since then, the network has grown quietly and steadily beneath the radar of the mainstream media and with very little public support. National and regional networks now cover most of the globe.

The ecovillage concept is very central to the task of real development under the umbrella of the Gaian Development Bank. GEN includes traditional villages in its definition of ecovillages, because, until being destroyed by "free market" economics and industrial agriculture, they were always sustainable, and many still are. It is not too late to begin to rebuild the traditional villages and reverse the flow of people from the villages to the slums of the big DC cities. Senegal is one country that has realized the potential of the ecovillage concept as a new approach to development—entirely consistent with their cultural traditions—to replace the exploitative World Bank development model, which has been of more help to IC consulting firms and the local elite than to the rural poor. Senegal established the first government agency specifically to support the ecovillage concept, as well as the first national ecovillage network in Africa, and initiated the establishment of an ecovillage network for all of West Africa.

Ecovillages may well form the core of the many eco-communities that will explode on the world scene when we enter the period of energy descent and economic chaos. They can be not only models for sustainable rural and urban communities both in the North and the South, but also as what GEN calls "living and learning centers," teaching sustainability principles in their local regions, for example, using their "Gaia Education" curriculum.[14]

Local Currencies

One of the characteristics of the current economic system is the centralization and internationalization of finance. In practice this is typically accomplished by a bank establishing a nationwide network of branch offices and sending the savings from local communities and towns to a financial center. From there it could go anywhere in the world and for any purpose, often into speculative instruments that are high risk and have high short-term profit expectations. Local communities will often experience this as a lack of capital for local investment, which contributes to job losses, a gradual dying of the community, and a flight of people, especially young people, to the cities. In the early days of banking, there were no national banks. Banks were primarily local and served the local community. Even in the United States, there were no national banks prior to 1997.

One of the prime objectives of Gaian society is to reestablish wealthy local communities with a high degree of local democracy and autonomy. A necessary condition for this to happen is the re-decentralization of finance, so that the money earned in local communities remains there and is invested in local projects that create jobs and local wealth rather than disappearing in foreign speculative schemes. Breaking up national banks and reestablishing local banking institutions is one way to accomplish this.

But there is a second way of accomplishing some of the same objectives, namely, by forming a local, complementary currency. Historically, such local currencies have often arisen spontaneously after a major crisis, when local communities, suffering from high unemployment and a lack of purchasing power, found that they could survive and even thrive in this way without any national currency. There are a number of ways it can be done. One way is to establish a mutual credit system, whereby every participant opens an account with the "bank." Any services provided between participants result in a credit and debit in the computer accounts. No physical money need exchange hands. Such is the local exchange trading system (LETS), which has been implemented in several countries, including Canada, the UK, Germany, and Australia. The LETS creates its own liquidity, and is similar in principle to the proposed Gaian Clearing Union system in that respect, but on a much smaller scale. Like the GCU, the problem is to avoid too great swings in the balances, in particular on the debit side, i.e., if someone goes deep into debt and suddenly disappears; the other participants are left with a loss. All such systems are based on trust, and for this reason normally limited in scope to a local region. We can expect to see an explosion of such systems when the next financial tsunami hits.[15]

A second approach is for some initiator to issue physical money "chits" (e.g., a distinctive paper) to all participants backed by domestic currency or some other physical goods. For example the local food store might play this role, provided that both its suppliers and customers were on board. In the United States, some local banks issue one local currency unit for $0.95, giving local citizens the incentive to buy locally. Some Americans have even called complementary currencies "recession breakers" because several such systems did quite well during the financial crisis of 2007–9. Some of the larger ecovillages have their own currency, for example Findhorn and Damanhur, while in the United States and Germany, whole towns have joined the trend, e.g., the town of Ithaca in New York State has run a successful system for twenty years.

Where appropriate—for example in small villages and towns, the Gaian Development Bank could have the option of issuing local complementary currency chits backed by its assets as a way of creating jobs, getting the local economy moving, and building real local wealth. In this way, there is a direct relationship between the foreign sponsor and the local citizens of the poorer communities, circumventing the traditional problems of corruption, foreign consultants, kickbacks, and permissions from government bureaucrats and other middlemen that tend to hijack 90% of the traditional foreign aid, while 10% may "trickle down" to the rural poor, if they are lucky.

Terms and Conditions

Just as the IMF's "structural adjustment programs" required a number of conditions to be satisfied before loans were made available, so too will the Gaian Development Bank require a number of conditions to be satisfied before setting up shop in a DC or making loans. But the conditions will be very different, with Gaian Development Bank's prime focus being on financing real and sustainable development rather than the IMF focus on how the hard currency loans are to be repaid to its private bank allies. A DC wishing to utilize the benefits of the Gaian Development Bank to finance development or to get temporary loans will work with the bank in developing programs that can convince the bank of the country's serious intentions and realistic plans; for example, a transition plan toward a sustainable society; a fiscally responsible national economic plan based on ecological economics; and a long-term program to control and reduce population. The details will vary considerably among participating countries, depending on local circumstances, but a closer look at some of the issues involved will clarify a lot.

Developing Country Reforms

Gaian League DC member countries will be faced with major reforms of the whole society. Some of the typical reforms that will have to be carefully considered include a shift from exporting a single cash crop based on chemical agriculture to becoming self-sufficient in food production based on organic farming and permaculture principles; a shift away from importing luxury goods and other goods that can be produced locally; a shift away from maximum possible export of mineral resources to planned decreases in resource extraction coupled with new value-added production industries where there is comparative advantage; a shift away from importing oil to energy saving and development of local sustainable energy sources like wind, solar, wave and geothermal.

Other policies to be implemented would include the establishment of new public institutions to regulate the economy and the reduction or annulment of odious foreign debt through the courts. Oil-exporting DCs will have to reduce their economic dependence on oil, in keeping with Gaian society's nonrenewable resource policies, and introduce similar reforms if real development is to begin. One way to do this would be to place foreign-exchange earnings in a sovereign fund whose earnings (but not the capital) could be used for present and future generations.

Economic Planning

The Gaian Development Bank should require that local currency loans by the bank will not result in currency devaluation due to imprudent economic planning by the member country. Ecological economics should be adopted as state policy and supported in educational institutions from kindergarten through university. Fiscal and monetary policies of the member state should require approval by the Gaian Development Bank. A shift of the tax base away from personal income and to property and resources is recommended in order to qualify for financial support. Economic performance should be monitored by well-being indices (e.g., "dashboard" reports, and so on) and not by "uneconomic growth" (GDP). A program to combat corruption should be implemented, as it is vital to the Gaian Development Bank's reputation that all transactions with the bank are free of corruption.

Population Control

In a society that has reached the limits to physical growth and is overloading the ecosystem with its unsustainable consumption habits, a reduction of population size is one of the two possibilities left to take the pressure off the ecosystem and to improve the standard of living at the same time. Therefore it is essential that Gaian society adopt population reduction as a major goal. It follows that this goal must be reflected in member countries' long-term planning. As a condition for its support, the Gaian Development Bank should require that a satisfactory plan is implemented. It is not enough to rely on a natural decrease in birth rates as standards of living increase, as has been observed in the ICs. The DCs are following a different path where this possibility is now out of the question. There is no way that 7 billion people can live sustainably in a post-peak-oil world at anything like ICs' current living standards. If we don't actively reduce population, nature will likely do it for us in a far more catastrophic and painful way through starvation and pandemics.

There are many ways to reduce population, and it is time this hitherto taboo subject rose to the top of the international agenda. All other species seem able to do it. Why is it so difficult for the most intelligent of all—*Homo sapiens sapiens*? One reason is the widespread attitude that having children is a basic human right and not a subject for government interference. A second—prevalent in many DCs—is the absence of any government guarantee of support for the elderly, leading to the rational conclusion for any young couple that their best insurance for old age is having many children. A third—in some DCs—is a simple lack of knowledge of, and/or access to, techniques of family planning. A fourth is the widespread gender inequality in the fastest growing countries. Improving the education level of women is probably the most cost-efficient way to improve overall living standards in developing countries, by simultaneously decreasing the perceived need for more offspring and increasing job opportunities. A fifth is the interest of the Empire in a larger population in order to sell more of its products.

In a fully developed Gaian society, all five reasons can be dealt with through government programs. Commercial interests will be regulated more closely. Lack of knowledge and access is a straightforward question of investment in education and distribution programs. The guaranteed care of the elderly can be handled as a quid pro quo for acceptance of restrictions on childbirth. The right to have children is backed by a UN resolution at the Cairo Population Summit in 1994 signed by 179 nations. This will be a difficult nut to crack, and will require widespread debate and dialogue to resolve. Barring any change, this means that any plan will have to be voluntary.

Sovereign states in a Gaian society will be free to choose whatever methods they prefer, but they will have to satisfy the Gaian Development Bank if they wish to access the bank's funds for development. The most effective program in the DCs will likely be a voluntary quid pro quo deal—guarantees of minimum income levels, including old-age support, in return for limits on childbirth. Such guarantees are completely consistent with the Gaian philosophy that all citizens have the right to a dignified existence. The Gaian Development Bank may even be willing to finance a portion of the costs and participate in the guarantee in some cases.

Some countries may opt for a more heavy-handed approach such as China's one-child policy, which includes financial penalties, social pressure, and forced sterilization in some cases. Although the policy only applies to urban Han Chinese, the birth rate has decreased over twenty-five years to just 1.7 births per woman, below the replacement rate of 2.1. The policy has had many negative consequences, from the murder of female children to stealing other peoples' children in broad daylight.

Vietnam chose a softer variant in 1988, the so-called two-child policy, whereby a woman should be at least nineteen before giving birth to her first child, and the second and last should be born three to five years later (a phenomenon that some wits call "slow sex").[16] This voluntary program had no official incentives or penalties, but a certain degree of social pressure has indeed reduced the birth rate somewhat, although it is still too high.

Singapore has one of the longest and best-documented records on birth control, going back to 1966, when the growth rate was 3% in this rather small territory and causing problems. Their approach was voluntary with a variety of incentives and penalties, and it was quite effective, as the birth rate was reduced to just 1.44 children per woman by 1987. The government then got concerned and reversed policy, encouraging more children for families that could afford them.[17]

One Large Family

Positive discrimination is another concept that existed under GATT, and that should be reinstated in the Gaian League. The dropping of this concept in the WTO charter was the major reason for the developing countries opposing the switch to the WTO in 1994. This policy recognizes the need to truly help the developing countries and not insist that every advantage they get must be paid for. In the Gaian League, the developing country members will be seen more as family needing assistance rather than as competitors or suppliers of cheap raw materials and labor. The Gaian Development Bank will work closely with the GTO to provide active support to developing countries where they really need it.

The developing countries have been left behind because of financial colonialism and have every right to participate fully in global society with self-determination and access to Gaian League IC markets where they have a comparative advantage. They will be given substantial support via the Gaian Development Bank, but will have to do a lot themselves if they want this assistance, including giving up unrealistic dreams of IC-level overconsumption and shifting to a more self-sufficient, less ambitious, sustainable, happier, more harmonious nation in charge of its own destiny within a commonwealth of diverse, independent, sovereign states.

SIXTEEN

A Gaian World

It may well be that the impossible at a given moment can become possible only by being stated at a time when it is impossible.

—Leszek Kolakowski

The practical functioning of ecological economics and the three proposed Gaian institutions—the Gaian Trade Organization, the Gaian Clearing Union, and the Gaian Development Bank—require major political reforms at the level of intergovernmental cooperation if they are to function as intended. We need five additional institutions.

The Gaian Congress

The key political reform needed is the establishment of an international institution that can adopt binding international law to regulate relationships among the sovereign states that are Gaian League members, in particular, regulations for environmental and human rights issues. Without such laws, the risk is that the ecosystem and social order may be destroyed beyond repair.

For the sake of reference let us call this fourth Gaian institution the Gaian Congress (GC), consisting of appointed representatives from member states. A necessary and closely associated fifth institution would be the Gaian Court of Justice to interpret the law. The sixth necessary institution is the Gaian Commission, which is the executive branch implementing the legislation passed by Congress. It would be led by a general-secretary, who would oversee the various agencies necessary to carry out policy, including but not limited to the Gaian Clearing Union, the Gaian Development Bank, and the Gaian Trade Organization. The commission would include the CEOs of each Gaian institution (except the Gaian Court of Justice, which must be an arms-length independent institution) plus some at-large members.

The Gaian Congress is *not* a world government. A centralized world government would not be consistent with Gaian principles, and would in all likelihood lead to the same kind of exploitation, corruption, and commercial domination that characterizes the world today. The GC is assumed to have a restricted mandate—with a strong environmental and human rights focus—to deal with the relationships among the Gaian League's diverse sovereign member states, which have control over their own economies and social policies consistent with the principles of the sovereign-trade regime discussed in a previous chapter, but operating within the restrictions of environmental and human rights policies that have been adopted by the Gaian Congress.

The resolutions adopted by the GC would, by definition, constitute the international law to regulate relations among member states. There is no universally accepted and operative set of international laws today, and certainly no enforcement agency. In the longer term, we can expect the initial laws adopted by the GC to include a major part of the existing body of international agreements and treaties and practices, including many of the resolutions by the United Nations and judgments by the International Court of Justice, in particular, the portions that are consistent with the Gaian paradigm and thus are in the interest of the entire global community. In addition, the GC will adopt enforceable and appropriate penalties for noncompliance.

A relevant question concerns the relationship of the Gaian Congress to the United Nations. Realistically speaking, not all members of the UN are likely to be members of the Gaian League, certainly not in the near term. There is no reason for Gaian League members to leave the UN, which has many useful functions. The UN is basically a forum for debate among member states, but without any real power beyond a certain influence on public opinion, although the UN has established a number of very useful and successful agencies that promote greater cooperation among member states, for example, UNESCSO, the ILO, the FAO, UNEP, the WHO, and many others. In the long run, if the Gaian League membership grows to encompass the great majority of states, a merger of the two might make sense. But for the foreseeable future, the Gaian Congress and the UN will play two very different roles and will have very different structures.

Structure of the GC

The real power of the Gaian Congress would be its role as a supranational legislative body to define a set of international laws applicable to member states, where noncompliance would have economic consequences. It is hoped that all nations would eventually become members. The Gaian Commission could issue directives based on adopted legislation to regulate any and all aspects of member activities that are relevant for long-term sustainability and the maintenance of human rights standards. Compliance could be made more attractive than noncompliance by the introduction of an "Economic Sanctions Protocol" that would override not only any national legislation, but the terms of any bilateral or multilateral treaty or agreement that was not part of the GC legal framework. In practice, the Economic Sanctions Protocol would mean that the Gaian League, or in some cases, a member nation, could impose appropriate economic sanctions on a member nation that failed to comply with a GC resolution or commission directive. Alternatively, a nation could demand and get compensation for any loss due to noncompliance of another state. Of course, the magnitude and duration of the sanctions and compensation must be reasonable and appropriate, and there should be a possibility for an appeal to the Gaian Court of Justice.

There are, of course, a number of organizational and procedural issues to be negotiated by the founding members and defined in the GC charter, and these details are beyond the scope of this work. For example, a democratic structure requires that there would be no veto rights, but what about the question of representation, e.g., should there be two chambers, one based on size, one independent of size, or perhaps one chamber with a weighting of votes? How many representatives should there be from each member state? What are the requirements for passage of new laws? What are the penalties for noncompliance? There is much to discuss.

The Gaian Resource Board

In Gaian society, the goal of ecological sustainability, together with the recognition of absolute scarcity in ecological economics, will require a completely new approach to the management of natural capital, particularly nonrenewable natural capital. No longer will it be acceptable for an individual nation to unilaterally control the use of its natural capital, as abuse could put the entire human race at risk. It will be necessary for all nations to cede a degree of sovereignty to a new international institution, which will have the mandate to administer resources in a way that is in the interest of the entire planet. For the sake of reference, let us call this seventh Gaian institution the Gaian Resource Board. There are three major subsets of natural capital management, each with its specific problems and solutions—nonrenewables (e.g., metals, fossil fuels), long-term renewables (e.g., forests, water aquifers, topsoil), and renewable resources (e.g., biomass, food).

Based on the principles of ecological economics and the laws of physics, the only way to be sure of achieving long-term sustainability for nonrenewable resources is to take a rationing approach, i.e., a specification of the maximum amount of the resource that can be used each year globally. Some critics of rationing may consider user taxes or voluntary guidelines as more attractive, less drastic approaches. But neither of these can guarantee that targets will be met. Only rationing can do that.

Recall from the second law of thermodynamics that the use of such limited resources is unidirectional, from low entropy (concentrated) to high entropy (dispersed and no longer useable). The rationing of such resources not only allows society to meet its sustainability target. In addition, the resulting higher prices will give the necessary incentive to the private sector to develop technologies that are both more efficient and more benign. Technological innovation, in particular a major shift in production technologies—e.g., from "cradle to grave" to "cradle to cradle," inspired by nature herself—will happen automatically once the higher prices are a reality.

It should be noted that it is not only metals and fossil fuels that must be managed, but also the sinks that absorb waste, such as rivers, lakes, oceans, and the biosphere, since these sinks are also limited capacity resources. The Resource Board would have the exclusive right to issue permissions to introduce nonrenewable resources into the global economy and to access resource sinks. The combination of a usage ceiling and permission trading is sometimes referred to as a "cap and trade" approach, while inclusion of the method of distribution is sometimes referred to as a "cap and share" approach. There are many variants of both.

The Wrong Approach

Unfortunately, the best-known implemented examples of "cap and trade"— the Kyoto Protocol and the EU emissions-trading system—have been poorly designed. A major problem with the Kyoto Protocol is the failure to account for the CO_2 content of imported goods. Clearly, it is the consumer and not the producer that should be charged with CO_2 emissions, but the Kyoto Protocol ignores this entirely. The bureaucratic and ineffective EU emissions-trading system was not really designed to solve global warming, but rather to make a modest start at a regional solution while satisfying the demands of powerful industrial polluters and financiers.

The hopelessness of the voluntary Kyoto approach was underscored by the International Energy Agency's latest report of May 2011, which states, "Energy-related carbon-dioxide (CO_2) emissions in 2010 were the highest in history," with 44% of the emissions from coal, 36% from oil, and 20% from natural gas.[1] The Kyoto Protocol is thus without any noticeable effect; by any objective measure it must be considered a failure.

There is just no political will in the Empire—the major polluter—to take the climate threat seriously. The chances of limiting the temperature rise to less than 2 degrees Celsius now look very bleak, especially as several major polluters (United States, Canada, Japan, and Russia), are now saying that they will not accept further commitments under the Kyoto Protocol beyond 2012 because China will not make a similar commitment.[2] This is completely ludicrous, as at least half of the Chinese emissions are for goods imported by the Empire and logically ought to be charged to it and not to China, which even including all emissions still has per capita emissions that are a small fraction of the industrialized states' emissions.

The result is that industrialized countries show CO_2 increases when they should be showing reductions. For example the United States, which promised a 7% reduction under Kyoto (but did not ratify) actually increased emissions in the period 1990–2008 by 25% when imports and exports are taken into account.[3] Other industrialized countries show the same pattern.

The Right Approach

Let me begin with defining what I think are the conditions to be fulfilled by an ideal rationing agreement. It should guarantee that the adopted target will be met with 100% certainty; it should be effective and cost-efficient; it should be equitable in order to get the backing of all 7 billion world citizens who are the ultimate owners of the resource; and it should be simple and transparent.

The Kyoto approach taken by the official UN climate negotiations *fails all four criteria*. And yet, three proposals have been put forward by the NGO community over the past four years that *fulfill all four criteria*! They are (1) the Earth Atmospheric Trust; (2) Kyoto2; and (3) the Carbon Board.[4] But they have been ignored by the political/economic establishment, and were not even on the table for discussion at the UN conferences in Copenhagen

(2009) and Cancun, Mexico (2010). While these three NGO proposals differ in minor aspects, they all fulfill the four conditions.

The same four conditions should apply to managing any nonrenewable resource, and the solutions are also similar. In all three CO_2 emissions proposals, the guarantee is fulfilled in the only way possible, by putting a global ceiling on the amount of the resource allowed to enter the economic system each year. Political promises and so-called binding targets are not good enough. Effectiveness and cost-efficiency is provided by a global auction among qualified, registered companies. An equitable solution is achieved by distributing the net revenues from the auction for the direct benefit of all 7 billion world citizens, and/or possibly for environmental mitigation projects. The three proposals differ here in the details, but all are equitable. Simplicity is guaranteed because the only political decision required is the annual ceiling, which is straightforward and based on science.

So why, if we have such obviously effective solutions to climate warming available, are they not on the table for discussion in the UN negotiations? During the Copenhagen conference I spoke to a colleague who was close to a number of the heads of delegations of several countries about these NGO proposals and why they were not being considered. The uniform answer from the negotiators was: "They are not politically feasible." Think about that for a moment! Not politically feasible? Does that mean that it is not politically feasible to save our civilization? Apparently, this is the case, because according to my colleague, the same negotiators admitted privately that the current Kyoto approach can never succeed in stopping runaway global warming. And they do not know what else to do.

Illustration: Fossil Fuels

I will illustrate the method with one of the three proposals, "The Carbon Board," which I published in November 2008 as my suggestion for the best way to solve the problem of global warming.[5] In the current world crisis, fossil fuels are important not only for long-term sustainability, but also because of the problems of global warming and imminent peak oil. But even if we had a much larger biosphere (and hence no immediate climate change problem) and much larger fossil fuel reserves (hence no immediate peak oil problem), we should still ration the use of this resource for the sake of future generations and long-term sustainability.

The first step is to establish a set of ceilings for the amount of CO_2 allowed to enter the global economy each year over a planning period of several years. For example, an initial level equal to the current level followed by annual declines by a fixed percentage each year. This gives industry time to adjust. These politically determined ceilings are assumed with all three approaches.

The second step assumes establishment of an international institution to manage the resource; for example, in the case of fossil fuels, it could be a division of the Gaian Resource Board designated as the Carbon Board. The Carbon Board auctions off the permissions to purchase fossil fuels, and hence to emit CO_2 into the biosphere, to the approved and registered private-sector companies that introduce fossil fuels into the global economy. The highest bidders will get the permissions. In every industry, those companies that are most innovative in reducing their CO_2 emissions will be most competitive in the bidding, gain market share, and increase profits. Those that cannot compete will disappear. In this way, the private sector will be working directly for the benefit of 7 billion world citizens, and not just for their shareholders, in a win-win scenario. The proposed method uses the private sector properly by putting a high price on CO_2 and allowing them to use their considerable ingenuity to solve the problem optimally and globally. There is no need for 190 sovereign nations to haggle for years about who pays what to whom, who reduces the most, who benefits, and who does not as in the dysfunctional ongoing negotiations. It is all taken care of by the private sector once the ceiling is set. There is no need for national emission targets, bureaucratic quota schemes, or intergovernmental negotiations. And there is no possibility for fraud or corruption as every single transaction has to go through an independent global agency similar to a central bank trading desk. Similar solutions can be implemented for all nonrenewable resources.

The Carbon Board and other such agencies could be set up by the Gaian League and offered to nonmembers as well as members, as the system is completely scalable up to the global level. Non-Gaian League members would have to adopt a sovereign-trade regime if they want to protect their domestic industries through tariffs on lower standard imports from countries not participating. They may have to leave the WTO unless the WTO makes an exception to the rules in this case.

More General Application

A natural extension of the above concept in Gaian society would be to price all internationally traded commodities in ecos. This will mean more stable prices, as the markets would avoid the effect today of currency fluctua-tions—especially the U.S. dollar—on commodity prices.

For renewable resources, similar solutions, restrictions, and appropriate prices must be established through negotiations at the GC level. The guiding principle is to limit the use of all resources, including waste sinks, to levels such that the ecosystem can regenerate renewable resources and absorb the wastes in a manner that is sustainable for an indefinite period. Some Gaian nations may choose an even more radical route than rationing oil and other resources. They may simply decide to leave the resource in the ground. Aside from the obvious quality-of-life value for future citizens, it could make a lot of economic sense also, because the price increases in a world of extreme scarcity may well be so large that the present value of the future asset in a world of scarcity is far greater than the extraction value today.

The Democratic Deficit

The Empire's institutions of global governance—the WTO/IMF/World Bank institutions—have been severely criticized by the antiglobalization move-ment for their lack of democratic accountability. This criticism is every bit as relevant for the proposed structure of the Gaian Congress, which is a legis-lature of government-appointed representatives. We have to assume that corruption, greed, and the desire to exploit will continue to be present to some extent at all levels of society for the foreseeable future, and we must deal with that. Perhaps, in the long run, corruption can be minimized as Gaian society becomes a more egalitarian society. This will be a natural consequence of the realization that the global economy is no longer growing, and resources must be shared, combined with the realization that greater equality means greater health, a more satisfied populace, and lower costs. The record of the Scandinavian countries, which have the least corruption and the greatest equality, is encouraging in this regard. However, in the short run, there is a substantial risk of a group of countries attempting to take effective control of the Gaian Congress with an agenda not in accordance with general planetary interests, in a "conspiracy against the public," as warned by Adam Smith. At the GC level, this could literally be disastrous for all of humanity. It could easily lead to a major international conflict and even global war.

Chapter 7 documented the way democracy has been hijacked by commer-cial interests in the United States—the very cradle of modern democracy. The United States' example was intended as a warning not to expect a body of state representatives in the Gaian Congress, nor any elected parliament for that matter, to necessarily act in the general interest. Winston Churchill is often quoted for the following: "It has been said that democracy is the worst form of government except all the others that have been tried." If this claim is true, then the time has come to go beyond democracy and attempt something that has not been tried before.

The Gaian Council

To counter the risk of the Gaian Congress getting hijacked by corruptible or power-hungry groups, or simply getting too far off the path toward sustainability, my suggested solution is to introduce a level of democratic global governance above the Gaian Congress, which, for the sake of reference I will call the Gaian Council, the eighth and final proposed Gaian institution, which we can think of as a council of wise elders.

The concept is for major regions of the planet to elect by popular vote—one from each region—a small council of incorruptible persons, who have demonstrated throughout their lives their dedication to the ideals of the Gaian paradigm and proven that their primary love is first and foremost for the entire planet, and not for any particular race, religion, culture, or geographical region. They should be incorruptible and no longer have any business interests or political position, and should have demonstrated high levels of integrity and ethical standards throughout their careers. Council members would have no agenda other than to serve all world citizens to the best of their abilities.

There are such persons. Every culture has them and knows who they are. They shall form the Gaian Council and have just one formal power, and that to be used sparingly—the power to veto or void any resolution passed by the Gaian Congress whenever they feel that things are moving in the wrong direction for the whole of humanity. Their major function would be to act as guardians of the entire planet, essentially protecting the interests of all of humanity, including the many minorities that are often victims of the tyranny of the majority, and giving direction to longer-term development. In addition, they could perform conflict-resolution services between nations when requested, and make suggestions to the Gaian Congress regarding future legislation. I would also recommend that Gaian Council approval should be necessary for every appointee to the Gaian Commission by the Gaian Congress, because of the importance of such positions for the entire planet.

The concept of such a council is not new. Many indigenous tribes bow to the decisions of the "elders" of their culture, who have a similar responsibility to keep the entire culture on the right track. The concept of a global council has been suggested by various groups in more recent times.

For example, Maurice Strong, former undersecretary of the UN and secretary-general of the UN Conference on Environment and Development in 1992, took the initiative to form an "Earth Council" to mobilize and support a network of citizen groups, NGOs, and other organizations committed to achieving the conference goals "to support and empower people in building a more secure, equitable, and sustainable future."[6] More than eighty regional Earth Councils have been set up since to monitor government compliance with commitments made to international agreements and facilitating partnerships for creative solutions to Agenda 21 issues. One of the major accomplishments of the Earth Council to date has been initiating the Earth Charter—a declaration of values, principles, and aspirations for a sustainable future shared by many individuals, groups, and countries. The Earth Charter was officially adopted in 2000 at the UNESCO Headquarters in Paris and articulates four guiding principles: respect for the Earth and each other; ecological integrity; social and economic justice; democracy, nonviolence, and peace.[7]

Another example is an initiative by Jakob von Uexkull, Swedish founder of the Right Livelihood Award, called the World Future Council, which brings the interests of future generations to the center of policy making and consists of fifty eminent members from around the globe. Founded as a charitable foundation in 2004, the council addresses challenges to our common future and provides decision makers with effective policy solutions. In-depth research underpins advocacy work for international agreements, regional policy frameworks, and national law making.[8]

More recently, in 2007, a group calling itself "The Elders" was constituted under the leadership of former South African president, Nelson Mandela.[9] While they have only an advisory role, and no formal powers, The Elders represent the type of people that would likely be elected in Gaian society. The Elders, including honorary and former members, include:

- *Desmond Tutu*, chairman of The Elders; he became the first black general secretary of the South African Council of Churches in 1979. In 1984, he was awarded the Nobel Peace Prize for his work in the struggle against apartheid. In 1986 he was elected Archbishop of Cape Town.

- *Nelson Mandela*, anti-apartheid activist, former elected leader of the ANC; .former president of South Africa, and winner of the Nobel Peace Prize in 1993.
- *Martti Ahtisaari*, former president of Finland, who, throughout his career, has been actively involved in conflict resolution, state building, and mediation; winner of the Nobel Peace Prize in 2008.
- *Kofi A. Annan* of Ghana, the seventh secretary-general of the United Nations, from 1997 to 2006 and the first to emerge from the ranks of United Nations staff; awarded the 2001 Nobel Peace Prize jointly with the United Nations.
- *Ela R. Bhatt*, widely recognized as one of the world's most remarkable pioneers and entrepreneurial forces in grassroots development. Known as the "gentle revolutionary," she has dedicated her life to improving the lives of India's poorest and most oppressed women workers, with Gandhian thinking as her source of guidance.
- *Lakhdar Brahimi*, Algeria, served his country as an ambassador, first to Egypt and then to the United Kingdom following Algeria's independence in 1962. He later served as foreign minister, and has led numerous UN missions. He lectures regularly on conflict resolution.
- *Gro Harlem Brundtland,* former prime minister of Norway and chair of the World Commission of Environment and Development (the Brundtland Commission) was director-general of the World Health Organization from 1998 to 2003. In March 2007, she was appointed as special envoy of the United Nations Secretary-General on Climate Change.
- *Fernando Henrique Cardoso* was president of Brazil from 1995 to 2002. He has a PhD in sociology and was a longtime professor of sociology and political science at the University of São Paulo, where he is now professor emeritus.
- *Jimmy Carter,* former president of the United States; his nonpartisan and nonprofit Carter Center works to advance peace and health worldwide. He was awarded the Nobel Peace Prize in 2002.
- *Graça Machel* is a renowned international advocate for women's and children's rights, and has been a social and political activist for decades. She was minister of education and

culture in Mozambique (1975–1989), and is today chancellor of the University of Cape Town, South Africa.

- *Mary Robinson* was the first woman president of Ireland (1990–1997) and former United Nations high commissioner for human rights (1997–2002); she has spent most of her life as a human rights advocate. She is honorary president of Oxfam International, and president of the International Commission of Jurists.
- *Aung San Suu Kyi* is one of the world's most renowned freedom fighters and advocates of nonviolence; she has been the figurehead for Burma's struggle for democracy since 1988.

Imagine for a moment what a different world it would be if such a council had existed in the past. For example, consider how a Gaian Council might have intervened to head off the invasion of Iraq in 2003, based on fabricated data and a dubious interpretation of a UN resolution in an aggression that the UN general-secretary declared was "illegal" and that was against the wishes of the great majority of world citizens, whose demonstrations in the streets across the planet were the biggest ever. Think of the unnecessary pain and suffering that could have been avoided.

Or take another example—the inability of the international community to act on global warming. A Gaian Council could suggest that the Gaian Congress urgently adopt a resolution to implement a climate solution that was in the public interest, such as one of the three proposals mentioned earlier that satisfy all the specified criteria, and thus possibly save humanity from destroying itself.

The exact number of members of the Gaian Council to be elected, their term, and the procedure for nomination and election must be negotiated by the founding members of the Gaian League, but it is important to maintain a procedure of popular election to give the Gaian regime democratic credibility. To avoid manipulation of the election procedure, I would suggest that all candidates for election would have to be screened and approved by a global committee of independent NGO activists in the fields of environmental protection and human rights.

I suspect that the establishment of such a council could well have an indirect effect that may in the long run be even more important than its formal powers, namely, the creation of new role models for the younger generation—a timely replacement for the billionaire hedge fund manager, the power-hungry politician, and the sexy film star, characteristic of the dying age.

The Gaian World Order

Figure 16.1 outlines the structure of a fully developed Gaian world order that hopefully would include all nations eventually. Initially, the structure can be the same, but for a much smaller membership. Fortunately, it is easily scalable. The initial, founding structure can be considered a prototype, a microcosm of the whole.

The time has now come to move beyond the vision of an ideal structure for a more just and sustainable world to the question of how we can realistically make the transition from the current society to the one envisioned.

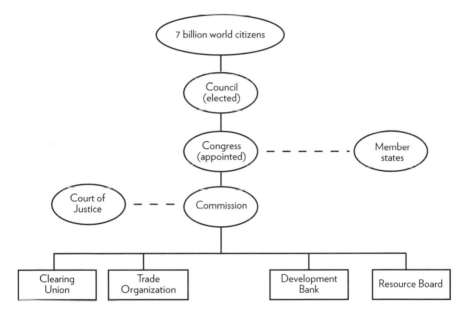

Figure 16.1. Gaian World Order.

PART SIX

Getting There

We must live together as brothers or perish together as fools.

—MARTIN LUTHER KING, JR.

SEVENTEEN

The Breakaway Strategy

Where there is no vision, the people perish.

—Proverbs 29:18

The Gaian world order is a realistic vision of the future that should be realizable in its full manifestation in the lifetimes of most of those living today if we really want it. The overarching principles of the Gaian civilization are ecological sustainability and human rights. These are what must be prioritized above everything else, before economic growth, before competiveness, before productivity, before everything. If the current generation establishes the embryonic beginnings of a new civilization based on just these two principles, then we will have laid the foundation not just for ourselves, our children, and grandchildren, but for all generations to come. No matter what the future may bring in technological progress or unexpected traumatic events, a dignified and just civilization will carry on.

The Gaian world order will not manifest all at once. It will involve a gradual process that in all likelihood will take many years to fully blossom. And the final form will undoubtedly differ from the rough outline in this book. But that is perfectly all right and is intended to be so. The best results will be achieved when as many people as possible contribute to the vision and the practical details of implementation. The greatest challenge facing us today is to plant the seed—to get the Gaian League off the ground so that it actually exists, can be seen, experienced, tested, criticized, and built upon, in the first instance as a prototype that can be modified, improved, and scaled up. This is also nature's way; start small and grow organically. There is a world of difference between an abstract vision and one that is on the ground and evolving.

The EU as Model

The closest I can come to a process similar to what I envisage for the Gaian League is the evolution of the European Union (EU), which went through several phases, gradually expanding the areas of cooperation and the membership. Today the EU has twenty-seven members and is still expanding. The original entity that later evolved into the EU of today was the European Coal and Steel Community, founded by only six countries in 1951 (France, Germany, Italy, Netherlands, Belgium, and Luxembourg) with the primary purpose of minimizing the chance of another European war by formally cooperating in two major industries, coal and steel. It took one year of negotiations to sign a treaty, including the establishment of four new institutions, and another year passed before it went into effect.

Seven years later, in 1958, after further extensive negotiations, the cooperation among the six countries was expanded to other economic sectors. The Treaty of Rome established new institutions (council, commission, and parliament) and created the European Economic Community (EEC) or "common market." The idea was for people, goods, services, and capital to move freely across borders without internal tariffs, but with common external tariffs. A twelve-year period of implementation was planned.

A number of amendments were made to the Treaty of Rome over the years, extending powers, modifying decision-making rules, and admitting new members. The major one was the Treaty on European Union in 1992 that extended and formalized cooperation in the areas of foreign policy, defense, police, and justice together under one umbrella, the European Union.

While the EU project has goals very different from the Gaian League project, the EU experience underscores the complexity of decision making and the time that can be required in negotiating and implementing international agreements among sovereign states. However, there are key differences between the two projects that should allow the Gaian League to evolve more quickly. One is the much more limited surrender of sovereignty, being limited to environmental protection and human rights. A second is the recommended absence of vetoes in the Gaian Congress, rather than the original EU model that required unanimity in all important decisions, later relaxed to a limited extent. A third difference is the existential need to react to the coming crisis of energy descent, negative growth, unemployment, and a continued deterioration of the environment. Citizens are going to demand radical action from their leaders. As the world we know begins to crumble, a functioning Gaian League may well become the stable center upon which to rebuild.

Taking the Initiative

Who can take the initiative? It can be taken as a given that the ruling elites of the United States and its closest allies who control the Empire have no interest in changing the status quo. Indeed, they may oppose the Gaian League initiative, although they will be on shaky ground if they do, if one-third of their citizens—the Cultural Creatives—actively support it, which I suspect they will.

What about the grass roots and thousands of NGOs around the world? Could they do it? We know from the ongoing demonstrations in the streets across the world that there are millions, if not billions, of people in every country and in every walk of life who would support an initiative to form the Gaian League or to have their country join such a league once it was a reality, simply because they are fed up with a world order that is not working for the great majority. Many potential supporters are found in the thousands of NGOs that promote a wide range of themes consistent with the Gaian vision. But many are also found in academic circles, in governments, in the business world, and, not least, among ordinary citizens. They are everywhere; not least in the most powerful states, such as the United States, Japan, and the EU. These Cultural Creatives are a minority, but a large minority, and they now constitute about 35% of the population in the West according to Paul Ray.

Could these minorities be effectively mobilized to take the initiative? Can civil society muster the necessary will and organizational ability to bring about real change in the face of resistance from the ruling elite? Dozens of authors, both from the ranks of Western intellectuals and from the NGO community, have in recent years deplored the current state of world affairs, written inspiring visions of a better world, and documented the unsustainability of our current path. Almost all conclude with an appeal to civil society to wake up to the dangers of passivity, to be active in their communities, to write to their congressmen, to take political action, to demonstrate in the streets, to start with themselves, to prepare for transition, to work for change within the NGO community, and so on. But none, to my knowledge, has yet put forward a plan of action that has any chance of creating real global change in the face of resistance from the Empire.

One problem is that those citizens who wish to change the status quo are fragmented into thousands of initiatives that are notoriously independent even though they have similar values. A second is that no single NGO has the resources to actually create a realistic alternative. The one area where civil society has had success in bringing about radical change is massive demonstrations in the streets where a particular well-defined objective was local, easily communicated, and doable. We saw this recently in Tunisia and Egypt, where the goal in both cases was simple and unifying: throw out the dictator. Another recent example was the Orange revolution in Ukraine. But there are other examples of failure: some of the largest demonstrations that the world has ever seen were the worldwide, coordinated, simultaneous protests in dozens of cities against the Empire's invasion of Iraq in 2003. The goal was simple and easily communicated. But the Empire had no trouble ignoring public opinion and carrying on with its plan as if nothing had happened. Why? *Because the goal was not local.* There are two lessons to be learned here that can be useful to tomorrow's street activists. Number one: civil society cannot do it alone. It needs allies. Number two: to be successful, demonstrations in the street must have a doable local objective that cannot be ignored. The basic dilemma facing us seems to be: those who can, will not; those who will, cannot.

The Small-State Alternative

But there is a third possibility, and it is the basis of my recommended strategy, namely, that the Gaian League be established and expanded by cooperation between top-down and bottom-up agents of change—a handful of small nations from the top and the grass roots of the world from the bottom. The top-down component involves a group of less than ten small nations that takes on the leadership responsibility by formally founding the Gaian League, with all its eight institutions—the Gaian Council, the Gaian Congress, the Gaian Commission, the Gaian Court of Justice, the Gaian Clearing Union, the Gaian Trade Organization, the Gaian Development Bank, and the Gaian Resource Board—as an alternative to the Empire, initially as a small prototype, but scalable. Once established, other nations will be invited to apply for membership. An initiative by a small number of sovereign states to form a new organization with an idealistic global motivation, while inviting others to join, will be a major world event that cannot be ignored. It is orders of magnitude more powerful than any conceivable action by civil society. And yet it can probably only succeed, in the face of Empire opposition, with massive support from civil society, not least from those within the Empire. This is the basic logic of the strategy.

The first action the founders must take—once the negotiating and paper work has been done—is to formally break away from the bondage of the Empire by leaving the WTO (with six months' notice); hence the name, "breakaway strategy." The founding nations do not have to leave the IMF, the World Bank, or the UN, as all relationships with these organizations are voluntary, and may continue to be useful, at least for the time being. The same is true of organizations of regional cooperation, provided only that there are no conflicts with the capital-controls/sovereign-state currency and trade regimes, as there would be in the EU, for example. The WTO is different because it involves compulsory arbitration of conflicts and a transfer of sovereignty that must be taken back if Gaian League members are to be self-determining and in charge of their own economies and cultural heritage. In practice, this first step is not as dramatic as it may appear at first glance. Trading patterns will not change overnight, but existing trade agreements will have to be renegotiated eventually. A transition period for compliance with the new rules will, of course, be necessary, just as it was for the EU project.

The bottom-up component comes into play later in the process and is the pressure coming from below by NGOs and ordinary citizens—the Cultural Creatives of this world, on the political leaders of nonmember nations once the Gaian League has been formally launched and is functioning. The key to success is the demonstrators in the streets, whose argument from below is simple and powerful: "The Gaian League represents everything we claim to stand for: freedom, justice, equality, democracy, human rights, self-determination, and a sustainable future for our children and grandchildren. WHY ARE WE NOT MEMBERS?" The argument is irrefutable. The objective is simple and easily communicated. And most important of all: the demonstrations in the streets will have a *local* objective—a binding *national referendum* on joining the Gaian League. And they should camp out until their demand is met.

If the initiative is launched properly, it should receive the support of a majority of world citizens, in some cases in opposition to their elected leaders. Grassroots support is critical. In time, other nations will join, contribute to the vision, and help to move the world in the direction of a truly sustainable and just global society. But to be convincing, it is absolutely essential that the founders present the Gaian League to the world as a prototype of a proposed global structure that is in the interest of *all* world citizens and that can be scaled up as required. *If it should degrade into just another international organization to promote and protect the interests of the founders, then the project will fail.* The founders must emphasize that the Gaian institutions are designed to meet the needs of a global civilization whose goals are sustainability, self-determination, democracy, and justice, and that all nations are invited to join when the time is right.

I believe a group of smaller nations working together has the best chance of success, because they have fewer ambitions and national agendas that could create resistance, as might be the case if one of the major powers, or even a major developing country were among the founders. And, of course, the small number makes negotiations much easier.

Founder Composition

Ideally, the founder states should represent the universal nature of the project, with a diversity of geographical regions, state of development, race, religion, and culture. They should have in common the will to take the lead as we shift from an unsustainable lifestyle toward an ecologically sustainable and just future. Ideally, the group should include both developing countries and at least one or two of the smaller industrialized countries. If possible, a significant oil-producing country would be a big asset for two reasons: to illustrate the principle of Resource Board rationing of fossil fuels and to illustrate the functioning of the Gaian Clearing Union for nonmembers who want to buy oil. Having some member states with significant raw-material resources would also be a big plus, in order to demonstrate the shift to value-added production for developing countries. Trade within the group will increase and external trade decrease on account of the shift to import substitution and external tariffs. Considering the possible risk of Empire resistance, it would be desirable if the initial group as a whole could constitute an economically viable entity that could manage with a minimum of imports from nonmembers if absolutely necessary. Hopefully, that will not be the case, and trade patterns will only change slowly.

In what follows, I will outline briefly how I could imagine the various phases in the evolution of the Gaian League. This will very likely be modified in practice once many people are involved and new ideas emerge.

Phase I: Dialogue

The first step is to establish a preliminary dialogue among a small number of potential candidate states that are willing to look into the idea more closely without necessarily making a commitment. At some stage, the hope is that one or two key national leaders will commit to the project, take on the leadership role, and personally invite other states to join in the dialogue. A charismatic state leader at this stage could make all the difference. A conference with invited participants would be a natural next step, resulting in the establishment of working groups on various aspects of the structure. The phase leading to the first conference could easily take one to two years.

Draft charters for the Gaian institutions will thereafter be developed and circulated for comment by the working groups. In time, probably an additional one to two years, a second conference will be called to adopt the charters, subject to ratification and approval by popular referendum in each participating country. A referendum is important both to stimulate debate about the whole project, to ensure citizen backing, and for dissemination of the goals of the project to the rest of the world.

Who Might Take the Lead?

It is pure speculation to guess from where a positive response to the breakaway strategy might come. There may be some surprises in store. Countries that might be interested are probably disillusioned with the consequences of the "free market" model on their economies, and are willing to try something radically different, especially if it means greater autonomy. They will also typically be interested in giving sustainability and human rights a higher political priority than further uneconomic growth, their major goal being the increasing well-being of all world citizens. Taking the lead on a project that is undertaken for the benefit of the entire global society can be an energizing, inspiring, meaningful, and rewarding experience for the participants, in spite of the unavoidable hardships, and in this challenge the initiating governments and their citizens will find an attractive and satisfying way to harness their collective energies in the service of a positive vision for the future.

Changing the economic, trade, and currency regime is going to affect almost everything in the founders' societies. However, the decision to join may be easier if they realize that radical change is coming to the entire globe in any case, and may well be far worse for those countries that choose to continue on a "business as usual" track until the growth bubble "suddenly" bursts and they discover how unprepared they are.

The EU is a special case, which demands comment. Sustainability and human rights are highly profiled values in the EU vision. Furthermore, the EU already has an established practice of issuing environmental directives to member states, similar to that envisaged for the Gaian League. In addition, the

EU members have a long tradition of democracy, intergovernmental institutions, and cooperation with the developing countries. Some of the EU countries, especially in the north, are among those that come closest to the Gaian ideal. I suspect that a majority of EU citizens would be enthusiastic about the idea of the EU taking on a new vision, namely, leadership of Gaian League on behalf of all humanity. At first glance, then, the EU would seem to be a natural core from which the Gaian vision could spring. But there is a problem.

The EU continues to promote economic growth and greater consumption as the major objective of every member state, even though such policies have been shown to be unsustainable. In other words, the EU is following a schizophrenic path. The two objectives—economic growth and sustainability—are mutually exclusive. Further growth and greater consumption will undermine and completely negate the goal of a sustainable future. The EU is going to have to decide on which side of history it will stand in the coming years. Will it continue to support the crumbling Empire built on a fantasy of unending growth or will it choose to support, or, even better, lead, the planet toward a seriously sustainable future?

If the EU chooses to continue on its current path, then the question arises whether some individual members might see their way to joining the Gaian League. Some countries, which ought to be ideal candidates based on their promotion of human rights, ecology, and democracy—Denmark, Sweden, Finland, and the Netherlands—are unfortunately hindered in joining because the EU does not allow member countries to implement a sovereign-trade regime or a capital-controls currency regime. In other words, they would have to leave the EU as well as the WTO—a really major hurdle. However, it is not out of the question, especially if the political leadership moves toward a centralized "United States of Europe" as a response to the eurozone crisis. Joining the Gaian League would allow them to return to their traditional cultural roots while in full control of their economies and priorities, while continuing to cooperate in the areas of environmental protection and human rights. Is this not a nobler vision than continuing on a path of uneconomic growth and overconsumption that is coming to an end in any case very soon?

The EU has served a useful historic purpose in bringing peace among states, which have been at war with each other for centuries, but perhaps the time has come to consider that goal as achieved and adopt a new, more appropriate vision for the twenty-first century based on sustainability, greater equality, and more local democracy, all of which require a reversal of current trends within the EU.

If the Gaian League is founded by other states, it is my hope that my adopted country, Denmark, will show leadership by leaving the EU and joining the Gaian League along with the other Nordic countries, while cutting its bonds to the euro. Such a move would be a strong signal for other countries to do the same, both within the EU and without. But my first preference would be for the EU to announce that it is dropping the pursuit of further economic growth and instead is leaving the WTO collectively and putting its full weight behind a single long-term goal—to lead the international community toward a sustainable and just future for all based on the Gaian vision. If the EU took the lead, I am sure many countries would quickly follow suit and the momentum would be unstoppable.

The following are some of the countries—in no particular order—where I can imagine there could well be some interest in taking the initiative in founding the Gaian League.

Bolivia

This land-locked, rather poor, socialist country has enormous resources, including the second largest natural gas reserves in South America, as well as substantial tin and massive lithium reserves. Bolivia is one of the few countries led by a native Indian—Evo Morales, who fought to free his country from the exploitation of foreign commercial interests. He nationalized all natural gas reserves and successfully renegotiated all foreign contracts with a higher tax income coming to the state. Morales also fought for and won a new constitution giving more power to the indigenous majority. The large number of different cultures within Bolivia has contributed greatly to a wide diversity in fields such as art, cuisine, literature, and music. As a member of ALBA, Bolivia is aligned with Gaian values.

Sri Lanka

This multiethnic, multireligious country is 70% Buddhist, very tolerant, and a socialist democracy. It is a fiercely independent developing country whose government has adopted a main theme of supporting rural and suburban small and medium enterprises, much in line with Gaian values and the coming need to decentralize. It also seeks to protect the domestic economy from external influences, such as oil prices, the World Bank, and the International Monetary Fund, also in keeping with the goals of the breakaway strategy. Sri Lanka has one of the most successful village networks anywhere in the South—the fifty-year-old Buddhist-based Sarvodaya—creating jobs and pleasant surroundings in 15,000 villages, thus slowing down the flight to the big city slums, and reestablishing pride in the people of the rural areas.

Costa Rica

In 2007 the Costa Rican government announced plans for this developing country to become the first carbon-neutral country by 2021. According to the New Economics Foundation, Costa Rica ranks first in the "Happy Planet Index" and is the "greenest" country in the world. The country is recognized as one of the few with true eco-tourism. Costa Rica has been cited by the UNDP as one of the countries that has attained much higher human development than other countries at the same income levels. Costa Rica has also developed a system of payments for environmental services. A main foreign-policy objective of Costa Rica is to foster human rights and sustainable development as a way to secure stability and grow through renewable sources, and is currently producing 90 percent of its electricity through renewable sources.

Iceland

This small but progressive island state was ranked number one on the UN's Human Development Index in 2009 and has a quite high standard of living. While it has applied for EU membership, joining is subject to a referendum, and there is much resistance due to fears of EU encroachment on Iceland's very important fishing industry. Iceland, with its substantial geothermal and hydroelectric energy resources, has the declared goal of becoming the first fossil-fuel-free country. This mainly Christian country has its own currency and an independent foreign policy.

Norway

As one of the two Nordic countries outside of the EU, and one of the world's wealthiest countries, Norway has an independent streak and a global consciousness that could make it a most interesting and valuable member of the Gaian League. Norway places a high priority on human rights as well as environmental protection, placing second in the 2008 Environmental Performance Index. As the third-largest net oil exporter, Norway could be a key player in bringing about key Gaian strategies, including the Clearing Union and the Carbon Board, with a really effective global CO_2 reduction program, possibly in cooperation with Venezuela, if both were members.

Venezuela

This important country has the longest record of uninterrupted democracy in South America—since 1958—and is the largest country in the candidate list at 29 million. Venezuela is dependent on oil, being the sixth-largest oil exporter and having some of the most extensive reserves of both conventional and nonconventional oil, and is a founding member of OPEC. Also a founding member of ALBA, Venezuela has made a great effort to free itself from IMF loans, is opposed to any North American free-trade zone, and prioritizes the well-being of its citizens above foreign and domestic commercial interests, all of which policies are in line with Gaian values.

Senegal

Senegal is one of the most advanced African states in information technology, and ranks fourteenth out of fifty-three on the 2010 Ibrahim Index of African Governance.[1] It is 90% Islam and 10% Christian, with close cultural ties to France. India is a major trading partner. Senegal has been somewhat disillusioned with the Western development model, and is trying to revitalize its rural communities. Senegal is a member of the West African Economic and Monetary Union with a common currency, the CFA franc, pegged to the euro. The fifteen-member union is working toward greater regional integration with a unified external tariff.

Bhutan

This primarily agricultural nation, with close economic ties to India and cultural ties to Tibet, is the only state on the candidate list that is not a member of the WTO, although it is considering applying. It is also the only state that measures the progress of its citizens on the basis of "Gross National Happiness" rather than GDP, demonstrating a high regard for personal well-being. Bhutan is primarily Buddhist, but exercises freedom of religion. The democratic state is increasingly making efforts to preserve and sustain the current culture and traditions of the country. Because of its largely unspoiled natural environment and cultural heritage, Bhutan has been referred to as "the Last Shangri-La."

New Zealand

Being a Western-oriented, prosperous, and developed market economy, New Zealand differs from many other developed economies in its widely recognized negative experience with neoliberal economics. Therefore it may well be ready to enter a new phase based on a much greater deal of self-determination and self-sufficiency and less dependence on "free trade," foreign investment, and foreign loans. With its considerable natural resources, high-quality institutions, and democratic traditions, New Zealand is well situated to take the lead in the movement toward a more sustainable and people-centered civilization.

Maldives

This low-lying island nation in the Indian Ocean attracted world attention during the Copenhagen Climate Summit in 2009, when President Mohamed Nasheed eloquently appealed to the industrialized countries to adopt an effective CO_2 reduction program as most of the Maldives would disappear beneath the waves if the sea rises by two meters. They would certainly support a project such as the Carbon Board. The major industries of this presidential republic are tourism and fishing. The Maldives has its own currency, and Islam is the official religion.

Tunisia

This North African state is formally a democratic republic that in 2009 was ranked the most competitive economy in Africa and the fortieth in the world by the World Economic Forum. After the 2011 revolt against the oppressive regime of Ben Ali, the future is open. Human rights and lack of democratic rule were highly criticized by the international NGO community, as well as by the successful 2011 revolutionaries, so the criticized policies are likely to be reversed. While the state religion is Islam, the country has a secular culture that encourages acceptance of other religions and religious freedom. Tunisia was ranked eighth out of fifty-three countries in the 2010 Ibrahim Index of African Governance.

Mauritius

The democratic republic of Mauritius earned the highest rank for "participation and human rights" and "sustainable economic opportunity," as well as earning the highest score in the overall Ibrahim Index of African Governance in 2010. Mauritius has followed a so-called dual-track approach to development, with equal focus on economic and human development. In religious terms, Hindus make up 52%, Christians 36%, and the rest are mostly Muslims. This developing country has close ties to France and India, and has the sixth-highest GDP per capita in Africa. The economy is mainly dependent on sugarcane plantations, tourism, textiles, and services.

Malaysia

A major component of Malaysia's government policy is national sovereignty and the right of a country to control its domestic affairs. Malaysia is a relatively open, state-oriented, and newly industrialized market economy. The state plays a significant but declining role in guiding economic activity through macroeconomic plans. Malaysia is a multiethnic, multicultural, and multilingual society. The Malaysian constitution guarantees freedom of religion and makes Islam the state religion; 60% of the population practices Islam; 19% Buddhism; 9% Christianity; 6% Hinduism; and the remainder Confucianism, Taoism, and other traditional Chinese religions. Substantial minority influence exists from Chinese and Indian culture. The country only has thirty-three years of natural gas reserves, and nineteen years of oil reserves, while the demand for energy is increasing. Because of this, the government is very aware of the need for switching to renewable energy sources.

Switzerland

This very wealthy European federal republic that prefers to remain outside the EU has a long history of independence, cultural integration, and decentralized local democracy, including frequent national referenda that can overturn parliamentary resolutions. A primarily Christian country, human rights and environmental protection are high on the list of Swiss priorities. Switzerland has implemented a form of protectionism in agriculture—a rare exception to Switzerland's free-trade policies. Being a wealthy country with a major world currency, Switzerland could be a powerful partner for the developing country members. The Swiss are a dark-horse candidate, having much in common with the Gaian vision, but also very tied into the ruling international elites.

Country	Population (mil)	GDP[1] ($ bil)	Trade Surplus[2] ($ mil)	Official Reserves[3] ($ bil)
Bolivia	10	23	690	10
Venezuela	29	294	22,070	33
Costa Rica	5	40	-1,349	5
Norway	5	479	60,230	53
New Zealand	4	153	-4,504	18
Tunisia	10	47	-1,389	11
Senegal	12	14	-1,046	2
Sri Lanka	21	58	-1,784	6
Bhutan	1	2	164	0
TOTALS	97	1,110	73,082	134

1. See en.wikipedia.org/wiki/List_of_countries_by_future_GDP_(nominal)_estimates.
2. See www.cia.gov/library/publications/the-world-factbook/rankorder/2187rank.htm.l.
3. See en.wikipedia.org/wiki/List_of_countries_by_foreign_exchange_reserves.

Table 17.1. One Gaian League Possibility.

An Example

To get a rough idea of what a combination of nine states from the above list with a good geographical and development spread might look like, table 17.1 summarizes a few statistics for just one possibility.

While the initial economic size is not important, it is quite possible that the Gaian League as a whole could quickly become the equivalent of a medium-sized country—in the example: 12th in population; 16th in GDP; 4th in trade surplus; and 11th in foreign-exchange reserves.

Phase II: The Founding

The founding charter of the Gaian League will presumably include the simultaneous founding of the eight institutions, although it may not include all from day one. In any case, there are a number of issues to consider for each institution. The charter of the Gaian Congress should be relatively straightforward, but will require some extensive committee work. There are a number of issues surrounding organization, voting rules, and membership rights and responsibilities to be negotiated. A related task is agreement on the resolutions that will establish the initial set of international laws that will apply to league members. Many of these can be adopted verbatim from various UN resolutions and international treaties. Others, particularly concerning overall goals and policies, such as sustainability, self-determination, and the adoption of ecological economics, capital controls, and sovereign-trade regimes, will no doubt be original.

Gaian Court of Justice

Member nations must be willing to resolve internal conflicts by presenting their cases to the Gaian Court of Justice, and to accept the court's decision as binding, including the use of the Economic Sanctions Protocol in cases of noncompliance. The latter will require some negotiations to define in more detail. The founders may want to allow for an appeal to the Gaian Council in some cases, provided that the council accepts the appeal as of principal nature. Alternatively, in some cases, members could ask the Gaian Council to undertake a binding or nonbinding mediation. League members will continue to be members of the UN's International Court of Justice (ICJ), which will continue to handle cases involving any conflicts between members and nonmembers of the league. The league should agree to accept ICJ decrees as binding as a matter of principle. In the long run, if and when league membership is broad enough, it may no longer be necessary to have two courts.

The Gaian Resource Board

This institution will not be able to function fully from the beginning. Resource rationing, especially as concerns metals, is controversial, requiring extensive negotiations among key players. Speaking realistically, it is not likely to come into effect before some of the nations with major resources have joined the league and are on board with the concept. However, the groundwork and principles can be developed, and the first resource rationed as an example.

In particular, a Carbon Board, or a similar-type institution, should have a high priority. Introducing a high price on CO_2 emissions is critical, not only for combating global warming, but also to provide incentives for the private sector to develop new low-carbon technologies. A small agency could function even with a limited initial membership, by applying the same principles to league members as would apply in a global agreement, with CO_2 targets simply scaled down proportionately based on the level of current CO_2 emissions among league members and global totals. The mechanics of the auction of CO_2 permissions and subsequent trading could be implemented as described earlier. This will make it quite easy for other states to take part quickly in the program. Nonmembers of the league should be encouraged to join the Carbon Board, or whatever it may be called. Because of the urgency of tackling global warming effectively as soon as possible, this initiative could even be launched before the Gaian League is founded, as league membership is not a condition for participating.

Primary fossil-fuel producers in the league should agree to cut back their production in proportion to the necessary global descent plan (e.g., 3% per annum), and only sell their oil and natural gas to nonmembers with a surcharge over world prices corresponding to the cost of permissions for Gaian League members, thus leveling the playing field. Some nonmember countries may actually be quite willing to pay a surcharge on Gaian League oil as an alternative to paying for a CO_2 quota at home, e.g., an EU country still operating under the EU quota system. The income from the nonmember surcharge should naturally go into the permissions pool for distribution to all league citizens. States that are not participating in the Carbon Board and are not following comparable CO_2-emissions-reduction programs will have to face price-leveling tariffs on their exports to league members if they want to do business. Any such tariff revenues should also be contributed to the permissions pool.

Gaian Clearing Union

Even with a small initial membership, the GCU structure can be put into effect, i.e., settling all trade debts with ecos, setting up the Ecofund, and abiding by the rules that are negotiated based on the draft framework described earlier. Internal league trade should progress smoothly, and will in all likelihood increase. There may be problems with settling trade debts with some obstinate nonmembers if they refuse to establish an eco credit account with the GCU and try to pressure league members to settle international trade with national currencies directly. In such cases, league members should try to avoid deviations from the GCU rules for nonmembers. They should have no major problem finding other trading partners in such cases. Those countries who want to sell their products to league members or import from league members will have to establish an eco trade account or see league business go elsewhere. It will simply make business sense for them to establish an account. The Ecofund will no doubt be small initially, but the principle will be established.

The Gaian Trade Organization (GTO)

The GTO charter will be far simpler than either the original GATT charter or the WTO rules and regulations. Both of those organizations were focused on reducing and equalizing tariffs, which led to very complicated and voluminous rules. In the GTO, each member country reserves the right to declare whatever tariffs, restrictions, or bans on imports that its national policies require within the directives laid down by the commission to achieve sustainability and protect human rights, so there will be few general rules.

Bilateral or multilateral agreements will eventually be negotiated with each trading partner, and the rules may vary widely for different partners. It would be natural for the founding league members to have "most favored nation" status with each other. It would also be natural, in order to simplify trade restrictions, for the league to develop a logo of environmental approval for different product categories, similar to the practice in several European countries for organic foods and organic cosmetics. Similar approval logos could be developed for other product categories, e.g., electronic products, toys, plastics, vehicles, household appliances, and so on. Criteria might include energy use in production, degree of recycling, biodegradability, nonpresence of heavy metals, GMOs, and undesired additives, for example. In a few cases, otherwise banned products may be admitted in limited quantities, but only for specified and controlled purposes, e.g., for use in medicinal applications.

In this connection, UK global justice author George Monbiot has put forward a proposal for what he calls a "Fair Trade Organization," which has some similarities to the GTO.[2] One of his suggestions in particular that I would recommend for the GTO is the concept of qualifying foreign corporations as potential importers to or direct investors in member states. To qualify, importers would have to live up to the standards specified by the league, for example, show that their product prices reflect all the costs that today are normally externalized in particular environmental costs (e.g., no felling of rainforests or dumping of dangerous chemicals) and social policies (e.g., no slave labor or underpaid sweatshops), and that they are not "dumping" at artificially low prices due to subsidies. Entire countries might eventually be awarded a qualification. Such a qualification policy, if generally adopted, would encourage corporations to develop more benign products, quite the opposite of what the WTO encourages. But, in the last analysis, it will always be up to each individual member to determine what products or investors it will admit at its sole discretion. Thus, qualification would be a necessary but not a sufficient condition for entry. For example, a particular member country may have a major focus on the precautionary principle and not allow anything in that is not on its positive list of approved products. Or it may cite cultural integrity or food security reasons for rejection.

The GTO will undoubtedly lead to less international trade, which traditional economists may see as a step backwards. But trade is not sacred. More of it is not necessarily a good thing, especially when there is no control over the environmental damage caused by production technologies, when growth is uneconomic, or when the same products are imported and exported, as is quite common today. The GTO will reduce the ability of many transnational companies to sell their products, but will increase the ability of more environmentally friendly domestic companies to do so, while increasing the freedom of sovereign peoples to determine what companies they will allow into their country, what products they want in their stores, and, more generally, what kind of society they want for themselves.

In many bilateral trade negotiations, members may well find that barter agreements with nonmembers provide the most efficient way to maintain export markets in the initial period when exports are less competitive than nonmembers' exports on account of higher CO_2 emission costs. Quid pro quo deals can be made with selective trading partners who will accept the member's exports in return for import preferences and thus greater market share on the imported goods that the member needs in a win-win trade. In this way imports and exports can be kept in balance and contribute to a sound economy. In time, energy costs will be reduced, driven by the incentive to save on CO_2 emission costs by developing more appropriate technologies. Exports will eventually be quite competitive and even be on the leading edge of green technologies. Nonmember countries that are not subject to the same pressures will risk finding themselves priced out of the market and far behind in technological development as resource prices increase relentlessly.

Gaian Council

It would be premature to think about elections to a Gaian Council before the league membership grows, not least geographically. Nevertheless, an initial Gaian Council should be established by appointment by the founding nations until elections are realistic. A good starting point for candidates would be the global institutions mentioned in chapter 16—the Earth Council, the World Futures Council and the Elders. Indeed, I would recommend that the founders invite each of these organizations to advise them on the charters of the various Gaian institutions. It would add credibility to the launch if these three organizations gave the project their blessings.

Gaian Development Bank

This is one institution that may have to wait until one or two major developing countries sign on, because a vital part of the concept is the pooling of central bank reserves to finance the founding of the bank. However, the groundwork can be laid, including a charter and a description of goals and policies.

Phase III: Expansion

Because of the desirability of a good geographical spread, the founding members are likely to be quite distant from one another and not major trading partners. Most trade, after all, is normally with close neighbors. This is a definite weakness in the beginning. Once the formalities are established, the next logical step will be to accept additional members, and these are likely to be major trading partners of the founders. Most countries are members of some regional groupings. For example, if Bolivia or Venezuela were among the founders, some of the other ALBA members might well join. If Senegal were a founding member, other states of the fifteen-member West African Economic and Monetary Union might like to join, and so on. From this point on, it becomes more and more difficult to foresee how things might develop. However, if all goes well, there is likely to be considerable interest, for example from the many developing countries in the Group of 77 that are dissatisfied with the domination of the Empire. If the league gets this far, it could well become an unstoppable dynamo with a life of its own.

The structure of the Gaian League allows for considerable flexibility in entering various forms of "associative" status for nonmembers. Three of the institutions—the Clearing Union, the Resource Board, and the Development Bank—do not require membership of the league to participate. This might be very attractive for some countries, especially some of the major ones. For example, China would not be likely to accept directives on human rights from the Gaian League, which membership would require, but may well be interested in joining the Gaian Clearing Union to promote an alternative to the dollar, the Carbon Board to promote the shift to renewable energy and earn enormous goodwill internationally, and the Gaian Development Bank to further its relationships with other developing countries. An associative status could be a useful path for many countries that wish to "test the waters" before making a full commitment. This is a path that the EU has used as well.

The Issue of Democracy

There can be no doubt that democracy is central to the Gaian vision. As far as the Gaian Congress is concerned, I am assuming that decisions will be made democratically, i.e., without veto rights and with reasonable rules for weighting votes and defining a qualified majority. But should "democracy" be a condition for membership in the Gaian League? It may be necessary to distinguish between the short term and the long term. The very nature of the Gaian worldview is the concept of inclusiveness—one large family. The idea of excluding some nation, for whatever reason, would not be consistent with this worldview, unless, perhaps, it was a temporary measure, while some issue was resolved. Furthermore, the goal of global sustainability—the overriding objective—requires that all states cooperate. These two considerations suggest that democracy should not be a condition. The United Nations is based on the same principle. Further support for this position is the avoidance of the problem of determining if a given country is truly a "democracy." As we saw in chapter 7 on the United States, there are many aspects to consider and no simple definition of the term. Perhaps the best way to extend true democracy to all peoples is to do it gradually, be a good example, and keep talking, trading, and promoting cultural exchange.

However, while democracy should not be a condition of membership in a fully developed and inclusive global Gaian regime, I think it is important that the founders are all indisputable democracies in order to create the greatest possible goodwill in the beginning.

Small Is Beautiful

If, at some point, the league becomes a significant and successful entity, with many small diverse states enjoying the luxury of being in control of their own resources and culture for the first time, it might well be tempting for bioregions or cultural regions of the larger states to consider seceding and joining the league in order to obtain for themselves the benefits of self-determination and cultural integrity. If so, this could be a major step toward a more stable and peaceful global society with a multitude of small states focused more on cooperation than on competition.

Figure 17.1 Europe as a Community of Small States.

Leopold Kohr points out that the key to a successful and peaceful federation such as Switzerland is that no members are so much larger than the others that they expect special treatment. This is a very important point. Whenever a few large states exist among several small ones, the chances of war grow immensely. In a world of only small states, war might well become obsolete, as no single state would have the means to force itself upon others against the wishes of the overwhelming majority. The very essence of democracy is that all members are equal, which is difficult in practice if some nations are very large and others very small. Indeed, the Gaian League might at some point in the distant future comprise mainly what are today smaller regions of the "great powers." For example, figure 17.1 shows Kohr's version of how Europe might eventually be split up into many small sovereign states based primarily on cultural boundaries.[3]

Civil Society Actions

As the league begins to expand, the bottom-up part of the breakaway strategy can manifest, as the grass roots of each nonmember country organize and put pressure on their political leaders to join the league and become part of the solution rather than part of the problem. This phase is critical and essential in order for the project to maintain momentum. Civil society will have a very powerful argument here that will be difficult for the establishment to counter because the grass roots can join together in the state capital and make a simple, reasonable, and doable demand for *local* action: a *binding referendum on joining the Gaian League*! And they should not leave until their demand is fulfilled, following the examples of Tunisia and Egypt. The breakaway strategy may well be the first operational strategy that can unite all the NGOs and ordinary citizens of the world behind a single proposal that has the potential to satisfy all of their different advocacy issues.

Conclusion

Humankind stands at a dangerous crossroads. In the worst case—if an irreversible global warming manifests, we may not survive. Even if this worst case does not materialize, we face a series of other threats—ecosystem overload, overpopulation, extinction of species, and a serious economic crisis when global oil production soon peaks and begins to decline. Time is running out. Political leadership at the global level has never been needed more, and yet the ruling elites are looking the other way, tending to their personal fortunes.

Like dinosaurs unable to adapt to changing conditions, they cling to their privileges, unwilling to act for the common good. Ironically, a large minority of the Empire's own citizens stands ready to support an initiative that could plant the seed of a new Gaian civilization based on sustainability, democracy, justice, and self-determination—all principles for which their political leaders claim to stand.

This critical situation calls for a fresh approach and new source of global leadership from a few of the smaller nations that have the flexibility to take action, the courage to rise to the occasion, and the sensitivity to hear that it is for them that the bell is tolling.

AFTERWORD

The Gaian League vision is nothing if not ambitious—some might say too ambitious. But we are living in unprecedented historic times, when the stakes could not be higher. A bold initiative is necessary to shake up the logjam that is preventing global solutions from emerging in our contemporary world. But help is needed.

The Gaian vision presented here is not a fully defined take-it-or-leave-it proposition. It is a framework that can only manifest if thousands of people around the world contribute to the vision and work actively for it in their local communities. It is purposely formulated as an open-ended proposal that can be debated, modified, refined, and improved. There are many ways to contribute. Only the imagination sets the limits.

I have established a Web site—www.occupyworldstreet.org—that will serve as a focal point for dialogue, blogs, articles, establishment of working groups, coordination of local initiatives, and all manner of input. Besides constructive ideas and suggestions for improving the Gaian framework, there will be a great need for assistance from people with experience in organizing, communication, social networks, forum management, Web design, and many other disciplines.

In addition, I hope to establish a small international working group among NGO colleagues that can help to establish personal contacts to key persons in the countries that might be considered possible candidates as founders, and thus get a "first-phase dialogue" going.

I would like to appeal to all who are excited by the possibilities that this initiative holds to take an active part in the follow-up. Only by working together can we make it happen.

See you soon.

Ross Jackson

NOTES

Chapter 1: The Assault on Nature

1. World Wildlife Fund, *Living Planet Report 2008*, www.panda.org.
2. Niles Eldredge, "The Sixth Extinction," www.ActionBioscience.org.
3. Mae-Wan Ho, *Genetic Engineering: Dream or Nightmare*, 2nd edition (Dublin: Gateway, 1999).
4. Ibid., p. 194.
5. Ibid., p. 1.
6. "Do Seed Companies Control GM Crop Research?" *Scientific American*, (August 2009).
7. See www.betterhealth.vic.gov.au/bhcv2/bhcarticles.nsf/pages/. Antibiotic_resistant_bacteria?; also see http://mslbra.com/ndm-1-the-untreatable-bacteria/.
8. World Health Organization, "Antimicrobial Resistance: A Global Threat," *Essential Drugs Monitor*, nos. 28 & 29 (2000).
9. Jeremy Laurence, "Drug-Resistant STD Now a Global Threat," *Times of India*, July 13, 2011.
10. Laura Sayre, "Organic Farming Combats Global Warming—Big Time," October 10, 2003, www.rodaleinstitute.org.
11. Union of Concerned Scientists. See ucsusa.org.
12. Donella Meadows, Jorgen Randers, Dennis Meadows, *The Limits to Growth: The 30-Year Update* (White River Junction, VT: Chelsea Green Publishing, 2004), pp. xx–xxi.

Chapter 2: Energy Descent

1. Terry Macalister, "Key Oil Figures Were Distorted by U.S. Pressure, Says Whistleblower," *Guardian* (UK), November 9, 2009.
2. John Vidal, "Wikileaks Cables: Saudi Arabia Cannot Pump Enough Oil to Keep a Lid on Prices," *Guardian* (UK), February 8, 2011.
3. Ibid.
4. Colin J. Campbell, *The Coming Oil Crisis* (Petroconsultants, in association with Multi-Science Publishing Co. Ltd, 1997).
5. Chris Nelder, "Tar Sands: The Oil Junkie's Last Fix, Part 2," *Energy and Capital* (2007); see www.energyandcapital.com.
6. Ibid.
7. "Art Berman Talks about Shale Gas," The Oil Drum, www.theoildrum.com.
8. Richard Heinberg, *Muse Letter* (July 2005).
9. Dave Rutledge, "Estimating Long-Term World Coal Production with Logit and Probit Transforms," *International Journal of Coal Geology* 85 (2011), pp. 23–33.
10. John Gever et al., *Beyond Oil*, (Boulder, CO: University Press, 1991).
11. Tad Patzek, "Thermodynamics of the Corn-ethanol Biofuel Cycle," *Critical Reviews in Plant Science* 23, no. 6 (December 2004).
12. "Wind Energy—the Facts," see www.wind-energy-the-facts.org.
13. Campbell, *The Coming Oil Crisis*.
14. Colin Campbell, letter to the *Guardian* (UK), November 2009; see www.theoildrum.com.

15. "Experts Underline Significant Future Role in Cutting Greenhouse Gas Emissions and Powering Sustainable Development, press release, Intergovernmental Panel on Climate Change (May 2011); see www.ipcc.ch.

Chapter 3: The Collapse of Civilizations

1. Wm. H. Kötke, *The Final Empire: The Collapse of Civilization* (Portland, OR: Arrow Point Press, 1993).
2. Jared Diamond, *Collapse: How Societies Choose to Fail or Survive* (London: Penguin Books, 2006).
3. Joseph Tainter, *The Collapse of Complex Societies* (Cambridge: Cambridge University Press, 1988).
4. Donella H. Meadows, Dennis L. Meadows, Jorgen Randers, William W. Behrens III, *The Limits to Growth* (London: Earth Island Ltd, 1972), p. 53.
5. Tainter, *The Collapse of Complex Societies*, p. 198.
6. See www.hdr.undp.org for UNDI; www.ciw.ca for Canada; www.grossnational happiness.com for Bhutan; and www.calvert-henderson.com for Calvert Henderson.
7. See www.ethicalmarkets.com; see "Beyond GDP" section.
8. "The Genuine Progress Indicator, 1950–2002" (2004 update), www.redefining progress.org/publications.
9. Giorgio Guenno and Silvia Tiezzi, "The Index of Sustainable Economic Welfare (ISEW) for Italy," working paper 5.98 (Fondazione Enrico Mattei, Milano, 1998).

Chapter 4: The Evolution of Economic Beliefs

1. Thomas S. Kuhn, *The Structure of Scientific Revolutions* (Chicago: University of Chicago Press, 1962).
2. Karl Polanyi, *The Great Transformation* (Boston: Beacon Press, 2001).
3. Adam Smith, *The Wealth of Nations*, books 1–3 (UK: Penguin Books, 1977), p. 232.
4. Radhakamal Mukerjee, *The Economic History of India* (Bombay, 1945).
5. George B. Curtiss, *The Industrial Development of Nations* (Binghamton, N.Y.: G.B. Curtiss Publication, 1912), vol. iii, p. 6 .
6. Richard Neuhaus, *In Defense of People: Ecology and the Seduction of Radicalism* (New York: MacMillan, 1971), p. 150.
7. John Kenneth Galbraith, "A Look Back: Affirmation and Error," *Journal of Economic Issues* 13, no. 2 (June 1989).
8. Robert U. Ayres and Benjamin Warr, *The Economic Growth Engine: How Energy and Work Drive Material Prosperity* (UK: Edward Elgar, 2009), p. 297.
9. Randi Pisani, "Kyoto-aftalens blinde øje" (The Kyoto Agreement's Blind Eye), *Dagbladet Information*, November 8, 2010, p. 18.
10. Signe Didde Frese, John Kornerup Bang, and John Nordbo "Dansk Forbrug, Global Forurening" (Danish Consumption, Global Pollution), "WWF Denmark (June 2008); see www.WWF.dk.
11. Mike Dash, *Tulipomania: The Story of the World's Most Coveted Flower and the Extraordinary Passions It Aroused* (London: Gollancz, 1999); John Carswell, *The South Sea Bubble* (London: Cresset Press, 1960).

Chapter 5: The Neoliberal Project

1. Milton Friedman and Rose D. Friedman, *Free to Choose* (New York, Harcourt, 1980), pp. 2–3.
2. Susan George, "A Short History of Neo-liberalism," Conference on Economic Sovereignty in a Globalizing World, Bangkok, March 1999; see www.globalexchange.org.
3. Joseph Stiglitz, *Globalization and Its Discontents* (London: Penguin Press, 2002), p. 13.
4. Michel Chossudovsky, *The Globalization of Poverty* (London: Zed, 1997), p. 48.
5. John Perkins, *Confessions of an Economic Hit Man* (San Francisco: Berrett-Koehler, 2004), p. 18.
6. Vandana Shiva, Stolen Harvest: *The Hijacking of the Global Food Supply* (London: Zed Books, 2000).
7. Interview of Joseph Stiglitz by *Trend Online Zeitung* (February 2004); see www.portland.indymedia.org.
8. Mark Weisbrot, Robert Naiman, and Joyce Kim, "The Emperor Has No Growth: Declining Economic Growth Rates in the Era of Globalization," Center for Economic and Policy Research (May 2001); see www.cepr.net.
9. Dani Rodrik, "Comments on 'Trade, Growth, and Poverty,' by D. Dollar and A. Kraay," (October 2000); see http://ksghome.harvard.edu/~.drodrik.academic.ksg/papers.html.
10. Paul Bairoch, *Economics and World History* (Chicago: University of Chicago Press, 1993).
11. John Kenneth Galbraith, *Money, Whence It Came, Where It Went* (London: André Deutsch Limited, 1975), p. 214.
12. Tim Lang and Colin Hines, *The New Protectionism* (London: Earthscan, 1993).
13. Donald L. Barlett and James B. Steele, "Corporate Welfare," *Time* 152, no. 19, November 9, 1998.
14. Stephen Moore, Cato Institute, "Corporate Subsidies in the Federal Budget," testimony before the Budget Committee, U.S. House of Representatives, June 30, 1999.
15. Charles M. Sennott, "The $150 Billion 'Welfare' Recipients: U.S. Corporations," *Boston Globe*, July 7, 1996.
16. Jean-Bertrand Aristide, *Eyes of the Heart* (Monroe, ME: Common Courage Press, 2000).
17. The U.S. WTO Agricultural Proposal: see http://www.fas.usda.gov.
18. "Farm Subsidies: U.S., EU," *Rural Migration News* 8, no. 3 (July 2002).
19. Mark Vaile, Australian minister for trade, media release, September 26, 2000.
20. Timothy Bancroft-Hinchey, Pravda On-line, www.pravda.ru, August 29, 2002.
21. André de Moor, *Subsidizing Unsustainable Development: Undermining the Earth with Public Funds* (Canada: Earth Council publication, 1997).
22. Mike Moore, "Farming Subsidies No Help to Peasants," *Guardian* (UK), August 5, 2002.
23. He Qinglian, Zhongguo de Xianjing, *The Pitfalls of Modernization* (Hong Kong, Mingjing Chubanshe, 1998).
24. Paul Krugman, "The Rich, the Right, and the Facts," *The American Prospect* 3, no. 11, (1992).
25. Paul Krugman, "The Spiral of Inequality," *Mother Jones* (Nov.-Dec. 1996).
26. Paul Stevenson, "Globalization and Inequity: The Negative Consequences for Humanity," 1999; see www.uwinnipeg.ca.

27. Richard Wilkinson and Kate Pickett, *The Spirit Level: Why Greater Equality Makes Societies Stronger* (New York, Bloomsbury Press, 2010).

28. Ibid., p. 25.

29. David Held, *Models of Democracy*, 2nd edition (UK: Polity Press, 1998), p. 215.

30. Nancy Birdsall, Thomas C. Pinckney, and Richard H. Sabot, "Why Low Inequality Spurs Growth: Savings and Investments by the Poor," Inter-American Development Bank, working paper 327 (March 1996); see www. Iadb.org.

31. John Gray, *False Dawn: The Delusions of Global Capitalism* (London: Granta Publications, 1999), p. 17–18.

32. Susan Rose-Ackerman, *Corruption and Government* (Cambridge: Cambridge University Press, 1999), p. 113.

33. Gray, *False Dawn*, p. 131.

Chapter 6: Financial Crises

1. See www.gaia.org.

2. Joseph Stiglitz, *Globalization and Its Discontents* (London: Penguin Press, 2002), p. 220, 16.

3. Ibid., p. 97.

4. Ethan Kaplan and Dani Rodrik, "Did the Malaysian Capital Controls Work?" National Bureau of Economic Research, Inc., working paper no. 8142, (February 2001).

5. Harlan Cleveland, Hazel Henderson, and Inge Kaul (eds.), *The United Nations: Policy and Financing Alternatives: Innovative Proposals by Visionary Leaders* (New York: Apex Press, 1995).

6. Ilan Moscovitz and Morgan Housel, "It's Time to End 'Too Big to Fail,'" *Motley Fool*, November 13, 2009; see www.fool.com.

7. Michael Kirk, producer, *The Warning*, video by *Frontline*, Public Broadcasting Service; see www.pbs.org.

8. F. William Engdahl, "Behind the Panic: Financial Warfare over Future of Global Bank Power," October 10, 2008; see www.engdahl.oilgeopolitics.net.

9. Raghuram G. Rajan, *Fault Lines: How Hidden Fractures Still Threaten the World Economy* (Princeton: Princeton University Press, 2010).

10. Ross Jackson, *And We ARE Doing It!: Building an Ecovillage Future* (San Francisco: Robert D. Reed, 2000), p. 96.

Chapter 7: The Kennan Doctrine

1. George F. Kennan, "Review of Current Trends, U.S. Foreign Policy," Policy Planning Staff, PPS no. 23. Top Secret. Included in the *U.S. Department of State, Foreign Relations of the United States*, 1948, vol. 1, part 2 (Washington, DC: Government Printing Office, 1976), 524–25); declassified June 17, 1974.

2. Noam Chomsky, "Consent without Consent," in *Profit Over People* (Seven Stories Press, 1999).

3. Noreena Hertz, *The Silent Takeover: Global Capitalism and the Death of Democracy* (New York: The Free Press, 2001), p. 108.

4. Frances Fox Piven and Richard Cloward, *Why Americans Don't Vote* (New York: Pantheon Books, 1988), p. 4.

5. Robert W. McChesney, "Noam Chomsky and the Struggle against Neo-liberalism," *Monthly Review*, April 1, 1999.

6. See www.pollingreport.com.

7. "Obama Angry over Campaign Funding Ruling," *San Francisco Sentinel*, January 23, 2010.

8. Dean McSweeney, "Parties, Corruption and Campaign Finance in America," in Robert Williams, ed., *Party Finance and Political Corruption* (London: Macmillan Press Limited, 2000), p. 47.

9. Thomas Mann, Anthony Corrado, Daniel Ortiz, and Trevor Potter, *The New Campaign Finance Sourcebook* (Washington: Brookings Institution Press, 2002), chap. 3.

10. Elizabeth Drew, *The Corruption of American Politics: What Went Wrong and Why* (Woodstock, NY: The Overlook Press, 1999), p. 84.

11. "Think Globally, Sabotage Locally," *Climate Action Network Europe* (October 2010); see www.climnet.org.

12. Drew, *The Corruption of American Politics*, p. 61.

13. Ibid., p. 83.

14. Ibid., p. 79.

15. Chalmers Johnson, *Nemesis: The Last Days of the American Republic* (New York: Metropolitan Books, 2006), p. 115, 264.

16. Marjorie Kelly, *The Divine Right of Capital: Dethroning the Corporate Aristocracy* (San Francisco: Berrett-Koehler, 2001).

17. Johnson, *Nemesis*, p. 260.

18. Kimberly Ann Elliott, ed., *Corruption and the Global Economy* (Washington, DC: Institute for International Economics, 1997).

19. "Keating Five," see www.en.wikipedia.org/wiki/Keating_Five.

20. Noam Chomsky and Edward S. Herman, *Manufacturing Consent: The Political Economy of the Mass Media* (New York: Pantheon Books, 1988).

21. David Edwards, *Free to Be Human: Intellectual Defense in an Age of Illusions* (Dartington, UK: Green Books, 2002), p. 13.

22. Johan Galtung, "The NATO War, the Ethnic Cleansing—Is There a Way Out?" The Transnational Foundation for Peace and Future Research, TFF PressInfo 70, June 10, 1999.

23. William Blum, *Rogue State: A Guide to the World's Only Superpower* (Monroe, ME: Common Courage Press, 2000).

24. Johan Galtung, *Searching for Peace* (London: Pluto Press, 2000), p. 91.

25. Ibid., pp. 91–102.

26. Ralph McGehee, *Deadly Deceit* (New York: Sheridan Square Press, 1983), p. 192.

27. William Blum, "A Brief History of U.S. Interventions: 1945 to the Present," *Z Magazine*, (June 1999).

28. Stephen Kinzer, *All the Shah's Men: An American Coup and Roots of Middle East Terror* (Hoboken, N.J.: John Wiley & Sons, Inc., 2003).

29. Hertz, *The Silent Takeover*, p. 78.

30. Kate Doyle and Peter Kornbluh, "CIA and Assassinations: The Guatemala 1954 Documents," www.gwu.edu, referring to National Security Archive Electronic Briefing Book No. 4 (Washington, DC: The Gelman Library, George Washington University).

31. William Blum, *Killing Hope* (Monroe, ME: Common Courage Press, 1995).

32. Jan Knippers Black, *United States' Penetration of Brazil* (Philadelphia: University of Pennsylvania Press, 1977).

33. Blum, *Killing Hope.*

34. Peter Gribbin, "Brazil and CIA," *Counter Spy* (April-May 1979), pp. 4–23.

35. Noam Chomsky, *Profit Over People* (New York: Seven Stories Press, 1999), p. 49.

36. Federation of American Scientists, "Allende's Leftist Regime," www.fas.org.

37. Peter Kornbluh, "Chile and the United States: Declassified Documents Relating to the Military Coup, September 11, 1973," www.gwu.edu, referring to National Security Archive Electronic Briefing Book No. 8 (Washington, DC: The Gelman Library, George Washington University).

38. Bill Miller, "Family of Slain Chilean Sues Kissinger, Helms," *Washington Post*, September 11, 2001, p. A22.

39. "Pinochet's Profiteers: Canadian Business in Chile," *Peace Magazine* (May/June 1997).

40. See www.powerinquiry.org.

Chapter 8: Who Is in Charge?

1. Edward N. Wolff, "Recent Trends in Household Wealth in the United States: Rising Debt and the Middle-Class Squeeze—An Update to 2007," working paper 589, Levy Economics Institute of Bard College (March 2010).

2. Chief Justice John Marshall, *Providence Bank v. Billings*, 29 U.S. 514 (1830).

3. See "IC-10 Guide for Mental Retardation," section F60.2; www.who.int.

4. Sheldon Wolin, *Democracy Incorporated: Managed Democracy and the Specter of Inverted Totalitarianism* (Princeton: Princeton University Press, 2008).

5. Naomi Wolf, *The End of America: Letter of Warning to a Young Patriot* (White River Junction, VT: Chelsea Green, 2007).

6. Johnson, *Nemesis*, p. 279.

7. G. William Domhoff, "Who Rules America: Wealth, Income, and Power," Sociology Department, University of California at Santa Cruz (January, 2011); see http://sociol ogy.ucsc.edu/whorulesamerica/power/wealth.html.

8. Gretchen Morgenson, "How to Slow Runaway Executive Pay," *New York Times*, October 23, 2005.

9. From the film *War Made Easy*; see www.warmadeeasythemovie.org.

10. George Kennan, preface to Norman Cousins, *The Pathology of Power*, (New York: W. W. Norton & Co., 1987).

11. Galtung, *Searching for Peace*, p. 91.

12. David Korten, "The Great Turning: From Empire to Earth Community," *YES! Magazine* (Summer, 2006).

13. Johnson, *Nemesis*, p. 138.

14. Walden Bello, "The IMF's Hidden Agenda," *Nation Newspaper* (Bangkok), January 25, 1998.

15. Andrew Harvey, *The Hope; A Guide to Sacred Activism* (New York: Hay House, 2009), pp. 174–75.

Chapter 9: The Emergent Worldview

1. Alain Aspect, Philippe Grangier, and Gérard Roger, "Experimental Realization of Einstein-Podolsky-Rosen-Bohm Gedankenexperiment: A New Violation of Bell's Inequalities," *Physical Review Letters* 49, no. 2 (July 1982).

2. James Lovelock, *Gaia: The Practical Science of Planetary Medicine* (London: Gaia Books Limited, 1991).

3. Lynn Margulis, *Symbiosis in Cell Evolution* (New York: W. H. Freeman, 1981).

4. John Brockman, *The Third Culture: Beyond the Scientific Revolution* (New York: Simon and Schuster, 1996), p. 144.

5. Paul H. Ray and Sherry Ruth Anderson, *The Cultural Creatives*, (New York: Harmony Books, 2000).

6. Paul Opuku-Mensah, "The Rise and Rise of NGOs: Implications for Research," www. svt.ntnu.no.

7. See www.forumsocialmundial.org.br.

8. Paul Hawken: *Blessed Unrest: How the Largest Movement in the World Came into Being and Why No One Saw It Coming* (New York: Viking Press, 2007).

9. Mohsen Al Attar and Rosalie Miller, "Toward an Emancipatory International Law: The Bolivarian Reconstruction," *Third World Quarterly* 31, no. 3 (2010), pp. 347–63.

10. Peter Allen, "French Foreign Secretary Resigns 'Over Her Close Friendship with Deposed Tunisian Dictator,'" February 28, 2011, www.dailymail.co.uk.

11. David Korten, *The Great Turning: From Empire to Earth Community* (San Francisco: Berrett-Koehler; and Bloomfield, CT: Kumarian Press, 2006), p. 295.

Chapter 10: Learning from Nature

1. From "Interview with Janine Benyus"; see www.biomimicryinstituite.org; see Janine M. Benyus, *Biomimicry: Innovation Inspired by Nature* (New York: HarperCollins, 1997).

2. William McDonough and Michael Braungart, *Cradle to Cradle: Remaking the Way We Make Things* (New York: North Point Press, 2002).

3. Keto Mshigeni and Gunter Pauli, "Brewing a Future: Zero Emissions in Namibia," *YES! Magazine* 2 (June 1997).

Chapter 11: Gaian Economics

1. Herman E. Daly, *Steady-State Economics* (San Francisco, W. H. Freeman & Co., 1977); Nicholas Georgescu-Roegen, *The Entropy Law and the Economic Process* (Harvard University Press, 1971); Kenneth Boulding, *Principles of Economic Policy* (New York: Prentice-Hall, 1958); E. F. Schumacher, *Small Is Beautiful: Economics as if People Mattered* (London: Blond and Briggs, 1973); Hazel Henderson, *The Politics of the Solar Age: Alternatives to Economics* (Indianapolis, Knowledge Systems, 1988).

2. Robert Costanza, "Ecological Economics Is Post-Autistic," *Post-Autistic Economics Review*, no. 20 (June 2003).

3. Alex Morales, "Fossil Fuel Subsidies Are 12 Times Support for Renewables, Study Shows," www.Bloomberg.com, July 29, 2010.

Chapter 12: Designing a Gaian World

1. Leopold Kohr, *The Breakdown of Nations* (Totnes, UK: Green Books, 2001).

2. Kirkpatrick Sale, *Human Scale* (New York: Coward, McCann & Geoghegan, 1980).

3. See, for example, Hazel Henderson, *Building a Win-Win World* (San Francisco: Berrett-Koehler, 1996).

Chapter 13

1. Quoted in J. W. Smith, *The World's Wasted Wealth 2* (Institute for Economic Democracy, 1994), p. 123.
2. Robert A. Mundell, *International Economics* (New York: Macmillan, 1968).
3. Dev Kar and Karly Curcio, "Illicit Financial Flows from Developing Countries: 2000–2009," *Global Financial Integrity* (January 2011); see www.gfip.org.
4. See www.imf.org.

Chapter 14: The Gaian Clearing Union

1. IMF Statistics Department COFER database, www.imf.org.
2. Michael Hudson, *Super Imperialism: The Origin and Fundamentals of U.S. World Dominance*, 2nd edition (Fortescue, Sidmouth, UK: Pluto Press, 2003).
3. Greg Canavan, "The Triffin Dilemma," http://www.dailyreckoning.com.au/.
4. Sha Zukang, speaking in Istanbul, October 5, 2009. Full text at www.un.org.
5. Zhou Xiaochuan, "Reform the International Monetary System," People's Bank of China, March 23, 2009; see www.pbc.gov.cn/.
6. John Maynard Keynes, "Proposals for an International Currency Union," in Elizabeth Johnson and Donald Moggridge, eds., *The Collected Writings of John Maynard Keynes* vol. 25 (London, MacMillan, 1980).
7. John Maynard Keynes, "National Self-Sufficiency" *The Yale Review* 22, no. 4 (June 1933), pp. 755–69.

Chapter 15: The Gaian Development Bank

1. Paul Bairoch, *Economics and World History: Myths and Paradoxes* (Chicago: University of Chicago Press, 1993).
2. John Perkins, *Confessions of an Economic Hit Man* (San Francisco: Berrett-Koehler, 2004); *The Secret History of the American Empire* (New York: Plume, 2007); John Perkins, *Hoodwinked* (New York: Broadway Books, 2009).
3. Robert Howse, "The Concept of Odious Debt in Public International Law," www.unctad.org, no. 185 (July 2007).
4. Alan Greenspan, "The Crisis," Brookings Institute working paper (April 2010); see www.brookings.edu.
5. Elisabet Sahtouris, *Earth Dance: Living Systems in Evolution* (Lincoln, NE: iUniverse Press, 2000).
6. Catherine Badgely et al., "Organic Agriculture and the Global Food Supply," *Renewable Agriculture and Food Systems* 22 (2007).
7. Peter Goerling, Helena Norberg-Hodge, and John Page, *From the Ground Up* (London: Zed Books, 1993).
8. Bill Mollison, *Permaculture: A Designers Manual* (Australia: Tagari Publications, 1988).
9. See "Permaculture," www.en.wikipedia.org.
10. See "Fukuoka," www.en.wikipedia.org.
11. Sepp Holzer, *The Rebel Farmer* (Graz-Stuttgart: Leopold Stocker, 2004).
12. Geoff Lawton, *Greening the Desert*; see video at www.soildoctor.org.
13. Hildur Jackson and Karen Svensson, eds., *Ecovillage Living: Restoring the Earth and Her Peoples* (Totnes, UK: Green Books, 2002).

14. See www.gaiaeducation.net.

15. See www.complementarycurrency.org.

16. H. T. Hoa et al., "Child Spacing and Two-Child Policy in Practice in Rural Vietnam: Cross-Sectional Survey," *British Medical Journal*, November 2, 1996; see www.bmj.com.

17. "Singapore: Population Control Policies"; see www.country-data.com.

Chapter 16: A Gaian World

1. "Prospect of Limiting the Global Increase in Temperature to 2°C Is Getting Bleaker," International Energy Agency, May 31, 2011; see www.iea.org.

2. "U.S., Russia, Japan to Nix New Kyoto Protocol: Diplomats," *AFP-news*, May 27, 2011.

3. Duncan Clark, "Carbon Cuts by Developed Countries Cancelled out by Imported Goods," *Guardian* (UK), April 25, 2011.

4. Peter Barnes, Robert Costanza, Paul Hawken, David Orr, Elinor Ostrom, Alvaro Umaña, and Oran Young, "Creating an Earth Atmospheric Trust: A System to Control Climate Change and Reduce Poverty" (January 2008); see article on www.grist.org; Oliver Tickell, *Kyoto 2: How to Manage the Global Greenhouse* (London: Zed Books, 2008); Ross Jackson, "An Ideal Climate Agreement?" *Permaculture*, no.58 (Winter 2008).

5. Ross Jackson, "Climate Solutions I" and "Climate Solutions II" in Jonathan Dawson, Ross Jackson, and Helena Norberg-Hodge, eds., *Gaian Economics: Living Well within Planetary Limits* (UK: Permanent Publications, 2010).

6. See www.earthcouncilalliance.org.

7. See www.earthcharterinaction.org.

8. See www.worldfuturecouncil.org.

9. See www.theelders.org.

Chapter 17: The Breakaway Strategy

1. The Ibrahim Index; see www.moibrahimfoundation.org.

2. George Monbiot, *Manifesto for a New World Order* (New York: The New Press, 2003).

3. Kohr, *The Breakdown of Nations*, p. 235.

INDEX

Sahtouris, Elisabet, 248
Sale, Kirkpatrick, 207
Saudi Arabia, 19
savings and loan crisis, 106–7, 133–35
self-regulating systems
    earth as, 166–67
    homeostasis, 167–68
    markets, 58, 90–91 (See also free
    markets/trade)
Senegal, 252–53, 285, 292
service society, 190–92, 197
Sha Zukang, 228
shale gas, 23
Shields, Elson J., 11
Shiva, Vandana, 84
Simberloff, Daniel, 9
Singapore, 258
Skakkebæk, Niels, 14
Smith, Adam, 55–56, 266
social order, neoliberalism and, 95–100
solar energy, 29, 32
Solow, Robert, 68–69
South Korea, 176
sovereign-trade regime, 212–13, 243, 260, 288
    European Union position, 282
    Gaian League members, adoption by, 222
    non-Gaian League members, adoption by,
    265
    trade balance, achieving, 240
species extinction, 9–10
speculation, 112–16
Sri Lanka, 283
steady-state economics, 193
Steelcase Inc., 186–87
Stevenson, Paul, 98
Stiglitz, Joseph, 80, 82, 85, 109
street demonstrations, xv, 278
Strong, Maurice, 268
Structure of Scientific Revolutions, The, 49
subsidies, 77, 79–80, 88–89, 91–95, 199, 211, 291
substitutability, 196–97
sugar subsidies, 93
sustainability, 4, 179–81, 191, 281, 293
    eco-communities, 181–82
    economic growth and, 87
    of economy, 196
    elite's attitude toward, 155–58
    European Union position, 282
    Gaian currency regime and, 222
    Gaian paradigm design and, 185–86
    Gaian Resource Board role, 261–62
    global governance for, 206, 207, 209, 212
    serious, 205–6
    waste, elimination of, 186–90
Suu Kyi, Aung San, 270

Sweden, 282
Switzerland, 287
symbiotic cooperation, 167

Tainter, Joseph, theory of, 34–40
tar sands, 22–23
tariffs, 89, 212
    Asian financial crisis and, 109
    Gaian League policy, 213, 280
    history of, 60–62
    International Monetary Fund (IMF) policy,
    79
    World Trade Organization policy, 85, 210
taxation, 200–201, 256
Thailand, 109–10
Thatcher, Margaret, 76, 78, 103
thermodynamics, second law of. See physics,
    laws of
totalitarianism, inverted, 148
trade deficits/surpluses, 37, 91, 155, 176, 217,
    224–28, 231–34
trade liberalization, 79
trade organizations. See Gaian Trade
    Organization; World Trade Organization
    (WTO)
Traditionals, 171–72
Triffin dilemma, 228, 229, 230
Truman, Harry, 138, 139
Tunisia, 177, 278, 286
Tutu, Desmond, 268
TWAIL (third world approaches to international
    law), 175
Type I ecosystem, oil-based economy as,
    23–24
Type III ecosystem (climax community), 24

Uexkull, Jakob von, 268
United Fruit Company, 139
United Kingdom, 143–44
United Nations, 172, 293
    Climate Conferences, xvi, 9, 286
    Gaian Congress and, 260
    Gaian League members in, 279
    Habitat Conference on Human Settlements,
    252–53
    International Court of Justice, 288
United States, 263. See also democracy, American
    budget deficit, 176
    climate change policy, 9
    dollar as reserve currency, 155, 158, 176,
    224–30, 240
    economic measures, 43–45
    foreign policy, 135–43, 155, 177–78
    gold standard, role in, 65, 77
    inequality in, 96–100

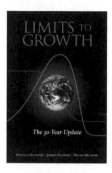

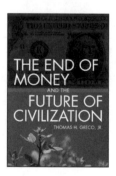